Welcome home Harvest Cookbook

QUICK-AND-EASY FARM-TO-TABLE DINNERS AND DESSERTS

Hope Comerford

Good Books

New York, New York

Good Books books may be purchased in bulk at special discounts for sales promotion, corporate gifts, fund-raising, or educational purposes. Special editions can also be created to specifications. For details, contact the Special Sales Department, Good Books, 307 West 36th Street, 11th Floor, New York, NY 10018 or info@skyhorsepublishing.com.

Good Books is an imprint of Skyhorse Publishing, Inc.®, a Delaware corporation.

Visit our website at www.goodbooks.com.

10 9 8 7 6 5 4 3 2 1

Library of Congress Cataloging-in-Publication Data is available on file.

Cover design by Mona Lin
Cover photos by Bonnie Matthews and Clare Barboza

Print ISBN: 978-1-68099-391-2
Ebook ISBN: 978-1-68099-393-6

Printed in China

Table of Contents

About *Welcome Home Harvest Cookbook*

Welcome to the *Welcome Home Harvest Cookbook: 450 Farm-to-Table Recipes for Easy Dinners, Desserts and More!* We've pulled together the BEST 450 farm-to-table recipes from stovetop, to oven, to slow cooker, and compiled them into one farm-healthy cookbook for you! You'll find all of these recipes contain fresh fruit, vegetables, herbs, eggs, and more.

As you begin journeying through this book, I always suggest reading from cover to cover. I can't tell you the good recipes I've passed on in the past by not following this advice. Don't become overwhelmed. Bookmark, or dog-ear the pages of the recipes that interest you the most as you go through. Then, when you've looked at everything, go back to those marked pages and pick 2–3 to start with. You may even consider choosing a recipe or two you already have the ingredients on hand for. If not, start that grocery list and get to your local farm-stand, farmers' market, co-op or personal garden to grab the rest of the ingredients you need.

Once you've made a couple recipes from this book, I challenge you to make one that seems "hard" for you! You may just surprise yourself at what you can accomplish with a little help from all your Fix-It and Enjoy-It and Fix-it and Forget-It friends!

Fresh Herbs vs. Dried Herbs

Because this is a farm-to-table cookbook, you'll find almost all of the herbs in this book are fresh. However, I know that some of you won't necessarily have access to fresh herbs year-round, so I wanted to make a little chart for you that would help you convert those fresh herbs into dried ones.

Herb	Fresh	Dried
Basil	2 teaspoons finely chopped	1 teaspoon dried
Bay Leaf	1 leaf fresh	1 leaf dried
Cilantro	3 teaspoons fresh	1 teaspoon dried
Cinnamon	1 cinnamon stick	½ teaspoon ground
Cumin	1 Tablespoon whole seed	1 Tablespoon ground
Dill	3 teaspoons fresh	1 teaspoon dried
Garlic (large)	1 clove fresh	½ teaspoon powder
Garlic (small)	1 clove fresh	⅛ teaspoon powder
Garlic minced	½ teaspoon minced	⅛ teaspoon powder
Garlic minced	1½ teaspoon minced	½ teaspoon powder
Ginger	1 tablespoon freshly grated	¼ teaspoon dry ground
Ginger	1 tablespoon minced	½ teaspoon dry ground
Marjoram	3 teaspoons fresh	1 teaspoon dried
Onion	1 medium onion	1 teaspoon onion powder
Oregano	3 teaspoons fresh	1 teaspoon dried
Parsley	2 teaspoons fresh	1 teaspoon dried
Rosemary	3 teaspoons fresh	1 teaspoon dried
Sage	2 teaspoons fresh	1 teaspoon dried
Thyme	3 teaspoons fresh	1 teaspoon dried
Thyme	1 teaspoon dried	¾ teaspoons ground
Vanilla	1 inch vanilla bean	1 teaspoon extract

Canned Tomatoes vs. Fresh Tomatoes

When do I use canned tomatoes and when do I use fresh tomatoes? From everything I learned over the years, it really depends on what you're using them for and when you're using them.

If you're using tomatoes on things like a sandwich, skewers or in a salad, you need to use fresh. I would never put canned tomatoes on top of a salad or try to skewer them for my kabobs!

If you're cooking with tomatoes for things like sauces, stews, etc. then canned tomatoes are usually best. Unless you are sure the tomatoes you have are in season, then it's best to use canned. Canned tomatoes are tomatoes that are picked at their freshest, and canned with a little bit of salt to help bring out and amplify their flavor. If you're avoiding salt altogether, then always using fresh tomatoes is going to be the best option for you.

When it comes to buying canned tomatoes, choose a high-quality brand. I recommend always buying whole, peeled tomatoes and chopping or slicing them, depending on what the recipe calls for. The cans of pre-diced or chopped tomatoes can have chemicals added to them to help the tomato chunks hold their shape.

Sometimes we're caught without canned tomatoes and need to use fresh. Sometimes we're caught without fresh tomatoes and need to use canned. I've created a little chart for you below to help you convert your tomatoes.

Fresh Tomatoes vs. Canned Tomatoes	
5–6 whole tomatoes, chopped	14.5 oz. can chopped tomatoes
10–12 whole tomatoes, peeled	28 oz. can whole, peeled tomatoes

Healthy Hummus

**Barbara Forrester Landis,
Lititz, PA**

Makes 1½ cups, or 8 servings
Prep. Time: 15 minutes

1½ cups drained canned great northern beans

¼ red onion, chopped

1 tsp. fresh minced garlic

1 tsp. fresh rosemary, finely chopped

1 tsp. Kosher salt, or to taste

1 tsp. black pepper, or to taste

½ cup extra-virgin olive oil

1. In a food processor, puree beans until they are halfway between chunky and smooth.

2. Add onion, garlic, rosemary, salt, and pepper.

3. Puree while drizzling in olive oil.

4. Add more or less olive oil, salt, and pepper to taste.

5. Serve with crackers or pita chips. Or spread in tortilla wraps with roasted vegetables, or with cheese and salsa.

Hummus from Scratch

**Melanie Thrower,
McPherson, KS**

Makes 24 servings; about
2 Tbsp./ serving
Prep. Time: 10 minutes
Soaking Time: 8 hours, or
overnight
Cooking Time: 1½ hours

16-oz. bag dried chickpeas (garbanzo beans)

⅔ cup lemon juice

3 cloves garlic

⅔ cup peanut butter, or tahini (sesame seed paste)

½ cup chopped cilantro

2-3 Tbsp. ground cumin

1 Tbsp. olive oil

TIP

You can freeze the hummus and use it up to a week later.

1. Place chickpeas in large stockpot. Cover with water. Let stand overnight.

2. In the morning, discard soaking water.

3. Cover with fresh water.

4. Cover and cook 1–1½ hours over low-medium heat, or until tender.

5. Drain off any liquid. Pour beans into food processor.

6. Add all other ingredients, except olive oil, to processor.

7. Blend until smooth. Add additional lemon juice and cumin to suit your taste.

8. Place hummus in serving dish. Drizzle with olive oil.

9. Serve as a dip with cut-up fresh vegetables, baked chips, or pita bread. Or use as a spread on a sandwich with vegetables.

Guacamole

Joyce Shackelford,
Green Bay, WI

Makes 5 cups; ½ cup/serving
Prep. Time: 15 minutes

3 avocados, peeled

¼ cup minced onion

¾ tsp. garlic powder

½ tsp. chili powder

2 Tbsp. lemon juice

1 large ripe tomato

1. Cut avocados in half and remove seed. With spoon scoop out insides and put in medium bowl. Add onion, garlic powder, chili powder, and lemon juice.

2. With a masher, squash avocados until creamy.

3. Chop tomato and fold in, mixing everything together well.

4. Serve as a dip, sandwich filling, or garnish.

Lightened-Up Spinach Artichoke Dip

Hope Comerford,
Clinton Township, MI

Makes 6–8 servings
Prep. Time: 10 minutes
Cooking Time: 3–4 hours
Ideal slow-cooker size: 3- or 4-qt.

10-oz. bag fresh baby spinach, roughly chopped

13.75-oz. can quartered artichoke hearts, drained and chopped

8-oz. brick reduced-fat cream cheese

1 cup nonfat plain Greek yogurt

1 cup shredded mozzarella cheese

½ cup grated Parmesan cheese

½ cup chopped onion

¼ cup chopped scallions

Serving suggestion:
Serve with brown rice crackers, gluten-free pita bread, or fresh carrot sticks. Garnish with thinly sliced red bell pepper.

1. Spray your crock with nonstick spray.

2. Combine all ingredients in crock, making sure everything is well-mixed.

3. Cover and cook on low for 3–4 hours, or until the cheese is melted and the dip is heated all the way through.

Fresh Salsa

**Barbara Kuhns,
Millersburg, OH**

Makes 3 cups; ½ cup/serving
Prep. Time: 20 minutes

3 tomatoes

½ cup green bell peppers

¼ cup onions, chopped

1 tsp. garlic powder

1 tsp. cumin

¼ tsp. ground red pepper

2 tsp. vinegar

1 tsp. olive oil

2 tsp. lemon juice

1. Chop vegetables.

2. Add remaining ingredients and mix well.

3. Serve.

Black Bean Salsa

**Barbara Tenney,
Delta, PA**

Makes 7½ cups; ⅓ cup/serving
Prep. Time: 15 minutes

2 15-oz. cans black beans, rinsed and drained

2 cups fresh corn, cooked or 16-oz. can whole-kernel corn, rinsed and drained

4 Roma/plum tomatoes, seeded and chopped

1 large avocado, peeled and chopped

½ cup red onion, finely chopped

¼ cup chopped fresh cilantro, according to your taste preference

3 Tbsp. lime juice

1 Tbsp. olive oil

1 Tbsp. red wine vinegar

½ tsp. freshly ground pepper

1. Combine all ingredients in large bowl.

2. Cover and chill. Serve with baked tortilla chips.

Fruit Salsa

**Maryann Markano,
Wilmington, DE**

Makes 4 servings; 1/3 cup/serving
Prep. Time: 15 minutes
Marinating Time: 20 minutes

3/4 cup chopped strawberries

1/3 cup chopped blueberries

2 Tbsp. chopped green bell pepper

2 Tbsp. chopped carrot

1 Tbsp. chopped onion

2 tsp. cider vinegar

1 tsp. minced jalapeño pepper*

1. Combine all ingredients in small bowl.

2. Let stand 20 minutes to allow flavors to blend.

NOTE

Wear gloves and wash hands after chopping jalapeño.

Pineapple Salsa

**Lorraine Stutzman Amstutz,
Akron, PA**

Makes 2½ cups
Prep. Time: 30 minutes

1½ cups fresh pineapple

1 cup cucumber

¼ cup red onion

2–4 tsp. jalapeño

1 tsp. garlic

2 Tbsp. chopped cilantro

¼ cup lime juice

1 tsp. grated lime peel

1 tsp. sugar

¼ tsp. salt

1. Pulse ingredients together in food processor until just chopped.

2. Serve with your favorite tortilla chips.

TIP

If you don't have a food processor, simply chop the pineapple, cucumber, onion, jalapeño, garlic, and cilantro. Combine with lime, sugar, and salt.

Dill Weed Dip for Vegetables

**Hannah D. Burkholder,
Bridgewater, VA**

Makes 1¼ cups
Prep. Time: 15 minutes

⅔ cup sour cream

⅔ cup mayonnaise

1 Tbsp. fresh chopped parsley

1 Tbsp. grated onion

3 Tbsp. fresh dill, chopped

¼ tsp. dry mustard

1. Mix all ingredients together; then refrigerate until ready to serve.

Dilly Crab Dip

**Joyce M Shackelford,
Green Bay, Wisconsin**

Makes 1½ cups
Prep. Time: 30 minutes
Chilling Time: 2–8 hours

½ cup mayonnaise or salad dressing

½ cup sour cream

1 cup flaked cooked crabmeat, *divided*

1 Tbsp. fresh chopped dill weed

2 tsp. finely chopped onion or scallion

½ tsp. finely shredded lime peel

1 tsp. fresh lime juice

dash of bottled hot pepper sauce

dash ground red pepper, optional

salt and pepper to taste

1. Stir together mayonnaise, sour cream, ⅔ cup crabmeat, dill weed, onion, lime peel, lime juice, hot pepper sauce, and red pepper. Season with salt and pepper to taste.

2. Refrigerate for 2 hours, or overnight.

3. Just before serving, sprinkle with reserved crabmeat.

4. Serve with warm or chilled artichokes or crackers.

Rose's Bread Dip

**Rose Hankins,
Stevensville, MD**

Makes 1+ cups, enough for
6–8 servings
Prep. Time: 3 minutes

1 cup extra-virgin olive oil

3 Tbsp. freshly snipped Italian herbs (for example, oregano, basil, thyme, or rosemary)

2 cloves garlic, minced

1 Tbsp. red wine vinegar

1. Mix all ingredients together and pour into small dipping bowls, 1 for each person.

2. Serve with crusty French, Italian, or artisan breads, sliced or cut into chunks for dipping.

Dill, Feta, and Garlic Cream-Cheese Spread

**Kathleen Rogge,
Alexandria, IN**

Makes about 3 cups
Prep. Time: 15 minutes
Chilling Time: 4 or more hours

2 8-oz. pkgs. cream cheese, softened

8-oz. pkg. feta cheese, crumbled

3 cloves garlic, peeled and minced

2 Tbsp. chopped fresh dill

1. In a medium bowl, thoroughly blend ingredients with electric mixer.

2. Cover and chill for at least 4 hours.

3. Serve in a dish alongside firm, raw veggies or crackers.

TIPS

1. Cut back the garlic if you prefer.
2. After mixing the ingredients together, chill them thoroughly, and then shape into a cheese ball before serving.

Tomato-Zucchini Ratatouille

**Barb Yoder,
Angola, IN**

Makes about 3½ cups, or
13 servings
Prep. Time: 20–30 minutes
Cooking Time: 7–8 hours
Ideal slow-cooker size: 4-qt.

1½ cups chopped onion

6-oz. can tomato paste

1 Tbsp. olive oil

2 cloves garlic, minced

1 Tbsp. fresh chopped basil

1½ tsp. fresh chopped thyme

15-oz. can chopped low-sodium tomatoes,
   with juice drained but reserved

1 large zucchini, halved lengthwise and sliced
   thin

salt and pepper to taste, optional

26 slices French bread or baguette

1. Mix all ingredients except bread in slow cooker.

2. Cover. Cook on low 7–8 hours.

3. If mixture is stiffer than you wish, stir in some reserved tomato juice.

4. Serve hot or cold on top of French bread or baguette slices.

Cranberry Cream-Cheese Appetizer

**Christie Detamore-Hunsberger,
Harrisonburg, VA**

Makes 12 servings
Prep. Time: 20–25 minutes
Cooling Time: 45–60 minutes

1 cup water

1 cup sugar

12-oz. fresh cranberries (if frozen, thaw)

½ cup apricot preserves

2 Tbsp. fresh lemon juice, optional

⅓ cup slivered almonds, toasted

8-oz. pkg. cream cheese

1. In pan over medium heat, bring water and sugar to a boil without stirring. Boil for 5 minutes.

2. Add cranberries and cook until berries pop and sauce is thickened, about 10 minutes. Remove from heat.

3. Cut apricots in the preserves into small pieces. Add to cranberry mixture.

4. Stir in lemon juice if you wish.

5. Cool cranberry-apricot mixture to room temperature.

6. Stir in almonds.

7. Spoon over cream-cheese block. Serve with crackers.

Feta Bruschetta

**Lena Sheaffer,
Port Matilda, PA**

Makes 10 servings
Prep. Time: 15 minutes
Baking Time: 20 minutes

¼ cup butter, melted

¼ cup olive or vegetable oil

10 slices French bread, cut 1" thick

4-oz. pkg. crumbled feta cheese

2-3 garlic cloves, minced

1 Tbsp. chopped fresh basil

1 large tomato, seeded and chopped

1. Combine butter and oil. Brush on both sides of bread. Place on baking sheet.

2. Bake at 350° for 8–10 minutes, or until lightly browned.

3. Combine feta cheese, garlic, and basil. Sprinkle over toast. Top with tomato.

4. Bake 8–10 minutes longer, or until heated through. Serve warm.

Variation:
Mix chopped red pepper into Step 3, along with any other of your favorite herbs.

Veggie Pizza

Jean Butzer, Batavia, NY
Julette Rush, Harrisonburg, VA

Makes 10–12 servings
Prep. Time: 20–30 minutes
Cooking Time: 9–12 minutes
Cooling Time: 30 minutes

2 8-oz. pkgs. refrigerated crescent rolls

8-oz. pkg. cream cheese, softened

½–¾ cup salad dressing or mayonnaise

1 Tbsp. fresh chopped dill

½ tsp. onion salt

¾–1 cup broccoli florets

¾–1 cup green pepper or mushrooms, chopped fine

¾–1 cup tomato, membranes and seeds removed, chopped fine

½ cup sliced ripe olives

¼ cup sweet onion or red onion, chopped fine

¾ cup cheddar cheese, shredded fine, optional

1. Separate dough into 4 rectangles.

2. Press onto bottom and up sides of 10 × 13 jelly roll baking pan to form crust.

3. Bake 9–12 minutes at 350° or until golden brown. Cool at least 30 minutes.

4. Mix cream cheese, dressing, dill, and onion salt until well blended.

5. Spread over cooled crust.

6. Top with chopped vegetables and optional cheese.

Fresh Tomato Crostini

**Marilyn Mowry,
Irving, TX**

Makes 4 servings
Prep. Time: 20 minutes
Marinating Time: 30 minutes

4 plum tomatoes, chopped

¼ cup minced fresh basil

2 tsp. olive oil

1 clove garlic, minced

freshly ground pepper

¼ lb. crusty Italian peasant bread, cut into 4
slices and toasted

1. Combine tomatoes, basil, oil, garlic, and pepper in good-sized bowl.

2. Cover and let stand 30 minutes.

3. Divide tomato mixture with any juices among the toast. Serve at room temperature.

Mini Eggplant Pizzas

**Maryann Markano,
Wilmington, DE**

Makes 4 servings
Prep. Time: 20 minutes
Cooking/Baking Time:
11–13 minutes

1 eggplant, 3" diameter

1½ tsp. fresh chopped oregano

½ tsp. fresh chopped basil

1 clove garlic, crushed

1 Tbsp. olive oil

⅛ tsp. black pepper

1 large ripe tomato, cut into 4 slices

¼ cup low-sodium, low-fat pizza sauce

½ cup shredded reduced-fat mozzarella
   cheese

1. Preheat oven to 425°.

2. Peel eggplant and cut into 4½"-thick slices.

3. Combine herbs and set aside.

4. Brush both sides of eggplant with oil and season with pepper.

5. Arrange on baking sheet and bake until browned, about 8 minutes. Turn once during baking to brown both sides.

6. Place a tomato slice on each eggplant slice and sprinkle with herb mixture. Drizzle each slice with 1 Tbsp. pizza sauce.

7. Top with cheese and bake until cheese melts, about 3–5 minutes. Serve hot.

Quesadillas

**Melanie Mohler,
Ephrata, PA**

Makes 8 servings
Prep. Time: 5 minutes
Cooking/Baking Time: 5 minutes

2 ozs. cheddar cheese, shredded

2 ozs. mozzarella cheese, shredded

2 10" flour tortillas

Optional ingredients:

1 small tomato, diced

¼ cup green pepper, finely chopped

¼ cup fresh mushrooms, sliced

picante sauce

sour cream

1. Sprinkle half the cheddar cheese, mozzarella cheese, and your choice of the optional ingredients (tomatoes, green pepper, fresh mushrooms) on half of each tortilla. Fold over and press edges to seal lightly.

2. Coat skillet with nonstick cooking spray. Turn burner to medium heat. Place tortillas in heated skillet.

3. Grill until browned and crisp. Turn over carefully with a spatula and continue to brown until cheese is melted.

4. Remove from skillet and cut into quarters.

5. Serve with picante sauce or sour cream for dipping, if you wish.

Cheesy Shrimp Melts

**Mary Seielstad,
Sparks, NV**

Makes 8–32 servings
Prep. Time: 10–15 minutes
Cooking/Baking Time:
15 minutes

1 lb. cooked and peeled small shrimp

1 cup shredded sharp cheddar cheese

3 Tbsp. chopped celery

3 Tbsp. chopped onion

¼ cup mayonnaise

4 English muffins

1. Mix first 5 ingredients together.

2. Heat oven to 350°.

3. Split English muffins. (To serve as a smaller appetizer, cut each half into halves or quarters.) Place on cookie sheet. Heat or toast 5 minutes, just until lightly browned.

4. Remove from oven and spread with shrimp mixture. Return to oven for 12–15 minutes, or until mixture is bubbly.

Hints from tester:
1. Sprinkle with a dash of freshly ground pepper in Step 4, just before placing in oven.
2. For the non-seafood eaters, substitute cooked chicken for the shrimp.
3. Top with a few cubes of fresh tomato just before serving.

Avocado Egg Salad

Melanie Mohler,
Ephrata, PA

Makes 4 servings
Prep. Time: 10 minutes

4 eggs, hard-cooked and chopped (reserve 2 yolks for another use)

1 clove garlic, minced

1 large avocado, chopped

pepper to taste

2 Tbsp. fresh lemon juice

1. In a serving bowl, combine eggs, garlic and avocado.

2. Sprinkle with pepper and lemon juice. Stir gently.

3. Use as topping for crackers or as sandwich filling. Eat immediately or store in fridge.

Shrimp Mousse on Cucumber

J. B. Miller,
Indianapolis, IN

Makes 36 slices
Prep. Time: 10 minutes

3 scallions

3-oz. pkg. cream cheese, at room temperature

1 lb. cooked baby shrimp

3 Tbsp. fresh lemon juice

10"-long seedless cucumber, or 2 smaller
   cucumbers

1. Trim the scallions and cut into small pieces. Place them in a food processor and pulse several times to chop.

2. Add the cream cheese and mix. Add the shrimp and lemon juice and puree until creamy and smooth.

3. Slice the cucumber about ¼" thick and place on serving platter.

4. Spoon 1 Tbsp. mousse on top of each cucumber slice, or place mousse in pastry bag and pipe onto cucumbers.

Ham Roll-Ups

Hope Comerford,
Clinton Township, MI

Makes about 40 pieces
Prep. Time: 10 minutes

8 oz. pkg. cream cheese, room temperature

1 Tbsp. fresh chopped dill

8-10 slices thinly sliced cooked ham

8-10 scallions, end trimmed

1. In a small bowl, mix together the cream cheese and chopped dill.

2. Lay out a piece of ham and dry off with a piece of paper towel.

3. Spread $\frac{1}{8}-\frac{1}{10}$ of the cream-cheese mixture over the slice.

4. Lay a scallion along the edge and begin rolling.

5. Cut each roll-up into 4–5½" pieces.

6. Repeat this process for each piece of ham.

Rhonda's Apple Butter

**Rhonda Burgoon,
Collingswood, NJ**

Makes 24 servings (2 Tbsp. each)
Prep. Time: 20 minutes
Cooking Time: 12–14 hours
Ideal slow-cooker size: 3-qt.

4 lbs. apples

2 tsp. cinnamon

½ tsp. ground cloves

1. Peel, core, and slice apples. Place in slow cooker.

2. Cover. Cook on high 2–3 hours. Reduce to low and cook 8 hours. Apples should be a rich brown and be cooked down by half.

3. Stir in spices. Cook on high 2–3 hours with lid off. Stir until smooth.

4. Pour into freezer containers and freeze, or pour into sterilized jars and seal.

Pear Honey Butter

Becky Fixel,
Grosse Pointe Farms, MI

Makes 45–50 servings
Prep. Time: 30
Cooking Time: 10 hours
Ideal slow-cooker size: 6½- or 7-qt.

10 lbs. ripened pears, peeled, cored, sliced

1 cup water

1 cup honey

1. Place your pear slices inside your slow cooker.

2. Add in the water and honey.

3. Cover and cook on low heat for 10 hours. You can stir if you want to but it's not necessary. When your pears are done, they will have darkened in color, but won't dry out through cooking.

4. Either use your blender and puree your softened pears in batches until it is done or use an immersion blender to make a smooth consistency.

Serving suggestion:
Serve on whole grain bread with cream cheese and top with cinnamon.

TIP

Freeze or can the extras in a water bath for 20 minutes.

Baked French Toast with Cream Cheese

Blanche Nyce,
Hatfield, PA

Makes 6–8 servings
Prep. Time: 15–20 minutes
Soaking Time: 8 hours, or overnight
Baking Time: 40–45 minutes

1-lb. loaf firm bread, *divided*

8-oz. pkg. cream cheese

10 eggs

½ cup half-and-half

¼ cup maple syrup, or pancake syrup

1 stick (½ cup) butter, melted

2 cup berries of your choice (strawberries, blueberries, or raspberries)

1. Cube bread and layer half in well-greased 9 × 13 baking pan.

2. Cut cream cheese into small pieces and scatter across bread.

3. Sprinkle with berries.

4. Cover berries with remaining half of bread.

5. In mixing bowl, beat together eggs, half-and-half, syrup, and melted butter.

6. Pour over bread contents of baking pan.

7. Press down until bread is submerged as much as possible.

8. Cover and refrigerate for 8 hours, or overnight.

9. Bake uncovered at 375°F for 40–45 minutes, or until lightly browned and puffy.

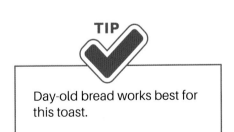

TIP

Day-old bread works best for this toast.

Overnight Apple French Toast

**Eileen Eash,
Lafayette, CO
Peggy C. Forsythe,
Memphis, TN**

Makes 9 servings
Prep. Time: 40–45 minutes
Soaking Time: 8 hours, or overnight
Baking Time: 35–40 minutes

¾ cup packed brown sugar

¾ stick (6 Tbsp.) butter

3–4 large tart apples, peeled and sliced ¼" thick

3 eggs

1 cup milk

1 tsp. vanilla

9 slices day-old French bread, ¾" thick

Syrup:
½ cup applesauce

¼ tsp. cinnamon

5-oz. jar apple or crabapple jelly

pinch of ground cloves

sprinkle of nutmeg, optional

maple syrup for serving, optional

whipped cream, optional

1. In a small saucepan, melt sugar and butter together about 3–4 minutes, stirring constantly, until slightly thick.

2. Pour into ungreased 9 × 13 baking pan.

3. Top with apple slices.

4. In a medium-sized mixing bowl, beat together eggs, milk, and vanilla.

5. Dip bread slices in egg mixture, one by one, and then lay over top of apples.

6. Cover and refrigerate overnight. Sprinkle with nutmeg if you wish.

7. Bake uncovered at 350° for 35–40 minutes.

8. Meanwhile, prepare syrup by cooking applesauce, cinnamon, apple jelly, and ground cloves in small saucepan until hot.

9. Serve over toast.

10. Offer maple syrup and whipped cream as toppings, too.

B&B Blueberry Coffee Cake

**Kim Rapp,
Longmont, CO**

Makes 18 servings
Prep. Time: 15–20 minutes
Baking Time: 55–65 minutes

4 cups flour

1½ cups sugar

5 tsp. baking powder

1 tsp. salt

1 stick (½ cup) butter

1½ cups milk

2 eggs

4 cups fresh blueberries

Topping:
¼ cup sugar

⅔ cup flour

1 tsp. cinnamon

½ tsp. nutmeg

1 stick (½ cup) butter, softened

1. In mixing bowl, mix together flour, sugar, baking powder, salt, butter, milk, and eggs. Using mixer, beat vigorously for 30 seconds.

2. Carefully fold blueberries into batter.

3. Pour into greased 9 × 13 baking pan.

4. For topping, combine sugar, flour, cinnamon, and nutmeg in a bowl.

5. Using a pastry cutter, or two knives, cut in butter until small crumbs form.

6. Sprinkle crumbs evenly over batter.

7. Bake 55–65 minutes, or until toothpick inserted in center of cake comes out clean.

Strawberry Pancakes

**Becky Frey,
Lebanon, PA**

Makes 15 medium-sized pancakes, or
4–5 servings
Prep. Time: 10–15 minutes
Cooking Time: 10 minutes

2 eggs

1 cup buttermilk

1 cup crushed strawberries＊

¼ cup oil

1 tsp. almond extract

2 cups whole wheat (or white) flour

2 Tbsp. brown sugar

2 tsp. baking powder

1 tsp. baking soda

1. In large mixing bowl beat eggs until fluffy.

2. Stir buttermilk, strawberries, oil, and almond extract into eggs.

3. In a separate bowl, combine flour, brown sugar, baking powder, and baking soda. Add to wet ingredients. Beat together with whisk just until smooth.

4. Heat skillet or griddle until a few drops of water sizzle when sprinkled on top. Fry pancakes until bubbly on top. Flip and continue cooking until browned. Strawberries can scorch, so keep checking to make sure they're not burning. Turn the heat lower if necessary.

NOTE

You can use fresh or frozen berries. If frozen, thaw them and drain them well before mixing into batter.

Serving Suggestion:
Top finished pancakes with vanilla yogurt and fruit sauce and serve for breakfast, brunch, a light lunch or supper, or as a dessert.

Apple Puff Pancake

**Wilma Stoltzfus,
Honey Brook, PA**

Makes 8 servings
Prep. Time: 20 minutes
Baking Time: 50 minutes

4 Tbsp. butter

2 large apples, peeled and thinly sliced

3 Tbsp. brown sugar

1 tsp. cinnamon

6 eggs

1½ cups milk

1 cup flour

3 Tbsp. sugar

1 tsp. vanilla extract

½ tsp. salt

½ tsp. cinnamon

confectioners' sugar

syrup, optional

1. Melt butter in a 9 × 13 pan. Arrange apples over butter. Mix brown sugar and cinnamon in small bowl and sprinkle over apples.

2. Bake at 375° about 10 minutes, or until apples soften.

3. Combine in blender eggs, milk, flour, sugar, vanilla, salt, and cinnamon. Blend thoroughly and pour over apples.

4. Return to oven and bake 40 minutes.

5. Sprinkle with confectioners' sugar and serve immediately. Serve with syrup if you like.

Blueberry and Oatmeal Breakfast Cake

Jean Butzer,
Batavia, NY

Makes 8 servings
Prep. Time: 15 minutes
Baking Time: 25 minutes

1½ cups whole wheat pastry flour

¾ cup uncooked rolled oats

⅓ cup sugar

2 tsp. baking powder

¼ tsp. cinnamon, optional

¾ cup skim milk

2 Tbsp. canola oil

2 Tbsp. mashed banana, or unsweetened
    applesauce

egg substitute equivalent to 1 egg, or 2 egg
    whites

1 cup fresh blueberries

1. Preheat oven to 400°. Spray 8" round baking pan with cooking spray.

2. Combine flour, oats, sugar, baking powder, and cinnamon if you wish, in medium-sized mixing bowl.

3. In 2-cup measure, mix milk, oil, mashed banana or applesauce, and egg.

4. Add wet ingredients to flour mixture. Stir until just moistened.

5. Gently fold in blueberries.

6. Spoon into baking pan.

7. Bake, uncovered, 20–25 minutes, or until tester inserted in center of cake comes out clean.

Lemon Almond Blueberry Breakfast "Cakes"

**Hope Comerford,
Clinton Township, MI**

Makes 4 servings
Prep. Time: 25 minutes
Cooking Time: 3½–4 hours
Ideal slow-cooker size: 3-qt. oval

2 Tbsp. liquid egg whites

¼ cup coconut sugar

1 Tbsp. unsweetened applesauce

⅓ cup fresh lemon juice

½ tsp. lemon zest

2 cups almond flour

¾ tsp. baking powder

¼ tsp. baking soda

¼ tsp. salt

½ cup blueberries

1. Spray 3–4 small ramekins or individual baking dishes (about 1 each) with nonstick spray.

2. Mix together the egg whites, coconut sugar, applesauce, lemon juice, and lemon zest in a large bowl.

3. In a separate bowl, mix together the almond flour, baking powder, baking soda, and salt.

4. Slowly mix the dry ingredients into the wet ingredients. Stir only until just combined, then carefully fold in the blueberries. Pour the batter evenly into the ramekins or baking dishes.

5. Place a trivet, rack, mason jar lids, or crumpled-up foil in the bottom of the crock, then arrange the ramekins or baking dishes on top in the crock.

6. Place paper towel on top of the opening of the slow cooker. Secure it with the lid, then cook on Low for 3½–4 hours.

7. Eat with a spoon right out of the dish.

Spiced Apple Twists

Janessa Hochstedler,
East Earl, PA

Makes 16 pieces
Prep. Time: 10–20 minutes
Baking Time: 30–35 minutes

¼ cup freshly squeezed orange juice, or water

8-oz. tube crescent rolls

2 large tart, firm apples, peeled and cored

2 Tbsp. butter, melted

½ tsp. cinnamon

¼ cup sugar

1. Pour juice into bottom of greased 9 × 9 baking dish.

2. Unroll crescent dough. Separate into 8 triangles. Cut each in half to make 16 triangles.

3. Cut each apple into 8 slices.

4. Place an apple slice at wide end of each triangle. Roll up.

5. Arrange filled pastries in pan.

6. Drizzle butter over tops.

7. In a small bowl, mix cinnamon and sugar together.

8. Sprinkle cinnamon-sugar mixture over pastries.

9. Bake at 400° for 30–35 minutes.

Variations:
1. If you wish, sprinkle a few raisins or currants over each apple slice before rolling up in Step 4.
2. If you wish, use a sprinkling of nutmeg and/or allspice with cinnamon in Step 7.

Fresh Apple Pockets

Janet Groff,
Stevens, PA

Makes 8 servings
Prep. Time: 30–40 minutes
Resting/Rising Time: 40 minutes
Baking Time: 20–25 minutes

Dough:

2–2½ cups flour, *divided*

1 pkg. (1 Tbsp.) fast-rising yeast

2 tsp. sugar

½ tsp. salt

⅔ cup water

½ cup oil

Filling:

½ cup sugar

2 Tbsp. flour

½ tsp. cinnamon

2 cups thinly sliced apples (about 2 apples)

Frosting:

1½ cups confectioners' sugar

water, enough to make the frosting of drizzling
consistency

1. In large bowl, combine 1 cup flour, undissolved yeast, sugar, and salt. Add very warm water (120–130°).

2. Stir in oil and enough additional flour to make a soft dough.

3. On floured surface, knead 4 minutes.

4. Cover and let rest 10 minutes.

5. Meanwhile, make filling in a mixing bowl by combining dry ingredients. Toss with apples. Set aside.

6. Divide dough in half. On lightly floured surface, roll each half into a 10" square. Cut each square into 4 squares.

7. Place ¼ cup filling onto center of each square. Bring corners up over filling, making a triangular "pocket." Pinch to seal.

8. Transfer to greased baking sheet. Let rise until double, about 30 minutes.

9. Bake at 350° until golden brown, about 20–25 minutes. Cool on wire rack.

10. Whisk frosting ingredients together and drizzle over apple pockets.

Breakfast Apples

Joyce Bowman,
Lady Lake, FL
Jeanette Oberholtzer,
Manheim, PA

Makes 4 servings
Prep. Time: 10–15 minutes
Cooking Time: 2–8 hours
Ideal slow-cooker size: 3-qt.

4 medium-sized apples, peeled and sliced

¼ cup honey

1 tsp. cinnamon

2 Tbsp. melted butter

2 cups dry granola cereal

Serving suggestion:
Serve as a side dish to bacon and bagels, or use as a topping for waffles, French toast, pancakes, or cooked oatmeal.

1. Place apples in your slow cooker.

2. Combine remaining ingredients. Sprinkle the mixture evenly over top of the apples.

3. Cover and cook on Low 6–8 hours or overnight, or on High 2–3 hours.

Apple Cinnamon Oatmeal

**Hope Comerford,
Clinton Township, MI**

Makes 2–3 servings
Prep. Time: 5 minutes
Cooking Time: 7 hours
Ideal slow-cooker size: 2-qt.

½ cup steel-cut oats

2 cups sweetened vanilla almond milk

1 small apple, peeled, cored, and diced

¼ tsp. cinnamon

1. Spray crock with nonstick spray.

2. Place all ingredients into crock and stir lightly.

3. Cover and cook on Low for 7 hours.

Apple Nut Ring

Naomi Cunningham,
Arlington, KS

Makes 10 servings
Prep. Time: 10 minutes
Baking Time: 25–30 minutes

2 7.5-oz. pkgs. refrigerated buttermilk biscuits

¼ cup butter or margarine, melted

⅔ cup sugar

2 Tbsp. ground cinnamon

3–4 medium-sized apples, peeled, cored, sliced and cut in half crosswise

⅓ cup nuts, chopped

1. Separate biscuits.

2. In a saucepan, melt the butter or margarine.

3. Combine sugar and cinnamon in a small bowl.

4. Dip biscuits in butter, and then roll in sugar mixture. Arrange biscuits, so that they overlap, around the edge and into the center of a greased 9 × 13 baking pan.

5. Place an apple slice between each biscuit and around the outer edge of the baking dish.

6. Mix the nuts with any remaining sugar mixture. Sprinkle over top of biscuits and apples.

7. Bake at 400° for 25–30 minutes, or until biscuits are a deep golden brown.

Berry Breakfast Parfait

Susan Tjon,
Austin, TX

Makes 4 servings
Prep. Time: 15 minutes

2 cups fat-free vanilla yogurt, sweetened with low-calorie sweetener

¼ tsp. ground cinnamon

1 cup sliced strawberries

½ cup blueberries

½ cup raspberries

1 cup low-fat granola

1. Combine yogurt and cinnamon in small bowl.

2. Combine fruit in medium bowl.

3. For each parfait, layer ¼ cup fruit mixture, then 2 Tbsp. granola, followed by ¼ cup yogurt mixture in parfait glass (or whatever container you choose).

4. Repeat layers once more and top with a sprinkling of granola.

Green Smoothie

**Hope Comerford,
Clinton Township, MI**

Makes 1 serving

¾ cup almond milk

½ cup nonfat plain Greek yogurt

2 tsp. honey

½ banana

¼ cup strawberries

1 cup spinach leaves

¼ cup ice

1. Place all ingredients into the blender and blend until smooth.

Variation:
Use any combination of fruit you would like.

TIP

Have bananas about to go bad and no time to make banana bread? Peel them and slice them in half. Freeze each half individually in Baggies, then use them when you're making smoothies.

Spinach Frittata

Shirley Unternahrer,
Wayland, IA

Makes 4-6 servings
Prep. Time: 15 minutes
Cooking Time: 1½–2 hours
Ideal slow-cooker size: 5-qt.

4 eggs

½ tsp. salt

1 tsp. fresh chopped basil

freshly ground pepper to taste

3 cups chopped fresh spinach, stems
 removed

½ cup chopped tomato, liquid drained off

⅓ cup freshly grated Parmesan cheese

1. Whisk eggs well in mixing bowl.
Whisk in salt, basil, and pepper.

2. Gently stir in spinach, tomato, and
Parmesan.

3. Grease interior of slow-cooker crock.
Pour mixture into cooker.

4. Cover and cook on High 1½–2 hours,
or until middle is set. Serve hot.

Fresh Veggie and Herb Omelet

Hope Comerford,
Clinton Township, MI

Makes 8 servings
Prep. Time: 20 minutes
Cooking Time: 4–6 hours
Ideal slow-cooker size: 6-qt.

12 eggs

1 cup unsweetened almond milk or milk

½ tsp. kosher salt

¼ tsp. pepper

3 cloves garlic, minced

1 tsp. fresh chopped basil

6 dashes hot sauce

2 cups broccoli florets

1 yellow bell pepper, diced

1 red bell pepper, diced

1 onion, diced

1 cup crumbled feta cheese

1 cup diced cherry tomatoes

½ cup fresh chopped parsley

1. Spray crock with nonstick spray.

2. In a bowl, mix together eggs, milk, salt, pepper, garlic, basil, and hot sauce.

3. Place broccoli, yellow pepper, red pepper, and onion in crock. Gently mix with a spoon.

4. Pour egg mixture over the top.

5. Cover and cook on Low for 4–6 hours, or until center is set.

6. Sprinkle feta over the top, then cook an additional 30 minutes.

7. To serve, sprinkle the omelet with the chopped tomatoes and fresh parsley.

Overnight Veggie Omelet

Doug Garrett,
Palmyra, PA

Makes 6 servings
Prep. Time: 30 minutes
Chilling Time: 4–8 hours, or overnight
Cooking Time: 3–4 hours
Ideal slow-cooker size: 4- or 5-qt.

6 slices whole-grain bread, torn into pieces

½ cup diced onion

1 medium carrot, pared and sliced thinly

¼ stick (2 Tbsp). butter

2 cups fresh broccoli florets, cut small

¾ cup grape tomatoes, sliced lengthwise

4 oz. cream cheese

1 cup grated Colby cheese

6 eggs

1½ cups milk

½ tsp. dry mustard

½ tsp. salt

dash cayenne pepper

1. Grease interior of slow-cooker crock.

2. Distribute torn bread in bottom of greased crock.

3. If you have time, sauté diced onion and carrots in butter in skillet, until onion is light brown and softened. If you don't have time, spread diced veggies over bread pieces in cooker.

4. Drop broccoli and grape tomatoes evenly over top of other vegetables.

5. Cut cream cheese into small pieces. Sprinkle it and grated cheese evenly over broccoli and tomatoes.

6. In a bowl, mix eggs, milk, mustard, salt, and cayenne together. Pour over all other ingredients in crock.

7. Cover. Refrigerate 4–8 hours, or overnight.

8. Cook on Low 3–4 hours, or until eggs are set in center.

9. Twenty minutes before end of cooking time, remove lid so that top of omelet can dry.

Serving suggestion:
Serve alongside breakfast pastries, such as sticky buns or muffins.

Mushroom Oven Omelet

Elaine Patton,
West Middletown, PA

Makes 4 servings
Prep. Time: 20 minutes
Baking Time: 20 minutes

½ lb. fresh mushrooms, cleaned and sliced

2 Tbsp. butter

2 Tbsp. flour

6 eggs

⅓ cup milk

⅛ tsp. pepper

¼ cup chopped onions, optional

¼ cup chopped green pepper, optional

1½ cups shredded cheddar cheese, *divided*

½ cup cooked, chopped bacon

1. In a small skillet, sauté mushrooms in butter until tender. Drain. Set aside.

2. In a bowl, combine flour, eggs, milk, and pepper until smooth. Add chopped vegetables if you wish.

3. Stir in 1 cup cheese, bacon, and mushrooms.

4. Pour into a greased 8"-square baking dish.

5. Baked uncovered at 375° for 18–20 minutes, or until eggs are completely set.

6. Sprinkle with remaining cheese, return to warm oven for 1 minute, and then serve.

Breakfast in a Bag

Donna Lantgen,
Golden, CO

Makes 1 serving
Prep. Time: 1–2 minutes
Cooking Time: 12 minutes

2 eggs

Optional ingredients:

¼ cup cooked sausage

1 slice cooked bacon, crumbled

¼ cup cooked and cubed ham

thin onion slices

several Tbsp. chopped red or green bell
   pepper

several Tbsp. sliced black olives

¼ cup sliced mushrooms

¼ cup grated cheese of your choice

¼ cup chopped fresh tomato

1. Place a 4-qt. saucepan, ⅔ full of water over high heat. Bring to a boil.

2. Meanwhile, break 2 eggs into a sturdy plastic bag. Holding it shut, mash the eggs a bit.

3. Add optional ingredients of your choice. Press the air out of the bag. Zip close, or tie shut with a twisty.

4. Place bag in boiling water and cook for 12 minutes.

5. Remove from water and slide egg right out of the bag.

California Egg Bake

**Leona M. Slabaugh,
Apple Creek, OH**

Makes 2 servings
Prep. Time: 10–15 minutes
Baking Time: 25–30 minutes

3 eggs

¼ cup sour cream

¼ tsp. salt

1 medium tomato, chopped

1 scallion, sliced

¼ cup shredded cheese

1. In a small bowl, beat eggs, sour cream, and salt.

2. Stir in tomato, scallion, and cheese.

3. Pour into greased 2-cup baking dish.

4. Bake at 350° for 25–30 minutes, or until a knife inserted in center comes out clean.

Baked Egg Muffins

Hope Comerford,
Clinton Township, MI

Makes 6 servings
Prep. Time: 15 minutes
Cooking Time: 10 minutes
Baking Time: 25–30 minutes

¼ cup diced baby bella mushrooms

¼ cup diced zucchini

¼ cup diced yellow squash

¼ cup diced onion

1 Tbsp. olive oil

½ cup chopped spinach

½ lb. ground turkey sausage, browned

12 eggs

¼ cup milk

¼ tsp. salt

⅛ tsp. pepper

4 dashes hot sauce

1. Preheat oven to 350°. Spray your muffin tin with nonstick spray.

2. Preheat the olive oil and over medium heat, cook the mushrooms, zucchini, yellow squash, and onion until just soft.

3. Add the spinach and cooked browned turkey sausage to the pan with the vegetables and mix together. Evenly divide this mixture among the 12 muffin cups.

4. In a bowl, whisk together the eggs, milk, salt, pepper, and hot sauce. Pour this evenly over the contents of each muffin cup.

5. Bake for 25–30 minutes, or until the middle is set. Let them cool, then run a knife around the outside of each muffin to help remove them.

Shirred Eggs on Spinach

Scarlett von Bernuth,
Canon City, CO

Makes 5-6 servings
Prep. Time: 15 minutes
Cooking/Baking Time: 20 minutes

1 lb. fresh spinach, chopped fine

1½ cups dry bread crumbs, *divided*

½ tsp. salt

dash of pepper

6 eggs

¼ cup grated cheese of your choice

1. Wash spinach. Shake off water and place spinach in a large saucepan. Cover and wilt over medium heat for 1–2 minutes.

2. Remove from heat and stir in 1 cup bread crumbs, salt, and pepper.

3. Spoon spinach mixture into a flat, shallow, greased baking dish.

4. Break eggs into a bowl, being careful not to break the yolks. Pour over spinach mixture.

5. Cover with the remaining ½ cup bread crumbs. Sprinkle the cheese over all.

6. Bake at 375° for 15 minutes, or until the eggs are well set and the bread crumbs are browned.

Greek Eggs

**Mrs. Rosanne Hankins,
Stevensville, Maryland**

Makes 4 servings
Prep. Time: 15 minutes
Cooking Time: 20 minutes

2 garlic cloves, sliced

¼ cup sliced white onion

1 Tbsp. oil

1 lb. fresh chopped spinach

8 eggs, beaten

1 Tbsp. fresh chopped oregano

4 ozs. feta cheese

1. In large skillet, sauté garlic and onion in oil for 3–4 minutes.

2. Stir in spinach and let wilt.

3. Pour eggs and oregano into hot skillet.

4. Cook, turning 2–3 times until eggs are lightly cooked, about 5 minutes.

5. Turn off heat, crumble cheese over top of spinach-egg mixture. Cover and let set for 2 minutes, or until cheese melts into eggs.

Variations:

1. For added color and flavor, stir half a red bell pepper, chopped, into Step 1.
2. For additional flavor, add ¼ tsp. black or white pepper and ⅛ tsp. salt in Step 3.

Potato-Bacon Gratin

**Valerie Drobel,
Carlisle, PA**

Makes 6 servings
Prep. Time: 15 minutes
Baking Time: 1 hour

6-oz. bag fresh spinach

1 clove garlic, minced

1 Tbsp. olive oil

4 large potatoes, peeled or unpeeled, *divided*

6-oz. Canadian bacon slices, *divided*

6-oz. Swiss cheddar, or Gruyere, cheese,
   grated, and *divided*

1 cup chicken broth

1. In large skillet, sauté spinach and garlic in olive oil just until spinach is wilted.

2. Cut potatoes into thin slices.

3. In 2-quart baking dish, layer ⅓ the potatoes, half the bacon, ⅓ the cheese, and half the wilted spinach.

4. Repeat layers ending with potatoes. Reserve ⅓ cheese for later.

5. Pour chicken broth over all.

6. Cover and bake at 350° for 45 minutes.

7. Uncover and bake 15 more minutes. During last 5 minutes, top with cheese.

8. Allow to stand 10 minutes before serving.

TIP

Leftovers are delicious. Make two of these at a time and freeze one.

Gold Rush Brunch

Trish Dick,
Ladysmith, WI

Makes 12 servings
Prep. Time: 2 hours
Baking Time: 40 minutes

4 large potatoes, peeled or unpeeled

half stick (4 Tbsp.) butter, *divided*

2 Tbsp. onion

1 lb. sausage, ham, or bacon

8 eggs

4 Tbsp. fresh-chopped parsley

1 lb. shredded cheddar cheese, *divided*

White Sauce:
half stick (4 Tbsp.) butter

¼ tsp. salt

1¾ cups milk

¼ cup cornstarch

1 cup sour cream, optional

1. Cook potatoes until just soft. Cool to room temperature. Then refrigerate until chilled through.

2. When potatoes are cold, grate.

3. Melt 2 Tbsp. butter in large skillet. Stir potatoes and onion into skillet. Cook until lightly browned.

4. Spread in well-greased 9 × 13 baking pan.

5. Brown sausage or bacon or ham in same skillet. Drain off drippings.

6. Crumble over potato layer in baking pan.

7. In a bowl, beat the eggs and then stir in the parsley.

8. Melt 2 Tbsp. butter in skillet. Pour eggs into skillet. Cook, stirring up from the bottom until eggs are scrambled and just set.

9. Layer eggs over meat.

10. Sprinkle with half of shredded cheese.

11. Make white sauce by melting butter in saucepan.

12. Stir in salt, milk, and cornstarch. Stir continually with a wooden spoon until bubbly and thickened.

13. Remove from heat. Stir in sour cream if you wish.

14. Pour white sauce over egg layer in pan.

15. Sprinkle with remaining shredded cheese.

16. Bake at 350° for 40 minutes. Insert knife blade in center. If it comes out clean, the dish is finished. If it doesn't, continue baking another 5 minutes. Test again with knife blade. Continue cooking—and testing—as needed.

17. Allow to stand 10 minutes before cutting and serving.

Fair Warning:
This is delicious, but time-consuming!

Turkey Sausage

**Becky Frey,
Lebanon, PA**

Makes 6 servings
Prep. Time: 10 minutes
Broiling Time: 10–15 minutes

¾ lb. extra-lean skinless turkey, ground

¼ tsp. pepper

½ tsp. fresh chopped basil

½ tsp. fresh chopped sage

¾ tsp. fresh chopped oregano

1 small clove garlic, minced

1 egg white

⅛ tsp. allspice

⅛ tsp. nutmeg

⅛ tsp. chili powder

⅛ tsp. Tabasco sauce, optional

2 Tbsp. water

TIP

1. This turkey sausage can be shaped into meatballs and used with spaghetti or another favorite sauce.
2. I often brown this sausage and use it in any casserole in which I want a sausage flavor, but without the extra fat or salt of commercially made sausage.

1. Mix all ingredients together in a large bowl.

2. Shape into 6 patties. Place on baking sheet.

3. Broil 2–3" from heat 5–7 minutes.

4. Flip burgers over. Broil 5–7 more minutes.

Spinach Mushroom Frittata

J. B. Miller,
Indianapolis, IN

Makes 6 servings
Prep. Time: 20 minutes
Cooking/Baking Time: 25–30 minutes

3 cloves garlic, minced

1 cup onion, chopped

1 tsp. olive oil

½ lb. fresh mushrooms, sliced

½ tsp. dried thyme

10-oz. bag fresh spinach

egg substitute equivalent to 10 eggs

1 Tbsp. fresh chopped dill

¼ tsp. black pepper

¼ cup feta cheese

1. Preheat oven to 350°.

2. In a large 10" or 12" nonstick skillet, sauté garlic and onion in 1 teaspoon olive oil for about 5 minutes.

3. Add mushrooms and thyme. Cook an additional 5 minutes. Remove skillet from stove.

4. Place spinach in a separate saucepan. Add 1 Tbsp. water. Cover and cook until just wilted.

5. Drain spinach and let cool in a colander.

6. Squeeze out any liquid. Chop leaves.

7. In a good-sized bowl, beat together egg substitute, dill, and pepper.

8. Stir in spinach, mushroom mixture, and feta cheese.

9. Clean nonstick skillet. Spray liberally with vegetable spray. Return skillet to stove over medium heat.

10. When skillet is hot, pour in egg mixture. Place in oven, uncovered.

11. Check frittata in 10 minutes. Check every 5 minutes thereafter until center of frittata is slightly firm. Do not overcook.

12. When frittata is done, place a large serving platter over skillet. Flip skillet over so frittata falls onto the plate.

13. Cut into six servings and serve.

Rosemary Romano Bread

Doyle Rounds,
Bridgewater, VA

Makes 14-16 servings
Prep. Time: 5 minutes
Optional Standing Time: 2-3 hours
Cooking/Baking Time: 15 minutes

1 stick (½ cup) butter, softened

½ cup grated Romano cheese

1 garlic clove, minced

1 tsp. minced fresh rosemary

1-lb. loaf French bread, halved lengthwise

1. In a mixing bowl, stir together the softened butter, cheese, garlic, and rosemary. Allow to stand for 2–3 hours to allow flavors to blend, if you have time.

2. Spread topping over cut sides of bread.

3. Place halves with cut side up on an ungreased baking sheet.

4. Bake at 400° for 15 minutes, or until lightly browned. (Check frequently to be sure the bread isn't getting too dark.)

5. Slice and serve warm.

Breads

Oatmeal Herb Bread

Stacy Stoltzfus,
Grantham, PA

Makes 1 loaf
Prep. Time: 20 minutes
Rising Time: 65-85 minutes
Cooking/Baking Time: 30-35 minutes
Standing Time: 30-45 minutes

2 Tbsp. brown sugar

1 cup warm water (110-115°)

1 Tbsp. yeast

1 egg, lightly beaten

3 Tbsp. olive oil

1 tsp. salt

½ cup quick oats

2 tsp. fresh minced parsley

2 tsp. fresh minced sage

1 Tbsp. fresh minced oregano

2 tsp. fresh minced basil

1 Tbsp. fresh minced thyme

3½-4 cups bread flour

1. Dissolve sugar in warm water in a large mixing bowl.

2. Sprinkle yeast over top.

3. Let stand 5–10 minutes until yeast begins to foam.

4. Stir in egg, olive oil, salt, oats, and herbs.

5. Gradually add in flour, one cup at a time, mixing until a ball forms that is not too dense. Dough should be soft but not sticky.

6. Knead about 5 minutes on floured surface.

7. Grease a large bowl. Place dough in bowl and cover with a tea towel.

8. Place in warm spot. Let rise until doubled, about 30–45 minutes.

9. Punch down. Form into a loaf.

10. Place in greased loaf pan. Let rise until dough comes to top of pan, about 35–40 minutes.

11. Bake approximately 30–35 minutes at 350°. Loaf should be golden brown and should sound hollow when tapped.

12. Cool 10 minutes before removing from pan.

13. Let cool until lukewarm before slicing to keep moisture in the loaf. Slice the loaf just before serving.

TIPS

1. I always use an instant-read thermometer to ensure the bread is completely baked through. It should register 190–200 when done.
2. This is my favorite herb blend; feel free to substitute other herbs. This bread also makes wonderful croutons!
3. You can use dried herbs instead of fresh herbs. The formula? 1 tsp. dried herbs for 3 tsp. fresh herbs.

Tomato Bread

Betty Hostetler,
Allensville, PA

Makes 2 loaves
Prep. Time: 35-40 minutes
Rising Time: 70-100 minutes
Baking Time: 20-25 minutes

2 cups tomato juice

2 Tbsp. butter

3 Tbsp. sugar

1 tsp. salt

1 tsp. fresh minced basil

1½ tsp. fresh minced oregano

¼ cup ketchup

¼ cup grated cheese

1 pkg. dry granulated yeast

¼ cup warm water (110-115°)

7 cups bread flour, sifted

1. In saucepan, heat tomato juice and butter together until butter is melted.

2. Stir in sugar, salt, herbs, ketchup, and cheese. Cool to lukewarm.

3. In a large electric mixer bowl, sprinkle yeast on warm water. Stir to dissolve.

4. Add tomato mixture and 3 cups flour to yeast. Beat at medium speed for 2 minutes or until smooth.

5. Gradually add enough remaining flour to make soft dough that leaves the sides of the bowl.

6. Turn onto slightly floured board. Knead for 8–10 minutes, until elastic and smooth.

7. Place in lightly greased bowl, turning once. Cover and let rise in warm place until double, about 1–1½ hours.

8. Punch down. Divide in half. Cover and let rest 10 minutes.

9. Shape into loaves. Place in greased loaf pans. Cover and let rise until doubled, about 1 hour.

10. Bake at 375° for 15 minutes. Cover with foil and bake an additional 10 minutes.

Wholesome Harvest Bread

Kathryn Good,
Dayton, VA

Makes 3 loaves, 17 slices/loaf, each sliced
½" thick
Prep. Time: 20–30 minutes
Rising Time: 4–5 hours
Baking Time: 30–35 minutes

½ cup cornmeal

½ cup honey

⅓ cup (5⅓ Tbsp.) butter, or olive oil

1 Tbsp. salt

2 cups boiling water

2 pkgs. yeast

½ cup warm water

1 tsp. sugar

4 egg whites

1 cup rye flour

2 cups whole wheat flour

3 Tbsp. poppy seeds

1 cup sunflower seed kernels

4 cups unbleached bread flour

1. In a small bowl, combine cornmeal, honey, butter or olive oil, salt, and boiling water. Let stand until mixture cools to lukewarm.

2. Meanwhile, in a large mixing bowl combine yeast, warm water, and sugar. Stir until yeast and sugar dissolve.

3. Beat eggs into yeast mixture.

4. When cornmeal mixture is lukewarm, mix into yeast mixture.

5. Stir in rye flour, wheat flour, and seeds.

6. On a lightly floured surface, knead in bread flour until dough is smooth and elastic.

7. Return dough to bowl. Cover and place in a warm spot. Let rise until double, about 2½–3 hours. Form into 3 loaves. Place each in a 2½ × 4½ × 8½ loaf pan that has been generously sprayed with cooking spray.

8. Cover pans and place in a warm spot.

9. Let rise until almost double in size, about 1½–2 hours.

10. Bake at 350° for approximately 30 minutes, or until tops are golden.

Refrigerator Butterhorns

Becky Frey,
Lebanon, PA

Makes 36–48 rolls
Prep. Time: 15–20 minutes
Rising Time: 7–9 hours
Baking Time: 10–12 minutes

1 Tbsp., or 1 pkg., fast-rise, dry yeast

½ cup sugar

1 tsp. salt

6 cups flour

¾ cup butter or margarine, cut in pieces, at room temperature

2 cups warm (120-130°) milk

1 egg, beaten

2 Tbsp. water

1. In a large mixing bowl, combine yeast, sugar, salt, and flour.

2. In a separate bowl, add butter to warm milk. Stir until butter melts. Beat in egg and water.

3. Pour liquid into flour mixture. Mix well, but do not knead. Dough will be sticky.

4. Cover with well-greased waxed paper. Refrigerate 4–5 hours.

5. Divide dough into three parts. Roll each into a 9"–10" circle on a lightly floured counter.

6. Cut each circle into 12–16 wedges. Roll each wedge up, beginning with the point and rolling toward the wide end, as you would to make a butterhorn. Place on greased cookie sheets, about 2 inches apart from each other.

7. Cover with waxed paper. Let rise 3–4 hours, or until double in size.

8. Bake at 375° for 10–12 minutes, or until golden brown.

Variations:

1. For whole wheat rolls: Replace flour with whole wheat flour. Add 1 Tbsp. wheat gluten to dry ingredients (in Step 1). Add 1 Tbsp. liquid soy lecithin to wet ingredients (in Step 2).
2. For part-whole wheat rolls: Use 3 cups white flour and 3 cups whole wheat flour.

NOTE

You do not have to refrigerate the dough. I'm usually in a hurry for them. Just let the dough rise until double. Roll out and shape. Let rise again until double and bake. The rising times are much shorter when the dough is warm.

Popovers

Barbara Sparks,
Glen Burnie, MD

Makes 12 popovers
Prep. Time: 10 minutes
Cooking/Baking Time: 30 minutes

1 cup sifted flour

2 eggs, beaten

1 cup milk

¼ tsp. salt

1 medium onion, diced, optional

1. Combine all ingredients in a large mixing bowl.

2. Beat at high speed with a mixer for 3 minutes.

3. Grease 12 muffin tins. Pour batter into tins, making each half-full.

4. Bake at 450° for 15 minutes. Then reduce heat to 350° and bake 15 more minutes. Do not open oven door while popovers are baking, or they will fall.

Breads

Zucchini Sandwich Buns

Phyllis Good,
Lancaster, PA

Makes 12 rolls
Prep. Time: 30 minutes
Cooking Time: 2–3 hours
Rising Time: 1 hour
Ideal slow-cooker size: 6-qt.

1½ cups shredded zucchini

⅓ cup warm water

⅓ cup warm milk

3 Tbsp. oil

2 Tbsp. instant yeast

⅓ cup sugar

2 tsp. salt

1 cup whole wheat flour

3 cups unbleached all-purpose flour, *divided*

1. In a mixing bowl, combine zucchini, water, milk, oil, yeast, sugar, salt, and whole wheat flour. Do not pour off any liquid from zucchini.

2. Add unbleached flour a cup at a time, stirring until soft dough forms.

3. Knead 5 minutes. The dough will be sticky, but persevere!

4. Pour a little oil on dough and bowl, turning dough ball to grease it. Cover with damp kitchen towel and set aside to rise until doubled, about 1 hour.

5. Divide dough into 12 pieces. Press and roll them into balls.

6. Grease a large square of parchment paper and tuck it into the slow cooker.

7. Place rolls inside slow cooker.

8. Cover and cook on High for 1½–3 hours, checking at 1½ hours by gently pulling apart two rolls in the middle and checking to make sure they are not doughy yet.

9. Wearing oven gloves to protect your knuckles, lift parchment with rolls out of cooker. Set it on wire rack to cool.

Herb Biscuits

Sharon Timpe,
Jackson, WI

Makes 7 2½" biscuits
Prep. Time: 10 minutes
Cooking/Baking Time: 14–15 minutes

2 cups self-rising flour

1½ tsp. fresh minced oregano

1 tsp. fresh minced basil

5⅓ Tbsp. (⅓ cup) butter, plus 2 Tbsp. butter, at room temperature

¾ cup buttermilk

1. Preheat oven to 450°.

2. Combine flour, oregano, and basil in a medium-sized mixing bowl.

3. Cut ⅓ cup butter into flour mixture with pastry blender until crumbly.

4. Add buttermilk, stirring just until moistened.

5. Turn dough onto a lightly floured surface and knead 3 or 4 times.

6. Place 2 Tbsp. butter in a 10" cast-iron skillet. Place skillet in the oven for 5 minutes to melt butter.

7. Meanwhile, pat or roll dough out until ½" thick. Cut out biscuits with a 2½"-round biscuit cutter. (Gather the scraps together and re-roll if needed.)

8. Remove skillet from oven and place dough rounds in skillet.

9. Bake for 14–15 minutes, until lightly brown.

Tips from Tester:
1. If you don't have self-rising flour, substitute the following for each cup of flour:
⅞ cup regular flour
1½ tsp. baking powder
½ tsp. salt
2. These biscuits are light and fluffy, but with crusty bottoms! Delicious!

Breads

Harvest Quick Bread

**Lorraine Pflederer,
Goshen, IN**

Makes 12 slices
Prep. Time: 20–30 minutes
Baking Time: 70 minutes

½ cup cut-up, pitted prunes

2 Tbsp. water

1 cup fresh cranberries, chopped

1 cup grated apple

½ cup apple juice

1 Tbsp. grated lemon peel

2 egg whites, lightly beaten

2 cups flour

½ cup sugar

½ cup brown sugar, firmly packed

1 tsp. baking powder

½ tsp. baking soda

½ tsp. cinnamon

½ tsp. nutmeg

½ cup chopped walnuts, optional

1. Place prunes and water in blender and puree.

2. Mix together prune puree, cranberries, apple, apple juice, lemon peel, and egg whites in a bowl.

3. In a separate large bowl, combine flour, sugar, brown sugar, baking powder, baking soda, cinnamon, nutmeg, and nuts, if you wish.

4. Stir the wet ingredients into the dry ingredients until just moistened. Transfer to a 9 × 5 loaf pan.

5. Bake at 350° for 1 hour and 10 minutes, or until toothpick inserted in center comes out clean. Cool in the pan for 10 minutes. Remove and finish cooling on a wire rack.

TIP

To reduce the baking time, bake in 2 smaller loaf pans. Bake 45–50 minutes, and then check with toothpick to see if the loaves are fully baked. If they are not, bake longer, checking every 5 minutes with a toothpick to see if they are finished.

Apricot Bread

Lauren Eberhard,
Seneca, IL

Makes 10 servings
Prep. Time: 10–15 minutes
Baking Time: 60 minutes

1 stick (½ cup) butter, softened

2 eggs

1 cup sugar

½ cup milk

1 tsp. orange extract

2¼ cups flour, or 1 cup whole wheat flour and
    1¼ cups flour

1 tsp. baking soda

1 cup chopped, pitted apricots

½ cup chopped nuts

1. In a large mixer bowl, cream together butter, eggs, and sugar.

2. Add milk and orange extract. Mix well.

3. Blend in flour and baking soda. Mix well.

4. Fold in apricots and nuts.

5. Pour into a greased 9 × 5 loaf pan.

6. Bake at 325° for 60 minutes, or until toothpick comes out clean.

7. Cool in pan 10 minutes. Remove from pan and place bread on wire rack.

Breads

Raspberry Chocolate-Chip Bread

**Rosanna Martin,
Morgantown, WV**

Makes 10 servings
Prep. Time: 25 minutes
Cooking Time: 3–4 hours
Ideal slow-cooker size: 6-qt.

Breads

1 cup whole wheat flour

⅔ cup all-purpose flour

¾ cup rolled oats

⅔ cup sugar

2 tsp. baking powder

1 tsp. baking soda

½ tsp. salt

½ tsp. cinnamon

½ cup fresh raspberries

⅔ cup chocolate chips

1 egg, lightly beaten

¾ cup buttermilk

⅓ cup canola oil

1 tsp. vanilla extract

1. In a large bowl, mix flours, oats, sugar, baking powder, baking soda, salt, and cinnamon. Gently stir in raspberries and chocolate chips.

2. Separately, mix egg, buttermilk, oil, and vanilla.

3. Gently stir wet ingredients into dry until just barely mixed—streaks of flour are fine.

4. Make sure your loaf pan fits in your oval 6-quart slow cooker. Grease and flour loaf pan. Set it on a jar ring or other heat-resistant item to keep it off the floor of the cooker.

5. Pour batter into prepared loaf pan.

6. Put lid on cooker, propping it open at one end with a chopstick or wooden spoon handle.

7. Cook on High for 3–4 hours, until a tester inserted in middle comes out clean.

8. Wearing oven mitts (to protect your knuckles!), remove hot pan from hot cooker and allow it to cool for 10 minutes. Run a knife around the edge and turn loaf out on a cooling rack to cool for an additional 30 minutes before slicing.

Blueberry Bread

Renee Baum,
Chambersburg, PA

Makes 1 loaf
Prep. Time: 10–15 minutes
Baking Time: 1 hour

1 egg

1 cup sugar

2 Tbsp. vegetable oil

⅔ cup orange juice

2 cups flour

1½ tsp. baking powder

½ tsp. baking soda

½ tsp. salt

1 cup fresh blueberries

1. Place egg in large mixing bowl and beat well.

2. Add sugar, oil, and orange juice, and continue beating till well mixed.

3. In a separate bowl, sift together flour, baking powder, baking soda, and salt. Add to wet ingredients and mix well.

4. Gently stir in blueberries.

5. Pour into greased 9 × 5 loaf pan.

6. Bake at 350° for 1 hour.

Strawberry Bread

**Sally Holzem,
Schofield, WI**

Makes 2 loaves
Prep. Time: 20 minutes
Baking Time: 45-60 minutes

3 cups flour

2 cups sugar

1 tsp. baking soda

1 tsp. salt

1 tsp. cinnamon

4 eggs beaten

1¼ cups vegetable oil

2 cups fresh strawberries, chopped

1 cup chopped pecans, optional

Frosting:

half an 8-oz. block of cream cheese, softened

1 tsp. vanilla

9-10 Tbsp. butter, softened

1½ cups confectioners' sugar

chopped nuts, optional

1. In a large bowl, combine flour, sugar, baking soda, salt, and cinnamon. When well mixed, form a well in the center of the mixture.

2. In a separate bowl, combine beaten eggs, vegetable oil, strawberries, and chopped pecans. Pour into well in dry ingredients and stir until evenly mixed.

3. Spoon mixture into 2 greased and floured 9 × 5 loaf pans.

4. Bake at 350° for 45–60 minutes, until a tester inserted in the center of the tops of the loaves comes out clean.

5. Let loaves cool in pans for 10 minutes. Remove to wire racks and let cool completely.

6. To make the frosting, beat cream cheese, vanilla, and butter together until creamy in a medium-sized bowl. Gently stir in confectioners' sugar and chopped nuts until well distributed. Spread frosting over cooled bread.

TIP

This bread freezes well.

Carrot 'n Spice Quick Bread

Sally Holzem,
Schofield, WI

Makes 1 loaf; ½" slice per serving
Prep. Time: 20 minutes
Baking Time: 45 minutes

½ cup sifted all-purpose flour

1 cup whole wheat flour

2 tsp. baking powder

½ tsp. baking soda

½ tsp. ground cinnamon

¼ tsp. ground ginger

⅓ cup trans-fat-free buttery blend, softened to room temperature

¼ cup, plus 2 Tbsp., firmly packed brown sugar

⅓ cup skim milk

2 Tbsp. unsweetened orange juice

2 egg whites, beaten

1 tsp. vanilla extract

1 tsp. grated orange rind

1½ cups shredded carrots

2 Tbsp. golden raisins

1 Tbsp. finely chopped walnuts

1. Combine first 6 ingredients in a small bowl. Set aside.

2. Using a mixer, or stirring vigorously by hand, cream buttery blend in a good-sized mixing bowl.

3. Gradually add brown sugar, beating well.

4. Beat in milk, orange juice, egg whites, vanilla, and orange rind.

5. Stir in carrots, raisins, and walnuts.

6. Add reserved dry ingredients. Mix well.

7. Spoon batter into 2½ × 4½ × 8½ loaf pan coated with cooking spray.

8. Bake at 375° for 45 minutes, or until wooden pick inserted in center comes out clean.

9. Cool in pan 10 minutes. Remove from pan and let cool completely on wire rack.

TIP

Slicing fruit breads is always easier after chilling the loaf in the refrigerator overnight.

Zucchini Bread

Esther J. Yoder,
Hartville, OH

Makes 10 servings
Prep. Time: 25 minutes
Cooking Time: 3–4 hours
Cooling Time: 40 minutes
Ideal slow-cooker size: 6-qt., oval

2 eggs

2 cups shredded zucchini (no need to peel zucchini)

1 cup brown sugar

⅔ cup oil

1 tsp. vanilla extract

1 cup chopped walnuts, optional

8-oz. pkg. cream cheese, at room temperature

1½ cups whole wheat flour

½ cup rolled oats

1 tsp. baking powder

1 tsp. baking soda

1 ½ tsp. ground cinnamon

½ tsp. nutmeg

1 tsp. salt

1. Mix eggs, zucchini, brown sugar, oil, vanilla, and nuts (if using) in a big bowl.

2. Cut cream cheese into cubes. Using an electric mixer or food processor, beat in until smooth.

3. Separately, mix flour, oats, baking powder, baking soda, cinnamon, nutmeg, and salt.

4. Combine wet and dry ingredients, mixing gently until just combined.

5. Make sure you have a loaf pan that fits in your oval 6-quart cooker. Grease and flour loaf pan.

6. Pour batter into prepared pan and place in cooker, either on the bottom or hanging from the top edge.

7. Prop lid open at one end with a chopstick or wooden spoon handle.

8. Cook on High 3–4 hours, or until tester inserted in middle comes out clean.

9. Wearing oven mitts to protect your knuckles, remove hot pan and allow to sit for 10 minutes.

10. Run knife around edges and turn loaf out to cool for 30 more minutes before slicing.

TIP

When the garden is really churning out zucchini, I make sure I shred some and put it in the freezer in 2-cup amounts. Then, in the winter, we enjoy the scent of this zucchini bread baking.

Breads

Morning Glory Muffins

**Mary Jane Hoober,
Shipshewana, IN**

Makes about 36 muffins
Prep. Time: 25–30 minutes
Baking Time: 20 minutes

3 eggs

1 cup vegetable oil

2 tsp. vanilla

1¼ cups sugar

2 cups, plus 2 Tbsp., flour

2 tsp. baking soda

2 tsp. cinnamon

½ tsp. salt

2 cups grated carrots

1 cup raisins

½ cup nuts, chopped

½ cup grated coconut

1 apple, peeled, cored, and grated, or
chopped finely

1. In a large mixing bowl beat eggs. Then add oil, vanilla, and sugar and combine well.

2. In a separate mixing bowl, stir together flour, baking soda, cinnamon, and salt. When well mixed, add remaining ingredients.

3. Pour dry-fruit ingredients into creamed ingredients. Blend just until everything is moistened.

4. Fill greased muffin tins ⅔ full. Bake at 350° for 20 minutes, or until tester inserted in center comes out clean.

Breads

Apple Cranberry Muffins

Judy Buller,
Bluffton, OH

Makes 12 servings
Prep. Time: 20 minutes
Baking Time: 15 minutes

1⅓ cups whole wheat pastry flour

⅓ cup brown sugar

2 tsp. baking powder

½ tsp. baking soda

½ tsp. cinnamon

⅛ tsp. nutmeg

pinch of cloves

4 egg whites

¼ cup canola oil

1 cup fat-free sour cream

1 large Granny Smith apple, peeled and shredded

½ cup fresh cranberries cut in half

½ cup chopped walnuts, optional

1. Heat oven to 400°. Spray nonstick canola spray on bottom of 12 muffin cups.

2. In large bowl, whisk together flour, sugar, baking powder, baking soda, cinnamon, nutmeg, and cloves.

3. In medium bowl, whisk together egg whites, oil, and sour cream until blended.

4. Stir apples and cranberries, and walnuts if you wish, into wet ingredients. Mix well.

5. Add wet mixture to dry mixture, stirring just until blended.

6. Divide batter among muffin cups.

7. Bake 15 minutes, or until toothpick inserted in centers of muffins comes out clean.

8. Cool 5–10 minutes before serving.

Orange Bran Flax Muffins

Alice Rush,
Quakertown, PA

Makes 24 servings
Prep. Time: 15–20 minutes
Baking Time: 18–20 minutes

1½ cups dry oat bran

1 cup all-purpose flour

¾ cup ground flaxseed

1 cup wheat bran

1 Tbsp. baking powder

½ tsp. salt

2 oranges, peeled and sectioned to remove membranes and seeds

1 cup brown sugar

1 cup low-fat buttermilk

⅓ cup canola oil

4 egg whites

1 tsp. baking soda

1½ cups raisins

1. Preheat oven to 375°. Line two 12-cup muffin pans with paper liners, or coat cups lightly with cooking spray.

2. In a large bowl, combine oat bran, flour, flaxseed, wheat bran, baking powder, and salt. Set aside.

3. In blender or food processor, combine orange sections, brown sugar, buttermilk, oil, egg whites, and baking soda. Blend well.

4. Pour orange mixture into dry ingredients. Mix until well blended.

5. Stir in raisins.

6. Divide batter evenly among muffin cups.

7. Bake 18–20 minutes, or until toothpick inserted in centers comes out clean.

8. Cool in pans 5 minutes and then remove muffins to cooling rack.

Zucchini Oatmeal Muffins

Donna Lantgen,
Arvada, CO

Makes 30 muffins
Prep. Time: 15 minutes
Baking Time: 20–25 minutes

2½ cups flour

1½ cups sugar

½ cup oats, quick or old-fashioned

1 Tbsp. baking powder

1 tsp. salt

1 tsp. cinnamon

1 cup chopped walnuts

4 eggs

1¼ cups shredded zucchini, peeled or
unpeeled

¾ cup oil

1. Mix flour, sugar, oats, baking powder, salt, cinnamon, and walnuts together in large mixing bowl.

2. In a separate bowl, combine eggs, zucchini, and oil.

3. Stir wet ingredients into dry ingredients, until just mixed. Do not over-stir.

4. Fill greased baking tins half-full. (Or use paper liners instead of greasing tins.)

5. Bake at 400° for 25 minutes, or until toothpick inserted in centers of muffins comes out clean.

TIP

Shredding zucchini in your food processor makes things easier.

Raspberry Chocolate Scones

**Vonnie Oyer,
Hubbard, OR**

Makes 12 servings
Prep. Time: 15 minutes
Baking Time: 10–12 minutes

1 cup whole wheat pastry flour

1 cup all-purpose flour

1 Tbsp. baking powder

¼ tsp. baking soda

⅓ cup trans-fat-free buttery spread

½ cup fresh raspberries

¼ cup miniature chocolate chips

1 cup, plus 2 Tbsp., plain nonfat yogurt

2 Tbsp. honey

½ tsp. sugar

¼ tsp. cinnamon

1. Mix flours, baking powder, and baking soda in a large mixing bowl.

2. Cut in buttery spread until crumbly.

3. Add berries and chocolate chips. Mix gently.

4. Mix yogurt and honey together in a small bowl.

5. Add yogurt mixture to flour mixture, mixing until just blended.

6. Place ball of dough on countertop. Knead one or two times.

7. Roll into a ½"-thick circle. Cut into 12 wedges. Place on lightly greased baking sheet.

8. Mix sugar and cinnamon together in small bowl.

9. Sprinkle over top of scones.

10. Bake at 400° for 10–12 minutes.

Soups

Creamy Asparagus Soup

**Mary E. Riha,
Antigo, WI**

Makes 4 servings
Prep. Time: 30 minutes
Cooking Time: 15–20 minutes

¼ cup sesame seeds

2 Tbsp. olive oil

1 medium onion, chopped

2 medium potatoes, cubed

4 cups chicken stock, *divided*

1 lb. raw asparagus, broken in 1" pieces

1 tsp. salt

dash of pepper

dash of nutmeg

sour cream

salted sunflower seeds, optional

1. In stockpot, sauté sesame seeds in olive oil until brown. Add onions and potatoes. Cook and stir until potatoes begin to stick.

2. Add 2 cups stock, asparagus, salt, and pepper. Bring to boil. Reduce heat and simmer until potatoes are done.

3. Carefully pour one-fourth of hot mixture into blender. Cover and blend until smooth. (Hold the lid on with a potholder to keep the heat from pushing it off.)

4. Put pureed soup back in stockpot. Continue blending cooked soup, one-fourth at a time. Continue to add pureed soup back into stockpot.

5. When all soup has been pureed, add 2 more cups chicken stock to soup in stockpot. Heat thoroughly.

6. Add a dash of nutmeg.

7. Top each serving with a dollop of sour cream and a sprinkling of sunflower seeds.

Butternut Squash Soup

Stephanie O'Conner,
Cheshire, CT

Makes 6-8 servings
Prep. Time: 15-20 minutes
Cooking Time: 35 minutes

1 shallot, finely chopped

4 Tbsp. butter

3-lb. butternut squash, peeled and cubed

11 whole leaves of fresh sage, washed, *divided*

4 cups chicken stock

½ tsp. salt

¼ tsp. pepper

⅓ cup heavy cream

½ cup light brown sugar

1 tsp. ground cinnamon

pinch of nutmeg

1. In stockpot, sauté the shallot in butter over medium heat.

2. Add squash, 3 sage leaves, chicken stock, salt, and pepper. Cover and bring to a boil. Simmer, covered, for 20–30 minutes, until squash falls apart when stuck with a fork.

3. Puree soup by portions in a firmly covered blender, 2 cups at a time. When you've finished, return pureed mixture to stockpot.

4. Stir in cream, brown sugar, cinnamon, and nutmeg over low heat. Taste the soup to determine whether or not to add more cinnamon, sugar, salt, and pepper.

5. Serve garnished with whole leaves of fresh sage.

Soups

Fresh Tomato Soup

Rebecca Leichty, Harrisonburg, VA

Makes 6 servings
Prep. Time: 20–25 minutes
Cooking Time: 3–4 hours
Ideal slow-cooker size: 3½- or 4-qt.

5 cups diced ripe tomatoes (your choice about whether or not to peel them)

1 Tbsp. tomato paste

4 cups salt-free chicken broth

1 carrot, peeled, grated

1 small onion, minced

1 Tbsp. fresh minced garlic

2 tsp. fresh chopped basil

Pepper, to taste

2 Tbsp. fresh lemon juice

1 dried bay leaf

1. Combine all ingredients in a slow cooker.

2. Cook on Low for 3–4 hours. Stir once while cooking.

3. Remove bay leaf before serving.

Apple Butternut Squash Soup

Ann Bender,
New Hope, VA

Makes 6 servings
Prep. Time: 30 minutes
Cooking Time: 30 minutes

3 cups butternut, or acorn, squash, peeled, seeded, and cubed

1 large apple, peeled and sliced

1½ Tbsp. chopped onion

1 clove garlic, minced

1 Tbsp. tub-style margarine, non-hydrogenated

2 Tbsp. flour

¾ tsp. fresh minced thyme

¼ tsp. salt, or North Woods seasoning

⅛ tsp. pepper

10½-oz. can low-fat low-sodium chicken, or vegetable, broth

2 Tbsp. fat-free sour cream

1. Steam squash and apple in steamer or microwave until very tender.

2. In large saucepan, sauté onion and garlic in margarine until onion is clear.

3. Stir flour and seasonings into saucepan.

4. Add broth. Heat, stirring continually until smooth and slightly thickened.

5. Pour broth and cooked vegetables into blender. Cover and blend carefully until smooth.

6. Serve immediately. Top each individual serving with 1 tsp. sour cream.

Slow-Cooker Tomato Soup

Becky Fixel,
Grosse Pointe Farms, MI

Makes 8 servings
Prep. Time: 15 minutes
Cooking Time: 6 hours
Ideal slow-cooker size: 6-qt.

6–8 cups chopped fresh tomatoes

1 medium onion, chopped

2 tsp. fresh minced garlic

2 tsp. fresh chopped basil

½ tsp. pepper

½ tsp. sea salt

½ tsp. red pepper flakes

2 Tbsp. chicken bouillon

1 cup water

¾ cup fat-free half-and-half

1. Combine tomatoes, onion, spices, chicken bouillon, and 1 cup of water in your slow cooker.

2. Cover and cook on low for 6 hours.

3. Add in ¾ cup fat-free half-and-half and combine all ingredients with an immersion blender. Serve hot.

Soups

Tomato Mushroom Soup

D. Fern Ruth,
Chalfont, PA

Makes 4-6 servings
Prep. Time: 15 minutes
Cooking Time: 30 minutes

2 cups sliced fresh mushrooms

⅓ cup chopped onion

2 garlic cloves, minced

4 Tbsp. butter

6 Tbsp. flour

2 14.5-oz. cans chicken broth

2 14.5-oz. cans diced tomatoes, undrained, or
   10-12 whole tomatoes, peeled, chopped

4 Tbsp. chopped, fresh basil leaves

1 Tbsp. sugar

1 tsp. salt

¼ tsp. pepper

1. In a large saucepan, sauté mushrooms, onion, and garlic in butter until tender. Remove vegetables from pan and set aside. Leave as much of the drippings as you can in the pan.

2. In the same pan, combine flour and chicken broth with drippings until smooth. Bring to boil and stir 2–4 minutes, or until thickened.

3. Return mushroom mixture to saucepan and stir into thickened chicken broth.

4. Add tomatoes, basil, sugar, salt, and pepper. Cook over medium heat 10–15 minutes, stirring occasionally.

5. Remove from heat. Cool slightly. Then puree in tightly covered blender (¼ of the mixture at a time) until smooth.

6. Garnish with basil leaves and serve hot.

TIP

Flavors blend nicely when you make the soup a day ahead and allow it to stand overnight.

Soups

Fresh Vegetable Soup

**Sandra Chang,
Derwood, MD**

Makes 4-6 servings
Prep. Time: 25-30 minutes
Cooking Time: 60-70 minutes
Standing Time: 1 hour

4 Tbsp. butter

½ cup diced celery

½ cup diced onions

½ cup small chunks of peeled carrots

½ cup chopped cabbage

½ cup diced zucchini

½ cup fresh whole-kernel corn

½ cup fresh cut-up green beans

2 cups canned whole tomatoes, or 2 cups
    fresh whole tomatoes, peeled

4 cups beef stock

2 Tbsp. sugar

salt to taste

pepper to taste

½ cup fresh or frozen petite peas

1. In 4-quart saucepan, melt butter. Sauté celery, onions, carrots, cabbage, and zucchini in butter until vegetables are soft but not brown.

2. Add rest of ingredients, except ½ cup peas.

3. Simmer gently for 30–45 minutes, or until vegetables are cooked but not mushy.

4. Take pan off heat and stir in peas. Allow soup to stand for one hour before serving.

5. Reheat just until heated through and serve.

Soups

Garden Vegetable Soup with Pasta

Jan McDowell,
New Holland, PA

Makes 6 servings
Prep. Time: 20 minutes
Cooking Time: 30 minutes

1 Tbsp. olive oil

1 chopped onion

1 tsp. chopped garlic

1 small zucchini, chopped

½ lb. fresh mushrooms, sliced or chopped

1 bell pepper, chopped

24-oz. can chopped tomatoes, no salt added,
    undrained, or 10–12 whole tomatoes,
    peeled and chopped

1 Tbsp. fresh basil

2 cups water

3 reduced-sodium vegetable bouillon cubes

2 cups whole-grain rotini, cooked

dash of hot sauce, optional

1. Heat olive oil in 4-quart saucepan.

2. Sauté onion and garlic in oil until tender.

3. Add zucchini, mushrooms, bell pepper, tomatoes, basil, water, and bouillon.

4. Bring to a boil. Cover and simmer 10 minutes.

5. Meanwhile, cook rotini and drain. Add to soup.

6. Cover and heat through.

7. Pass hot sauce to be added to individual servings, if desired.

Soups

Veggie Minestrone

**Dorothy VanDeest,
Memphis, TN**

Makes 8 servings
Prep. Time: 15 minutes
Cooking Time: 25–30 minutes
Standing Time: 5–10 minutes

1 large onion, chopped

1 garlic clove, minced

4 cups fat-free low-sodium chicken, or vegetable, broth

16-oz. can kidney beans, rinsed and drained

½ cup elbow macaroni, uncooked

14½-oz. can diced tomatoes, undrained, no salt added, or 5–6 whole tomatoes, peeled and chopped

2 medium carrots, sliced thin

¾ tsp. fresh chopped oregano

1 lb. fresh spinach, chopped

½ cup grated Parmesan cheese

1. Lightly spray inside bottom of stockpot. Sauté onion and garlic until tender.

2. Add broth, beans, macaroni, tomatoes, carrots, and oregano.

3. Cover and cook until vegetables and macaroni are tender, about 20 minutes.

4. Stir in spinach. Bring to a boil.

5. Remove pan from heat. Let stand, covered, 5–10 minutes before serving.

6. Sprinkle 1 Tbsp. grated Parmesan on each individual bowl of this comfort soup.

Soups

Vegetarian Split Pea Soup

Colleen Heatwole, Burton, MI

Makes 6 servings
Prep. Time: 30 minutes
Cooking Time: 5–6 hours
Ideal slow-cooker size: 6-qt.

1 lb. split peas, sorted and rinsed

2 quarts gluten-free low-sodium
    vegetable broth

2 cups water

1 large onion, chopped

2 cloves garlic, minced

3 ribs celery, chopped

3 medium carrots, chopped finely

2 bay leaves

1 tsp. kosher salt

1 tsp. black pepper

Serving suggestion:
If creamy texture is desired, blend with immersion blender.

1. Combine all ingredients and add to slow cooker.

2. Cover and cook on low 5–6 hours. Remove bay leaves and serve.

Soups

Vegetable Minestrone

**Marcia S. Myer,
Manheim, PA**

Makes 12 servings
Prep. Time: 20 minutes
Cooking Time: 6¼–8¼ hours
Ideal slow-cooker size: 5-qt.

4 cups low-fat, low-sodium chicken broth

4 cups low-sodium tomato juice

2 Tbsp. fresh minced basil

1 tsp. salt

1½ tsp. fresh chopped oregano

¼ tsp. black pepper

2 medium-sized carrots, sliced

2 ribs celery, chopped

1 medium-sized onion, chopped

1 cup fresh mushrooms, sliced

2 cloves garlic, crushed

28-oz. can low-sodium diced tomatoes, or
    10–12 whole tomatoes, peeled and diced

1½ cups uncooked rotini pasta

1. Combine all ingredients except pasta in slow cooker.

2. Cover. Cook on low 6–8 hours.

3. Add pasta.

4. Cover. Cook on high 15–20 minutes.

Soups

Spring Pea Soup

**Ary Bruno,
Stevenson, MD**

Makes 4-6 servings
Prep. Time: 15 minutes
Cooking Time: 4 hours
Ideal slow-cooker size: 4-qt.

2 cups fresh shelled peas

3 cups chicken stock

1 rib celery, minced

2 scallions, minced

1 Tbsp. fresh chopped mint, *divided*

pinch dried thyme

salt, to taste

1 cup milk, room temperature

2 Tbsp. flour

1. Place peas, stock, celery, scallions, ½ Tbsp. mint, and thyme in slow cooker. Add salt to taste.

2. Cover and cook on Low for 3 hours, until peas are tender.

3. Add remaining ½ Tbsp. mint.

4. Use immersion blender to puree soup.

5. Whisk together milk and flour. Whisk into soup and cook on High for 30–40 minutes, until thickened. Add salt to taste.

Soups

Carrot Ginger Soup

Jean Harris Robinson,
Pemberton, NJ

Makes 8–10 servings
Prep. Time: 30 minutes
Cooking Time: 3¼–4¼ hours
Ideal slow-cooker size: 4-qt.

1 Tbsp. olive oil

3 lbs. carrots, peeled and thinly sliced

2 Tbsp. chopped ginger

2 Tbsp. minced scallion

3 ribs celery, chopped

49½-oz. can low- sodium, fat-free
   chicken broth

1 tsp. kosher salt

1 tsp. ground pepper

2 Tbsp. honey

1 cup fat-free half-and-half

1. Pour olive oil into slow cooker. Swirl to cover bottom of cooker.

2. Add carrots, ginger, scallion, and celery.

3. Pour in broth. Add salt, pepper, and honey. Stir to mix all ingredients well.

4. Cover. Cook on high 3–4 hours, or until carrots are soft.

5. Pulse with an immersion blender to purée.

6. Stir in half-and-half. Heat Soup 15–20 minutes until heated through, but don't let it boil. Serve immediately.

Orange Soup

**Carolyn Spohn,
Shawnee, KS**

Makes 4–6 servings
Prep. Time: 15 minutes
Cooking Time: 3–4 hours
Ideal slow-cooker size: 4-qt.

4 cups chopped orange vegetables such as
carrots, winter squash, red or orange bell
pepper, sweet potato, etc.

4 cups broth of choice

1 small onion, chopped

1 tart apple, cored and chopped

date syrup or brown sugar, to taste

1. Place all ingredients in slow cooker.

2. Cover and cook until vegetables are soft,
3–4 hours on High.

3. Puree with immersion blender, or
transfer soup to stand blender and puree with
lid slightly ajar for steam to escape.

TIP

This soup is best with
a variety of vegetables.

Soups

Spinach and Potato Soup

**Jane S. Lippincott,
Wynnewood, PA**

Makes 9 servings
Prep. Time: 30 minutes
Cooking Time: 45–50 minutes

2 ribs celery, chopped

1 medium onion, chopped

1 clove garlic, minced

6 cups chopped fresh spinach

2 Tbsp. olive oil

4 potatoes, unpeeled and sliced ¼" thick

32 ozs. low-fat, low-sodium chicken, or
   vegetable, stock, or less, depending upon
   how thick you like your soup

1 tsp. mustard seeds

1 Tbsp. white wine vinegar

pepper to taste

chopped chives for garnish

1. Chop celery, onion, garlic, and spinach
first so they're ready. Set aside, keeping
vegetables separate from each other.

2. In large stockpot heat olive oil on low or
medium. Add onion. Cook until soft, about
10 minutes.

3. Add garlic and cook just until slightly
softened.

4. Add celery, sliced potatoes, stock,
and mustard seeds. Cover and simmer
25–30 minutes, or until potatoes are soft.

5. Use a potato masher to mash the
mixture up a bit.

6. Add chopped spinach and vinegar.
Simmer uncovered for 10 minutes more.

7. Serve with pepper and chives sprinkled
on top of individual servings.

TIP

Try Swiss chard, collards, or
kale instead of spinach. If
using one of those greens,
add in Step 4.

Soups

Roasted Red Peppers, Vegetables, and Sweet Potato Soup

Melanie Mohler,
Ephrata, PA

Makes 6 servings
Prep. Time: 40 minutes
Cooking Time: 1 hour and 40 minutes

2 Tbsp. extra-virgin olive oil

1 medium onion, diced

2 red bell peppers, halved and seeded

2 cups peeled and cubed sweet potatoes

3–4 cloves garlic, minced

15-oz. can pinto beans, rinsed and drained

15-oz. can diced tomatoes with herbs, no salt added, undrained

4 cups low-sodium, fat-free chicken broth

croutons and grated cheese for garnish, optional

1. In large stockpot, heat oil and brown onion.

2. Meanwhile, roast peppers in toaster oven at 450°, or broil. Lay cut-side down on baking tray. Roast until skin is blackened, about 15–20 minutes.

3. Put roasted peppers in paper bag for 15 minutes until cool. Peel off skin. Chop peppers.

4. Add peppers, sweet potatoes, garlic, beans, tomatoes, and broth to pot. Bring to a boil.

5. Reduce heat, cover, and simmer 90 minutes.

6. Puree soup carefully and in small batches in blender until smooth, or leave partially chunky.

7. If you wish, garnish individual servings with croutons and/or grated cheese.

Soups

Good Old Potato Soup

Jeanne Hertzog, Bethlehem, PA
Marcia S. Myer, Manheim, PA
Rhonda Lee Schmidt, Scranton, PA
Mitzi McGlynchey, Downingtown, PA
Vera Schmucker, Goshen, IN
Kaye Schnell, Falmouth, MA
Elizabeth Yoder, Millersburg, OH

Makes 8–10 servings
Prep. Time: 15 minutes
Cooking Time: 3–6 hours
Ideal slow-cooker size: 6-qt.

6 potatoes, peeled or not, and cubed

2 leeks, chopped

2 onions, chopped

1 rib celery, sliced

4 chicken bouillon cubes

5 cups water

1 Tbsp. salt

pepper to taste

5⅔ Tbsp. (⅓ cup) butter

13-oz. can evaporated milk

2 Tbsp. fresh chopped parsley

1. Grease interior of slow-cooker crock.

2. Combine all ingredients except milk and parsley in slow cooker.

3. Cover. Cook on Low 4–6 hours, or on High 3–4 hours.

4. Stir in milk during last hour.

5. Stir in parsley just before serving.

TIP

Mash the potatoes with an immersion blender or a potato masher for a thicker consistency soup.

Variations:
1. Add one carrot, sliced, to vegetables in Step 2.
2. Instead of water and bouillon cubes, use 4–5 cups chicken stock.

TIP

Garnish with chopped chives and/or bacon bits.

Soups

Simple Potato Soup

Joyce Cox,
Port Angeles, WA

Makes 6 servings
Prep. Time: 10 minutes
Cooking Time: 6 hours
Ideal slow-cooker size: 4-qt.

6 potatoes, peeled and diced

5 cups low-sodium vegetable broth

2 cups diced onions

½ cup diced celery

½ cup diced carrots

¼ tsp. ground pepper

1½ cups evaporated milk

3 Tbsp. chopped fresh parsley

1. Combine potatoes, broth, onions, celery, carrots, and pepper in slow cooker.

2. Cover and cook on Low for 6 hours or until vegetables are tender.

3. Stir in evaporated milk and parsley. Taste to correct seasonings. Allow to heat on Low an additional 30 minutes.

Soups

Hearty Lentil and Barley Soup

Sherri Grindle,
Goshen, IN

Makes 10 servings
Prep. Time: 15 minutes
Cooking Time: 65 minutes

2 ribs celery, thinly sliced

1 medium onion, chopped

1 clove garlic, minced

2 Tbsp. olive oil

6 cups water

28-oz. can diced tomatoes, no salt added, undrained, or 10–12 whole tomatoes, peeled and diced

¾ cup uncooked lentils, rinsed

¾ cup uncooked pearl barley

2 Tbsp. (or 3 cubes) low-sodium chicken bouillon granules

1½ tsp. fresh chopped oregano

1½ tsp. fresh chopped rosemary

¼ tsp. pepper

1 cup thinly sliced carrots

1 cup (4 ozs.) shredded low-fat Swiss cheese, optional

1. In Dutch oven or soup kettle, sauté celery, onion, and garlic in oil until tender.

2. Add water, tomatoes, lentils, barley, bouillon, oregano, rosemary, and pepper.

3. Bring to a boil. Reduce heat, cover, and simmer 40 minutes, or until lentils and barley are almost tender.

4. Add carrots. Cover and simmer 15 minutes, or until carrots, lentils, and barley are tender.

5. If you wish, sprinkle each serving with 1 rounded Tbsp. cheese.

Tomato and Barley Soup

**Lizzie Ann Yoder,
Hartville, OH**

Makes 6 servings
Prep. Time: 20–30 minutes
Cooking Time: 1–1½ hours

½ cup uncooked medium barley

1 cup chopped onion

2 ribs celery, including tops, cut up

3 cups chopped fresh tomatoes

2 Tbsp. fresh basil

6 cups low-sodium, fat-free chicken, or
vegetable, stock

1–2 cups sliced fresh mushrooms, optional

1. In large stockpot combine all ingredients.

2. Bring to a boil and simmer, covered, 1 to 1½ hours, or until barley is tender.

3. If you wish, stir in mushrooms 30 minutes before end of cooking time.

Lentil, Spinach, and Rice Soup

**Jean Harris Robinson,
Cinnaminson, NJ**

Makes 10 servings
Prep. Time: 15 minutes
Cooking Time: 1¾ hours

1 large onion, diced

2 carrots, diced

1 celery rib, diced

3 Tbsp. extra-virgin olive oil

1 cup uncooked lentils

6 cups low-fat low-sodium
chicken, or vegetable, stock

4 cups water

1 cup diced tomatoes

¼ cup uncooked brown rice

1 bag (about 8 cups) fresh spinach, washed,
   dried, and chopped (with large stems
   removed)

1. In large stockpot over medium heat, sauté onion, carrots, and celery in oil for 10 minutes.

2. Add lentils and sauté another 5 minutes. Stir often.

3. Add stock and water. Cover and simmer 45 minutes. Stir occasionally.

4. Add tomatoes and brown rice.

5. Cover and simmer another 40 minutes.

6. Stir in chopped fresh spinach.

7. Cover and cook 5 minutes more.

Wild Rice Mushroom Soup

Kelly Amos,
Pittsboro, NC

Makes 4 servings
Prep. Time: 15–20 minutes
Cooking Time: 35 minutes

1 Tbsp. olive oil

half a white onion, chopped

¼ cup chopped celery

¼ cup chopped carrots

1½ cups sliced fresh white mushrooms

½ cup white wine, or ½ cup low-sodium, fat-free chicken broth

2½ cups low-sodium, fat-free chicken broth

1 cup fat-free half-and-half

2 Tbsp. flour

¾ tsp. fresh chopped thyme

black pepper

1 cup cooked wild rice

1. Put olive oil in stockpot and heat. Carefully add chopped onion, celery, and carrots. Cook until tender.

2. Add mushrooms, white wine, and chicken broth.

3. Cover and heat through.

4. In a bowl, blend half-and-half, flour, thyme, and pepper. Then stir in cooked wild rice.

5. Pour rice mixture into hot stockpot with vegetables.

6. Cook over medium heat. Stir continually until thickened and bubbly.

Beans 'n Greens Soup

Teri Sparks,
Glen Burnie, MD

Makes 10 servings
Prep. Time: 30 minutes
Cooking Time: 6–8 hours
Ideal slow-cooker size: 4- or 5-qt.

1 lb. dried 13-bean mix

5 cups gluten-free vegetable broth

¼ cup scallions, chopped

½ tsp. black pepper

¼ cup fresh chopped parsley

1 yellow onion, coarsely chopped

3 cloves garlic, chopped

1 Tbsp. olive oil

6 cups fresh kale, torn in 2-inch pieces

Greek yogurt or sour cream, optional

1. Rinse and place beans in 4-quart slow cooker.

2. Add broth, scallions, pepper, and parsley.

3. In skillet, sauté yellow onion and garlic in oil. Add to beans in slow cooker.

4. Pile kale on top of bean mixture and cover with lid (crock will be very full).

5. Cook on high for 1 hour. Greens will have wilted some, so stir to combine all ingredients. Replace lid. Cook on low for 6–8 hours.

6. Top individual servings with dollops of Greek yogurt or sour cream if you wish.

Soups

Hearty Beef Barley Soup

Karen Gingrich,
New Holland, PA

Makes 4–5 servings
Preparation Time: 5–10 minutes
Cooking Time: 35 minutes

1 lb. beef tips

2 cups sliced fresh mushrooms

1 clove garlic, minced

32-oz. can (3½ cups) beef broth

2 medium-sized carrots, sliced

¾ tsp. fresh chopped thyme

dash of pepper

½ cup quick-cooking barley

1. Cook beef in nonstick saucepan until browned and juices evaporate, about 10 minutes, stirring often.

2. Add mushrooms and garlic powder and cook until mushrooms begin to wilt, about 5 minutes.

3. Add broth, carrots, thyme, and pepper.

4. Heat to boiling. Stir in barley. Cover and cook over low heat for 20 minutes, or until barley is tender.

Soups

Barley Cabbage Soup

Betty K. Drescher,
Quakertown, PA

Makes 8 servings
Prep. Time: 20 minutes
Cooking Time: 4–10 hours
Ideal slow-cooker size: 3½- or 4-qt.

¼ cup dry pearl barley

6 cups fat-free, low-sodium meat, or vegetable, broth

1 cup chopped onion

3-4 cups green cabbage, finely chopped

¼ cup fresh parsley, chopped

½ tsp. celery salt

½ tsp. salt

⅛ tsp. black pepper

1 Tbsp. minute tapioca

1. Combine all ingredients in slow cooker.

2. Cover. Cook on low 8–10 hours or on high 4–5 hours.

Cheeseburger Soup

Marcella Heatwole, North Lawrence, OH
Jean Hindal, Grandin, IA
Beverly High, Ephrata, PA
Sherlyn Hess, Millersville, PA

Makes 8 servings
Prep. Time: 30 minutes
Cooking Time: 20-30 minutes

½ lb. ground beef

¾ cup chopped onions

¾ cup shredded carrots

¾ cup diced celery

½ tsp. fresh chopped basil

2 tsp. fresh chopped parsley

4 Tbsp. butter or margarine, *divided*

3 cups chicken broth

2 cups diced potatoes, peeled or unpeeled,
    your choice

¼ cup flour

1½ cups milk

¾ tsp. salt

¼-½ tsp. pepper

8 ozs. cheddar cheese, grated

¼ cup sour cream

1. In saucepan, brown beef. Drain. Set aside.

2. In same saucepan, sauté onions, carrots, celery, basil, and parsley in 1 Tbsp. butter until vegetables are tender.

3. Add broth, potatoes, and beef. Bring to boil. Reduce heat, cover, and simmer for 10–12 minutes, or until potatoes are tender.

4. While meat and potatoes cook, in small skillet melt 3 Tbsp. butter. Stir in flour until smooth. Cook and stir 3–5 minutes.

5. Reduce heat to low. Add milk, salt, and pepper. Stir until mixture thickens and becomes smooth.

6. Slowly stir in grated cheese, about ½-cupful at a time. Continue to stir until cheese is fully melted and blended into white sauce.

7. Blend in sour cream. Heat, but do not boil.

8. When vegetables are tender and cheesy white sauce is finished, pour the white sauce into the vegetable mixture and gently stir together.

9. When well mixed and heated through, serve.

Soups

Italian Sausage Soup

Esther Porter,
Minneapolis, MN

Makes 6-8 servings
Prep. Time: 15-25 minutes
Cooking Time: 65-70 minutes

1 lb. Italian sausage, casings removed

1 cup chopped onions

2 large garlic cloves, sliced

5 cups beef stock, or 3 14.5-oz. cans beef broth

2 cups chopped tomatoes

8-oz. can tomato sauce

1½ cups zucchini, sliced

1 carrot, thinly sliced

1 medium-sized green bell pepper, diced

1 cup fresh green beans

¼ cup fresh chopped basil

¼ cup fresh chopped oregano

8-10-oz. pkg. cheese tortellini

salt to taste

pepper to taste

freshly grated Parmesan cheese for topping

1. Sauté sausage in heavy Dutch oven over medium heat until cooked through, about 10 minutes, breaking it up as it browns with a wooden spoon.

2. Using a slotted spoon, transfer sausage to a large bowl. Pour off all but 1 Tbsp. drippings from Dutch oven. Add onions and garlic to the 1 Tbsp. drippings and sauté until clear, about 5 minutes.

3. Return sausage to pan. Add beef stock, tomatoes, tomato sauce, zucchini, carrot, pepper, green beans, basil, and oregano. Simmer 30–40 minutes, or until vegetables are tender.

4. Add tortellini and cook 8–10 minutes. Season to taste with salt and pepper.

5. Ladle hot soup into bowls and sprinkle with Parmesan cheese.

Variations:

1. Use leftover meat and vegetables from your refrigerator, instead of the sausage and the vegetables listed above.
2. Substitute V-8 juice for half of the beef stock or tomatoes.
3. When you're in a hurry, use Italian-style frozen vegetables instead of fresh beans, carrot, and zucchini.
4. Instead of tortellini, use ½-lb. package small pasta shells, uncooked.

   —Michelle Scribano, Harrisonburg, VA

Soups

Healthy Hamburger Soup

Chris Peterson,
Green Bay, WI

Makes 8 servings
Prep. Time: 20 minutes
Cooking Time: 1–2 hours

2 lbs. ground chuck

14½-oz. can stewed tomatoes

1 cup sliced mushrooms

2 cups sliced cabbage

1 cup sliced carrots

2 cups chopped celery

2 cups green beans

6 cups tomato juice

2 tsp. basil

2 Tbsp. fresh chopped oregano

1 Tbsp. Worcestershire sauce

salt and pepper to taste

1. In a soup pot, fry beef until brown, stirring often to break up clumps. Drain off the drippings.

2. Add rest of ingredients.

3. Simmer 1–2 hours.

TIP

This is a great recipe for cleaning out your refrigerator. Whatever leftover veggies you have in there—throw them in the soup. I've added broccoli or rice and it's great.

Soups

Kielbasa Soup

Janie Steele,
Moore, OK

Makes 6–8 servings
Prep. Time: 20 minutes
Cooking Time: 5 hours
Ideal slow-cooker size: 4 qt.

1 lb. kielbasa, sliced thin

8 cups chicken broth

2 14-oz. cans cannellini beans with juice

1 onion, diced

1 bay leaf

1 Tbsp. fresh chopped thyme

¼ tsp. red pepper flakes

8 oz. rainbow rotini, uncooked

3 cloves garlic, minced

1 lb. chopped fresh spinach

salt and pepper, to taste

1. In skillet, brown kielbasa slices over high heat until some edges are brown.

2. Transfer kielbasa to slow cooker.

3. Add broth, beans, onion, bay leaf, thyme, and red pepper to slow cooker.

4. Cover and cook on Low for 4 hours.

5. Add rotini and garlic. Cook an additional hour on Low, or until pasta is as tender as you like it.

6. Stir in chopped spinach. Add salt and pepper to taste. Remove bay leaf.

Soups

Pork and Vegetable Soup

Kristi See,
Weskan, KS

Makes 6 servings
Prep. Time: 30–45 minutes
Cooking Time: 3–8 hours
Ideal slow-cooker size: 3- or 4-qt.

1 lb. lean uncooked pork, or chicken, cut in ½" cubes

2 medium-sized carrots, cut in julienne strips

4 medium-sized scallions, chopped

1 clove garlic, finely chopped

3–4 Tbsp. low-sodium soy sauce, according to your taste preference

½ tsp. finely chopped ginger

⅛ tsp. black pepper

10¾-oz. can fat-free, reduced-sodium beef broth

1 cup fresh mushrooms, sliced

1 cup bean sprouts

1. Cook meat in large nonstick skillet over medium heat 8–10 minutes. Stir occasionally.

2. Mix meat and remaining ingredients, except mushrooms and bean sprouts, in slow cooker.

3. Cover. Cook on low 5–7 hours or on high 2–3 hours.

4. Stir in mushrooms and bean sprouts.

5. Cover. Cook on low 1 hour.

Soups

Green Bean Soup

Carla Keslowsky,
Hillsboro, KS

Makes 4 servings
Prep. Time: 20 minutes
Cooking Time: 1–1½ hours

1 ham hock

1½ cups water

ham broth and water to equal 6 cups

2 potatoes, peeled and cubed

½ cup onions, chopped

1 sprig fresh dill, chopped

1 lb. fresh beans

½ tsp. black pepper

½ cup fat-free milk

1. In large stockpot, cook hock over medium heat in about 1½ cups water. Meat is finished cooking when it pulls away from bone.

2. Pour broth into tall glass or cylinder. Fat can be skimmed off as broth cools. Or place in refrigerator until broth is congealed. Remove fat, which rises to the top.

3. Debone and cut up meat. Set aside.

4. Return broth, with fat removed, to stockpot. Add potatoes, onions, dill weed, beans, and pepper to broth mixture.

5. Cook, covered, until potatoes and beans are tender.

6. Add milk and ham. Heat through and serve.

Soups

Green Bean Soup for the Slow Cooker

Hope Comerford,
Clinton Township, MI

Makes 4 servings
Ideal slow-cooker size: 4-qt.

1 ham hock

2 potatoes, peeled and cubed

1 cup onions, chopped

1 sprig dill weed

3 cloves garlic, minced

½ tsp. fresh chopped rosemary

6 cups water

2 tsp. salt

¼ tsp. black pepper

1 lb. green beans

1. Combine all ingredients except green beens in slow cooker.

2. Cover. Cook on low 4–5 hours.

3. Remove ham hock, scrape meat off bone. Discard bone and chop any large pieces of meat. Stir the meat back through the soup.

4. Stir in the green beans, cover, and cook for an additional 30 minutes.

Soups

Black Bean and Pumpkin Soup

**Bev Beiler,
Gap, PA**

Makes 4–6 servings
Prep. Time: 30 minutes
Cooking Time: 45 minutes

2 medium onions, chopped

½ cup minced shallots

4 cloves garlic, minced

4–5 tsp. ground cumin

1 tsp. salt

½ tsp. ground pepper

1 stick (½ cup) butter

3 15½-oz. cans black beans, drained

1 cup chopped tomatoes

4 cups beef broth

1½ cups cooked pumpkin

½ lb. cooked ham, diced

3 Tbsp. vinegar

1. In a large soup pot, sauté onions, shallots, garlic, cumin, salt, and pepper in butter until vegetables are tender.

2. Stir in beans, tomatoes, broth, and pumpkin.

3. Simmer 25 minutes, uncovered, stirring occasionally.

4. Add ham and vinegar. Simmer until heated through.

Ham and Split Pea Soup

**Mary C. Casey,
Scranton, PA**

Makes 6–8 servings
Prep. Time: 25–30 minutes
Cooking Time: 6–8 hours
Ideal slow-cooker size: 5-qt.

2 cups cooked ham, diced

1 bay leaf

16-oz. pkg. dried split peas

2 ribs celery, sliced

1 small onion, chopped

¼–½ tsp. black pepper, according to your taste preference

½ tsp. salt

¼–½ tsp. dried marjoram, according to your taste preference

½ cup carrots, shredded

2 10¾-oz. cans reduced-sodium, low-fat chicken broth

5 cups water

1 cup potatoes, cooked and diced, optional

1. Combine all ingredients in slow cooker.

2. Cover. Cook on low 6–8 hours, or until peas are tender.

3. To thicken, remove 4 cups of soup after potatoes have been added and purée in blender.

4. Return to soup. Stir.

Bean Soup with Turkey Sausage

Dorothy Reise,
Severna Park, MD
D. Fern Ruth,
Chalfont, PA

Makes 4 servings
Prep. Time: 15–20 minutes
Cooking Time: 15–20 minutes

8 ozs. turkey kielbasa

4 cups chicken broth

2 15-oz. cans cannelloni beans, drained and rinsed

½–1 cup onion, chopped

2 tsp. fresh minced basil

¼ tsp. coarsely ground pepper

1 clove garlic, minced

1 carrot, peeled and sliced, or 1 cup baby carrots

half a red, yellow, or orange bell pepper, sliced

3 cups fresh spinach, cleaned

¼ dup fresh chopped parsley

1. Cut turkey kielbasa lengthwise, and then into ½" slices. Sauté in Dutch oven or large saucepan until browned, stirring occasionally so it doesn't stick.

2. Combine all ingredients in pan except spinach and parsley.

3. Bring to boil, and then reduce heat. Cover and simmer 10–15 minutes, or until onion and carrots are tender.

4. If you're using frozen spinach, add it to the soup and let it thaw in the soup pot. Stir occasionally to break up spinach and to have it heat through.

5. If you're using fresh spinach, remove stems from fresh spinach, stack, and cut into 1" strips. Remove soup from heat and stir in spinach and parsley until spinach wilts.

6. Serve immediately.

Variation:
For a thicker soup, remove 1 cup of hot soup after Step 3 and carefully process in firmly covered blender or food processor until smooth. Stir back into soup and continue with Step 4.

Soups

Turkey Sausage and Cabbage Soup

Bonita Stutzman,
Harrisonburg, VA

Makes 8 servings
Prep. Time: 20 minutes
Cooking Time: 1 hour, or more

1½ cups chopped onions

2 cloves garlic, finely chopped

¾ lb. turkey sausage, chopped in small pieces

6 cups green cabbage, shredded

3 lbs. canned tomatoes, no salt added, undrained

1½ quarts water

2 Tbsp. fresh chopped basil

2 Tbsp. fresh chopped oregano

¼ tsp. black pepper

1. Spray inside bottom of stockpot lightly with cooking spray. Sauté onions and garlic until tender.

2. Add chopped sausage. Cook until lightly browned.

3. Stir in remaining ingredients.

4. Cover. Simmer until cabbage is very tender.

Tuscany Peasant Soup

**Alice Valine,
Elma, NY**

Makes 8 servings
Prep. Time: 20 minutes
Cooking Time: 25 minutes

½ lb. bulk turkey sausage

1 onion, chopped

2–3 cloves garlic, minced

2 15-oz. cans cannellini beans, or great
   northern beans, rinsed and drained

2 14½-oz. cans diced tomatoes, no salt added,
   undrained, or 10–12 whole tomatoes,
   peeled and diced

2 14-oz. cans low-fat, low-sodium chicken
   broth

2 tsp. no-salt Italian seasoning

3 medium zucchini, sliced

4 cups fresh spinach leaves, chopped, or baby
   spinach, whole leaf

shredded Parmesan, or Romano, cheese,
   optional

1. In Dutch oven or stockpot, cook sausage over medium heat until no longer pink. Drain off drippings.

2. Add onion and garlic. Sauté until tender.

3. Stir in beans, tomatoes, broth, seasoning, and zucchini. Cook uncovered 10 minutes.

4. Add spinach and heat until just wilted.

5. Serve with cheese, if you wish.

Turkey and Garbanzo Soup

Michele Ruvola,
Vestal, NY

Makes 7 servings
Prep. Time: 10 minutes
Cooking Time: 6–8 hours
Ideal slow-cooker size: 5- or 6½-qt.

1 lb. lean ground turkey

1 yellow onion, chopped

2 garlic cloves, chopped

3 Tbsp. chopped poblano pepper

1 cup diced carrots

1 cup diced celery

28-oz. can petite diced tomatoes, or 10–12 whole tomatoes, peeled and diced

2 15-oz. cans garbanzo beans, drained

2 cups low-sodium, 99% fat-free chicken broth

2 tsp. turmeric

2 tsp. paprika

1 tsp. ground coriander

2 bay leaves

½ tsp. crushed red pepper flakes

2 tsp. coarse salt

2 Tbsp. chopped fresh Italian parsley or spearmint

1. Cook turkey in skillet for 10–12 minutes, until no longer pink. Transfer to slow cooker.

2. Add onion, garlic, pepper, carrots, celery, tomatoes, garbanzos, chicken broth, turmeric, paprika, coriander, bay leaves, red pepper flakes, and salt.

3. Cover and cook on Low for 6–8 hours. Remove bay leaves.

4. Stir in parsley or spearmint.

TIP

Serve with warm crusty bread.

Turkey Rosemary Veggie Soup

**Willard E. Roth,
Elkhart, IN**

Makes 8 servings
Prep. Time: 30 minutes
Cooking Time: 8 hours
Ideal slow-cooker size: 6-qt.

1 lb. 99% fat-free ground turkey

3 parsley stalks with leaves, sliced

3 scallions, chopped

3 medium carrots, unpeeled, sliced

3 medium potatoes, unpeeled, sliced

3 celery ribs with leaves, sliced

3 small onions, sliced

2 cups whole-kernel corn

2 cups fresh green beans

16-oz. can low-sodium diced Italian-style tomatoes

3 cups vegetable broth

3 Tbsp. fresh chopped rosemary

1. Brown turkey with parsley and scallions in nonstick skillet. Drain. Pour into slow cooker sprayed with nonstick spray.

2. Add vegetables, tomatoes, vegetable broth, and rosemary.

3. Cover. Cook on Low 8 hours, or until vegetables are done to your liking.

Chicken Noodle Soup

Mary Martins,
Fairbank, IA

Makes 12 servings
Prep. Time: 1 hour
Cooking Time: 3–3¼ hours

4-lb. stewing chicken, skin removed and cut up

2 quarts water

2 14½-oz. cans low-fat low-sodium chicken broth

5 celery ribs, coarsely chopped, *divided*

3 medium carrots, sliced, *divided*

2 medium onions, quartered, *divided*

⅔ cup coarsely chopped green bell pepper, *divided*

½ tsp. pepper

1 bay leaf

2 tsp. salt

8 ozs. uncooked whole wheat noodles

1. In large stockpot, combine chicken, water, broth, half the celery, half the carrots, half the onions, half the green pepper, ½ teaspoon pepper, and bay leaf. Bring to a boil.

2. Reduce heat. Cover and simmer 2½ hours, or until chicken is tender.

3. Meanwhile, chop remaining onion. Set aside.

4. Remove chicken from broth. When cool enough to handle, remove meat from bones and cut into bite-size pieces. Discard bones and skin. Set chicken aside. (This will equal about 3 lbs. cooked meat.)

5. Strain broth and skim fat.

6. Return broth to kettle. Add salt, chopped onion and remaining celery, carrots, and green pepper.

7. Bring to a boil. Reduce heat. Cover and simmer 10–12 minutes, or until vegetables are crisp-tender.

8. Add noodles and chicken.

9. Cover and simmer 12–15 minutes, or until pasta is tender.

Soups

Ground Turkey Soup

Betty K. Drescher,
Quakertown, PA

Makes 12 servings
Prep. Time: 20–30 minutes
Cooking Time: 8–9 hours
Ideal slow-cooker size: 5- or 6-qt.

1 lb. 99% fat-free ground turkey

1 cup onions, chopped

1 clove garlic, minced

15-oz. can kidney beans, drained

1 cup sliced carrots

1 cup sliced celery

¼ cup long-grain rice, uncooked

1 qt. low-sodium diced Italian tomatoes

2 cups fresh green beans

2 tsp. fresh chopped parsley

half a green bell pepper, chopped

1 tsp. salt

⅛ tsp. black pepper

1 Tbsp. Worcestershire sauce

1 bay leaf

3 cups water

1. Brown turkey in a large nonstick skillet.

2. Combine with remaining ingredients in slow cooker.

3. Cover. Cook on low 8–9 hours.

Soups

Roasted Chicken Noodle Soup

Janie Steele,
Moore, OK

Makes 8 servings
Prep. Time: 30 minutes
Cooking Time: 5½–6½ hours
Ideal slow-cooker size: 5-qt.

1 cup chopped onions

1 cup chopped carrots

1 cup chopped celery

1 clove garlic, minced

2 tsp. olive, or canola, oil

1 tsp. flour

1½ tsp. fresh chopped oregano

1½ tsp. fresh chopped thyme

¼ tsp. poultry seasoning

6 cups fat-free chicken broth

4 cups diced potatoes

1 tsp. salt

2 cups skinless roasted chicken, diced

2 cups uncooked wide noodles

1 cup fat-free evaporated milk

1. Brown onions, carrots, celery, and garlic in oil in skillet.

2. Stir in flour, oregano, thyme, and poultry seasoning and blend well. Pour into slow cooker.

3. Mix in broth, potatoes, and salt.

4. Cook on low 5–6 hours, or until potatoes are soft.

5. Add chicken, noodles, and milk. Cook until noodles are tender. Do not bring to a boil after milk is added.

Soups

Tex-Mex Soup with Crunchy Tortillas

**Deb Kepiro,
Strasburg, PA**

Makes 6 servings
Prep. Time: 10 minutes
Cooking Time: 5–7 hours
Ideal slow-cooker size: 3-qt.

2 boneless, skinless chicken breasts, cubed

1 onion, chopped

1 clove garlic, crushed

14.5-oz. can chopped tomatoes, or 5–6 whole tomatoes, peeled and chopped

4 cups chicken broth

¼ tsp. salt

⅛ tsp. pepper

1 mild green chile, seeded and chopped

2 Tbsp. vegetable oil

4 corn tortillas, cut in half and then in ¼" strips

shredded Monterey Jack cheese, for serving

chopped fresh cilantro, for serving

1. Combine chicken, onion, garlic, tomatoes, broth, salt, pepper, and green chile in slow cooker.

2. Cover and cook on Low 5–7 hours.

3. Heat oil in large skillet and add tortilla strips. Cook, stirring, over medium heat until crisp. Drain strips on paper towels.

4. If desired, put 1 tablespoon or 2 of shredded Monterey Jack cheese in each serving bowl.

5. Ladle soup into bowls and top with tortilla strips. Sprinkle with chopped cilantro.

Chicken and Vegetable Soup with Rice

Hope Comerford,
Clinton Township, MI

Makes 4-6 servings
Prep. Time: 20 minutes
Cooking Time: 6½–7½ hours
Ideal slow-cooker size: 3-qt.

1½–2 lbs. boneless, skinless chicken breasts

1½ cups chopped carrots

1½ cups chopped red onion

4 cloves garlic, chopped

1 Tbsp. onion powder

2 tsp. salt (you can omit the salt if you're using regular stock rather than no-salt)

¼ tsp. celery seed

¼ tsp. paprika

⅛ tsp. pepper

1 dried bay leaf

8 cups no-salt chicken stock

1 cup fresh green beans

3 cups cooked rice

1. Place chicken into the bottom of crock, then add rest of the remaining ingredients, except green beans and rice.

2. Cover and cook on Low for 6–7 hours.

3. Remove chicken and chop into bite-sized cubes. Place chicken back into crock and add in green beans. Cover and cook another 30 minutes.

4. To serve, place approximately ½ cup of the cooked rice into each bowl and ladle soup over top of the rice.

Soups

Wild Rice Soup

Joyce Shackelford,
Green Bay, WI

Makes 8 servings
Prep. Time: 25 minutes
Cooking Time: 3–4 hours
Ideal slow-cooker size: 4-qt.

2 Tbsp. butter

½ cup dry wild rice

6 cups fat-free, low-sodium chicken stock

½ cup minced onions

½ cup minced celery

½ lb. winter squash, peeled, seeded, cut in
    ½ cubes

2 cups chicken, chopped and cooked

½ cup browned, slivered almonds

1. Melt butter in small skillet. Add rice and sauté 10 minutes over low heat. Transfer to slow cooker.

2. Add all remaining ingredients except chicken and almonds.

3. Cover. Cook on low 3–4 hours, or until vegetables are cooked to your liking. One hour before serving, stir in chicken.

4. Top with browned slivered almonds just before serving.

Stews

Colorful Beef Stew

Hope Comerford,
Clinton Township, MI

Makes 6 servings
Prep. Time: 20 minutes
Cooking Time: 8–9 hours
Ideal slow-cooker size: 4-qt.

2 lbs. boneless beef chuck roast, trimmed of fat and cut into ¾-inch pieces

1 large red onion, chopped

2 cups gluten-free low-sodium beef broth

6-oz. can tomato paste

4 garlic cloves, minced

1 Tbsp. paprika

2 tsp. dried marjoram

½ tsp. black pepper

1 tsp. sea salt

1 red bell pepper, sliced

1 yellow bell pepper, sliced

1 orange bell pepper, sliced

1. Place all ingredients in the crock, except the sliced bell peppers, and stir.

2. Cover and cook on low for 8–9 hours. Stir in sliced bell peppers during the last 45 minutes of cooking time.

Stews

Mushroom Stew

**Lauren Bailey,
Mechanicsburg, PA**

Makes 10 servings
Prep. Time: 20 minutes
Cooking Time: 30–35 minutes

5 Tbsp. butter, *divided*

1 Tbsp. oil

2 bay leaves

1 large onion, chopped

2 cloves garlic, minced (use more if you wish)

2 Tbsp. flour

1 cup chicken broth

1 cup tomato juice, or fresh puree

2 cups cut-up tomatoes

1 Tbsp. fresh chopped thyme

1½ lbs. fresh mushrooms, chopped

salt and pepper to taste

1½ cups red wine

1. In medium-sized saucepan melt 2 Tbsp. butter and oil. Add bay leaves and onion. Sauté until onions are golden. Stir in garlic and sauté one more minute.

2. Stir in flour and lower the heat. Cook several minutes on low, stirring constantly.

3. Add broth and tomato juice. Stir with whisk to remove all lumps. Add cut-up tomatoes.

4. In larger pot, sauté mushrooms in 3 Tbsp. butter. Add thyme over high heat. Add tomato mixture, salt, and pepper. Lower heat and simmer for 20 minutes.

5. Add wine and stir for one minute.

Stews

Can't Beet Beef Stew

Bob Coffey,
New Windsor, NY

Makes 6–8 servings
Prep. Time: 30 minutes
Cooking Time: 6 hours
Ideal slow-cooker size: 5- or 6-qt.

4 large beets, roasted in the oven at 425° until tender, then cooled, peeled, and diced

2 large onions, diced

3 garlic cloves, diced

2 large carrots, peeled and diced

2 large parsnips, peeled and diced

2 ribs celery, diced

15½-oz. can petite diced tomatoes, undrained, or 5–6 whole tomatoes, peeled and diced

1 bay leaf

2 lbs. boneless beef chuck roast, cut into 1½-inch pieces

4 cups beef broth

¼ cup finely chopped fresh dill

coarse salt and pepper to taste

1. Grease interior of slow-cooker crock.

2. If roasting beets yourself, halve them. Place face down in single layer in greased baking pan. Cover and bake at 425° until tender, about 20 minutes. Uncover and allow to cool until you can handle them. Peel. Dice.

3. Place onions and garlic in crock. Stir in beets.

4. Add rest of ingredients, except dill, salt, and pepper, to crock.

5. Cover. Cook on Low 6 hours, or until meat and vegetables are tender.

6. Stir in dill. Season to taste with salt and pepper.

7. Remove bay leaf before serving.

TIPS

1. When making recipes with bay leaves, I keep an index card next to my slow cooker and make a note on it, saying how many I used. Then I know how many to fish out later on.
2. The same beet pigment that will turn this stew a beautiful deep ruby color will turn your fingertips pink for days when handling them. Plan ahead and have disposable gloves ready so you won't be caught red-handed!
3. From the tester: This is a great recipe. If you're wary about red beets, you barely taste them, if at all. But they help to make the stew a wonderful rich color.
   —A. Catherine Boshart

Cider Beef Stew

Jean Turner, Williams Lake, British Columbia

Makes 8 servings
Prep. Time: 30 minutes
Cooking Time: 8 hours
Ideal slow-cooker size: 3-qt.

2 lbs. stewing beef, cut into 1" cubes

6 Tbsp. flour, *divided*

2 tsp. salt

¼ tsp. pepper

¾ tsp. fresh chopped thyme

3 Tbsp. cooking oil

4 potatoes, peeled and quartered

4 carrots, quartered

2 onions, sliced

1 rib celery, sliced

1 apple, cored and chopped

2 cups apple cider or apple juice

1-2 Tbsp. vinegar

½ cup cold water

1. Stir together beef, 3 Tbsp. flour, salt, pepper, and thyme. Brown coated in oil in skillet. Do in two batches if necessary to avoid crowding the meat.

2. Place vegetables and apple in slow cooker. Place browned meat cubes on top.

3. Pour over apple cider and vinegar.

4. Cover and cook on Low for 8–10 hours.

5. Turn slow cooker to High. Blend cold water with remaining 3 Tbsp. flour. Stir into hot stew.

6. Cover and cook on High for 15 minutes or until thickened.

TIP

Great served with garlic bread or cheese bread.

Stews

Zucchini Stew

**Colleen Heatwole,
Burton, MI**

Makes 6 servings
Prep. Time: 30 minutes
Cooking Time: 4–6 hours
Ideal slow-cooker size: 6-qt.

1 lb. Italian sausage, sliced

2 ribs of celery, diced

2 medium green bell peppers, diced

1 medium onion, chopped

2 28-oz. cans diced tomatoes, or 20–22 whole
  tomatoes, peeled and diced

2 lbs. zucchini, cut into ½-inch slices

2 cloves garlic, minced

1 tsp. sugar

1 Tbp. Fresh chopped oregano

1 tsp. Italian seasoning

1 tsp. salt, optional (taste first)

6 Tbsp. grated Parmesan cheese

1. Brown sausage in hot skillet until brown and crumbly, about 5–7 minutes. Drain and discard grease.

2. Mix celery, bell peppers, and onion into cooked sausage and cook and stir until they are softened, 10–12 minutes.

3. Combine remaining ingredients, except Parmesan cheese, and add to slow cooker.

4. Cook on Low 4–6 hours. Garnish each serving with 1 Tbsp. Parmesan cheese.

Serving suggestion:
Croutons can be added to individual bowls for some crunch.

Stews

Weney's Chicken and Vegetable Stew

Becky Frey,
Lebanon, PA

Makes 8 servings
Ideal slow-cooker size: 4-qt.

To make this stew from scratch, you'll need two days. On Day One you'll cook the chicken for 6–8 hours. On Day Two, you'll add the vegetables to the chicken broth and the deboned chicken and allow the Stew to cook 7–8 hours. You can reduce the cooking to a total of 7–8 hours by using a deboned rotisserie chicken, chicken you've already cooked (and may have in the freezer), or canned chicken. And you can use boxed or canned chicken broth from the grocery store if you don't have your own. If you choose to use already-prepared chicken and broth, begin with "On the next day" below, Step 2.

4 chicken legs or thighs, skinned

2 carrots, diced

4-6 medium-sized potatoes, diced

2-3 garlic cloves, minced

half a medium-sized head of cabbage, cut in chunks

1 green bell pepper, coarsely chopped

1 medium-sized onion, coarsely chopped

2 cups fresh diced tomatoes

1 tsp. ground coriander

1 tsp. ground annatto

½ tsp. salt

¼ tsp. black pepper

The day before serving the Stew:
1. Place chicken in slow cooker, sprinkle lightly with salt, and cover with water.
2. Cover. Cook on low 6–8 hours, or until tender.
3. Remove chicken from bones and reserve.
4. Strain and chill broth.

On the next day:
1. Remove fat from broth.
2. Place broth, deboned chicken, vegetables, and seasonings into slow cooker.
3. Cover. Cook on low 7–8 hours or until vegetables are tender.

Stews

Chicken Mushroom Stew

Bernice A. Esau,
North Newton, KS
Carol Sherwood,
Batavia, NY

Makes 6 servings
Prep. Time: 25 minutes
Cooking Time: 4 hours
Ideal slow-cooker size: 3½- or 4-qt.

6 boneless, skinless chicken breast halves (about 1½ lbs.), uncooked

2 Tbsp. cooking oil, *divided*

8 ozs. sliced fresh mushrooms

1 medium-sized onion, diced

3 cups diced zucchini

1 cup diced green bell peppers

4 garlic cloves, diced

3 medium-sized tomatoes, diced

6-oz. can tomato paste

¾ cup water

2 tsp. salt, optional

1 Tbsp. fresh chopped thyme

1 Tbsp. fresh chopped oregano

1 tsp. dried marjoram

2 tsp. fresh chopped basil

1. Cut chicken into 1-inch cubes. Brown in 1 Tbsp. oil in a large skillet. Transfer to slow cooker, reserving drippings.

2. In same skillet, sauté mushrooms, onion, zucchini, green peppers, and garlic in drippings, and remaining 1 Tbsp. oil if needed, until crisp-tender. Place in slow cooker.

3. Add tomatoes, tomato paste, water, and seasonings.

4. Cover. Cook on low 4 hours, or until vegetables are tender.

Stews

Chilis

Garden Chili

Stacy Schmucker Stoltzfus,
Enola, PA

Makes 10 servings
Prep. Time: 45 minutes
Cooking Time: 6–8 hours
Ideal slow-cooker size: 3½- or 4-qt.

¾ lb. onions, chopped

1 tsp. garlic, minced

1 Tbsp. olive oil

¾ cup celery, chopped

1 large carrot, peeled and thinly sliced

1 large green bell pepper, chopped

1 small zucchini, sliced

¼ lb. fresh mushrooms, sliced

1¼ cups water

14-oz. can kidney beans, drained

14-oz. can low-sodium diced tomatoes with juice, or 5–6 whole tomatoes, peeled and chopped

1 tsp. fresh lemon juice

½ tsp. fresh chopped oregano

1 tsp. ground cumin

1 tsp. chili powder

1 tsp. salt

1 tsp. black pepper

1. Sauté onions and garlic in olive oil in large skillet over medium heat until tender.

2. Add remaining fresh veggies. Sauté 2–3 minutes. Transfer to slow cooker.

3. Add remaining ingredients.

4. Cover. Cook on low 6–8 hours.

Vegetarian Chili

Lois Hess,
Lancaster, PA

Makes 8 servings
Prep. Time: 30 minutes
Cooking Time: 30 minutes

1 cup tomato juice, no salt added

½ cup raw bulgur

4 cloves garlic, chopped

1½ cups chopped onion

1 Tbsp. olive, canola, or saffron, oil for sauté

1 cup chopped celery

1 cup chopped carrots

1 cup chopped tomatoes

1 tsp. cumin

2 tsp. fresh chopped basil

1-1½ tsp. chili powder, depending upon your taste preferences

1 cup chopped green bell peppers

2 16-oz. cans red kidney beans, rinsed and drained

juice of half a lemon

3 Tbsp. tomato paste, no salt added

dash cayenne pepper, or ¼ tsp. coarsely ground black pepper

chopped fresh parsley for garnish

1. Heat tomato juice to a boil. Pour over bulgur in a bowl. Cover and let stand 15 minutes.

2. Meanwhile, sauté garlic and onion in oil in large stockpot.

3. Add celery, carrots, tomatoes, and spices.

4. When vegetables are almost tender, add peppers. Cook until tender.

5. Stir in all remaining ingredients. Cover and heat gently.

6. Top individual servings with parsley.

Chilis

Summer Chili

Hope Comerford,
Clinton Township, MI

Makes 6 servings
Prep. Time: 15 minutes
Cooking Time: 3½–4 hours
Ideal slow-cooker size: 3-qt.

28-oz. can Red Gold sliced tomatoes and
  zucchini

15-oz. can tomato sauce

14-oz. can petite diced tomatoes with green
  chilies

15½-oz. can chili beans

15¼-oz. can black beans, drained and rinsed

1 medium onion, roughly chopped

3 small yellow squash, halved, quartered, and
  chopped

4 large cloves garlic, minced

¼ cup diced onion

1 tsp. salt

⅛ tsp. pepper

2 cups water

1. Place all ingredients into crock and stir.

2. Cover and cook on Low for 3½–4 hours.

Beef and Sausage Chili

Dorothea K. Ladd,
Ballston Lake, NY

Makes 6–8 servings
Prep. Time: 15 minutes
Cooking Time: 4–5 hours
Ideal slow-cooker size: 6- or 7-qt.

1 lb. ground beef

1 lb. bulk pork sausage

1 Tbsp. oil, optional

1 large onion, chopped

1 large green pepper, chopped

2–3 ribs celery, chopped

2 15½-oz. cans kidney beans

29-oz. can tomato purée

6-oz. can tomato paste

2 cloves garlic, minced

2 Tbsp. chili powder

2 tsp. salt

1. Grease interior of slow-cooker crock.

2. If you have time, brown ground beef and sausage in skillet. Drain and place meats in crock. If you don't have time, place meats in crock and use a wooden spoon to break them into small clumps.

3. Combine all remaining ingredients in slow cooker.

4. Cover. Cook on Low 4–5 hours.

Serving suggestion:
Top individual servings with shredded sharp cheddar cheese.

TIP

While it takes longer to brown the beef and sausage in a skillet before putting them into the slow cooker, the advantage is that it cooks off a lot of the meats' fat. When you drain off the drippings, you leave the fat behind and put far less into the crock, and therefore into your chili.

Chilis

No Beans Chili

**Sharon Timpe,
Jackson, WI**

Makes 10-12 servings
Prep. Time: 35 minutes
Cooking Time: Low 9-10 hours; High
6-7 hours
Ideal slow-cooker size: 5-6 qt.

¼ cup fresh chopped oregano

1 Tbsp. fresh chopped parsley

1 cup red wine

2-3 Tbsp. oil

1½ lbs round steak, cubed

1½ lbs. chuck steak, cubed

1 medium onion, chopped

1 cup chopped celery

1 cup chopped carrots

28-oz. can stewed tomatoes, or 10-12 whole
    tomatoes, peeled

8-oz. can tomato sauce

1 cup beef broth

1 Tbsp. vinegar

1 Tbsp. brown sugar

2 Tbsp. chili powder

1 tsp. cumin

¼ tsp. pepper

l tsp. salt

1. Place oregano and parsley in red wine and set aside, ideally for about 15 minutes.

2. Heat oil in a skillet and brown the beef cubes. You may have to do this in two batches.

3. Put browned beef in slow cooker.

4. Add wine mixture to skillet and stir, scraping up browned bits. Scrape mixture into slow cooker.

5. Add rest of ingredients to slow cooker.

6. Cook on Low 9–10 hours or High 6–7 hours, until meat is very tender.

Chilis

Turkey Chili

**Julette Rush,
Harrisonburg, VA**

Makes 5 servings
Prep. Time: 15 minutes
Cooking Time: 30 minutes

½ lb. ground turkey breast

1 cup chopped onions

½ cup chopped green bell pepper

½ cup chopped red bell pepper

14½-oz. can diced tomatoes, no salt added, undrained, or 5–6 whole tomatoes, peeled and diced

15-oz. can solid-pack pumpkin

15½-oz. can pinto beans, rinsed and drained

½ cup water

2 tsp. chili powder

½ tsp. garlic powder

¼ tsp. black pepper

¾ tsp. ground cumin

14½-oz. can low-sodium, fat-free chicken broth

1 cup low-fat shredded cheddar cheese

1. In large stockpot, sauté turkey, onions, and bell peppers until turkey is browned and vegetables are softened.

2. Mix in tomatoes, pumpkin, beans, water, seasonings, and broth. Reduce heat to low.

3. Cover and simmer 20 minutes. Stir occasionally.

4. Top individual servings with cheese.

Chicken Chili

Sharon Miller,
Holmesville, OH

Makes 6 servings
Prep. Time: 15 minutes
Cooking Time: 6 hours
Ideal slow-cooker size: 4-qt.

2 lbs. boneless, skinless chicken breasts, cubed

2 Tbsp. butter

2 14-oz. cans diced tomatoes, undrained, or 10–12 whole tomatoes, peeled and diced

15-oz. can red kidney beans, rinsed and drained

1 cup diced onion

1 cup diced red bell pepper

1–2 Tbsp. chili powder, according to your taste preference

1 tsp. ground cumin

1 Tbsp. fresh minced oregano

salt and pepper, to taste

TIP

Can be served with shredded cheddar cheese and sour cream.

1. In skillet on high heat, brown chicken cubes in butter until they have some browned edges. Place in greased slow cooker.

2. Pour one of the cans of tomatoes with its juice into skillet to get all the browned bits and butter. Scrape and pour into slow cooker.

3. Add rest of ingredients, including other can of tomatoes, to cooker.

4. Cook on Low for 5–6 hours.

Chilis

Chowders

Broccoli Chowder

**Ruth E. Martin,
Loysville, PA**

Makes 6 servings
Prep. Time: 15-20 minutes
Cooking Time: 20 minutes

2 cups diced potatoes, peeled or unpeeled,
your choice

½ cup water

2 cups chopped broccoli

2 Tbsp. diced onion

1 cup corn

¼–½ cup cooked, diced ham, optional

3 cups milk

½ tsp. salt, optional

⅛ tsp. pepper

1 tsp. powdered chicken bouillon, or 1 chicken
bouillon cube

½ cup Velveeta cheese, cubed

1. In medium-sized saucepan, cook potatoes in water. When potatoes are almost soft, add broccoli and onion. Cook until tender.

2. Add corn, ham, if you wish, milk, seasonings, and bouillon. Heat, but do not boil.

3. Turn off and add cubed cheese. Let cheese melt for about 3–4 minutes. Stir and serve.

Sweet Potato Chowder

Deborah Heatwole,
Waynesboro, GA

Makes 6 servings
Prep. Time: 15 minutes
Cooking Time: 25–30 minutes

1 rib celery, chopped

½ cup cooked, finely chopped, lean ham

2 Tbsp. olive oil

2 14½-oz. cans low-fat low-sodium chicken
   broth

3 medium potatoes, peeled and cubed

2 large sweet potatoes, peeled and cubed

¼ cup fresh minced onion

½ tsp. garlic powder

¾ tsp. fresh chopped oregano

1 tsp. fresh chopped parsley

¼ tsp. black pepper

¼ tsp. crushed red pepper flakes

¼ cup flour

2 cups skim milk

1. In large stockpot, sauté celery and ham in oil.

2. Stir in broth. Add white and sweet potatoes and seasonings.

3. Bring almost to a boil. Reduce heat, cover, and simmer for 12 minutes, or until potatoes are tender.

4. Combine flour and milk in a bowl until smooth. Stir into soup.

5. Bring to a boil. Cook, stirring continually, for 2 minutes, or until thickened and bubbly. Be careful not to scorch or curdle milk.

Creamy Potato Chowder

**Sylvia Beiler,
Lowville, NY**

Makes 4 servings
Prep. Time: 5 minutes
Cooking Time: 30–35 minutes

1 tsp. olive oil

½ cup chopped onion

½ cup chopped celery

2 garlic cloves, minced

1 carrot, diced

2 cups cubed unpeeled potatoes

2 Tbsp. flour

2 cups skim milk

1½ cup reduced sodium, low-fat chicken, or vegetable, broth

1 cup corn

pepper to taste

1. Heat oil in large saucepan over medium heat. Add onion, celery, and garlic. Sauté 2 minutes.

2. Add carrot and potatoes. Sauté 3 minutes.

3. Sprinkle flour over carrot and potatoes. Cook 1 minute, stirring continually.

4. Add remaining ingredients and bring to a boil.

5. Lower heat, cover, and simmer 20–25 minutes, or until carrot and potatoes are soft.

6. To thicken soup, mash vegetables somewhat before serving.

Shrimp Chowder

Kristi See,
Weskan, KS
Karen Waggoner,
Joplin, MO

Makes 8 servings
Prep. Time: 20–25 minutes
Cooking Time: 3¼–4¼ hours
Ideal slow-cooker size: 5- or 6-qt.

1 lb. red potatoes, cubed

2½ cups fat-free, reduced-sodium chicken broth

3 celery ribs, chopped

8 scallions, chopped

½ cup chopped red bell peppers

1½ cups fat-free milk

1½ lbs. medium-sized shrimp, uncooked, peeled, and deveined

¼ cup all-purpose flour

½ cup fat-free evaporated milk

2 Tbsp. fresh minced parsley

½ tsp. paprika

½ tsp. Worcestershire sauce

⅛ tsp. cayenne pepper

⅛ tsp. black pepper

1. Combine potatoes, broth, celery, scallions, and red bell peppers in slow cooker.

2. Cover. Cook on low 3–4 hours, or until vegetables are done to your liking.

3. Stir in 1½ cups milk and gently mash vegetables with potato masher. Leave some small chunks of potato.

4. Stir in shrimp.

5. Combine flour and evaporated milk. Mix until smooth. Gradually stir into soup mixture. Add remaining ingredients.

6. Cook and stir uncovered on high until thickened.

Chowders

Gazpacho and Bisque

Roasted Vegetable Gazpacho

J. B. Miller,
Indianapolis, IN

Makes 6 servings
Prep. Time: 30 minutes
Baking Time: 20–25 minutes
Chilling Time: 4 hours

2 red bell peppers, left whole

2 yellow bell peppers, left whole

2 large red onions, quartered

2 Tbsp. extra-virgin olive oil

pepper to taste

1-lb. (about 4 cups) medium zucchini, cut in
½"-thick slices

2 lbs. (about 7 medium) vine-ripened
tomatoes, cored, quartered, and seeds
removed

3 cloves garlic, chopped

2 Tbsp. chopped fresh basil

1 Tbsp. chopped fresh oregano

1 cup cold water

2 Tbsp. fresh lime juice, or more to taste

1. Preheat oven to 375°.

2. Place peppers and onions in large
mixing bowl. Toss with olive oil and black
pepper.

3. Spoon peppers and onions into large
shallow baking dishes or onto cookie sheets
with sides. Allow seasoned olive oil to remain
in mixing bowl. Place peppers and onions in
oven.

4. Meanwhile, stir zucchini and tomatoes
into large mixing bowl with remaining
seasoned olive oil.

5. After peppers and onions have roasted
10–12 minutes, add zucchini and tomatoes to
baking dishes.

6. Roast 10–12 minutes, or until peppers
are soft and vegetables have browned along
the edges and wrinkled. Total roasting time
will be 20–25 minutes.

7. Remove baking dishes from oven. Lift
out peppers and place in bowl. Cover with
plastic wrap. Let cool 10 minutes. Then peel
and seed peppers over a bowl, saving the
juices.

8. Coarsely chop all vegetables.

9. Place chopped vegetables in food processor together with garlic, basil, oregano, and 1 cup cold water.

10. Blend at high speed until smooth. Strain through a fine mesh sieve.

11. Place mixture in covered container. Refrigerate 4 hours before serving.

12. Adjust seasoning with pepper to taste.

13. Mix in lime juice just before serving.

TIP

Be sure gazpacho is chilled thoroughly before serving. It's best served in a chilled bowl or glass.

Gazpacho and Bisque

Crab Bisque

**Jere Zimmerman,
Reinholds, PA**

Makes 4 servings
Prep. Time: 15 minutes
Cooking Time: 20 minutes

1 stick (½ cup) butter, *divided*

½ cup finely chopped onion

½ cup finely chopped green pepper

2 scallions, finely chopped

¼ cup fresh chopped parsley

8 ozs. fresh mushrooms, chopped

¼ cup flour

2 cups milk

1 tsp. salt

¼ tsp. pepper

3 cups half-and-half

16-oz. can (2½ cups) claw crabmeat

grated carrot for color, optional

1. Melt half a stick of butter in stockpot. Add onion, green pepper, scallions, parsley, and mushrooms. Cook until tender. Remove vegetables from heat and set aside.

2. In the same stockpot, melt remaining half stick of butter over low heat. Add flour and stir until smooth. Add milk, stirring until thickened.

3. Add reserved vegetable mixture, salt, pepper, half-and-half, crabmeat, and grated carrot, if desired.

4. Heat through over low heat, but do not boil.

Chicken

Chicken Baked with Red Onions, Potatoes, and Rosemary

**Kristine Stalter,
Iowa City, IA**

Makes 4 servings
Prep. Time: 10–15 minutes
Baking Time: 45–60 minutes

2 red onions, each cut into 10 wedges

1¼ lbs. new potatoes, unpeeled and cut into chunks

2 garlic bulbs, separated into cloves, unpeeled

salt

pepper

4 Tbsp. extra-virgin olive oil

2 Tbsp. balsamic vinegar

approximately 5 sprigs rosemary

4-lb. chicken cut into 8 pieces, or 8 chicken thighs

1. Spread onions, potatoes, and garlic cloves in single layer over bottom of large roasting pan so that they will crisp and brown.

2. Season with salt and pepper.

3. Pour over the oil and balsamic vinegar and add rosemary, leaving some sprigs whole and stripping the leaves off the rest.

4. Toss vegetables and seasonings together.

5. Tuck chicken pieces among vegetables.

6. Bake at 400° for 45–60 minutes, or until chicken and vegetables are cooked through.

7. Transfer to a big platter, or take to the table in the roasting pan.

Chicken

Savory Slow-Cooker Chicken

Sara Harter Fredette,
Williamsburg, MA

Makes 4 servings
Prep. Time: 10–15 minutes
Cooking Time: 8–10 hours
Ideal slow-cooker size: 4- or 5-qt.

2½ lbs. chicken pieces, skinned

1 lb. fresh tomatoes, chopped

2 Tbsp. white wine

1 bay leaf

¼ tsp. pepper

2 garlic cloves, minced

1 onion, chopped

½ cup chicken broth

1 Tbsp. fresh chopped thyme

1½ tsp. salt

2 cups broccoli, cut into bite-sized pieces

1. Combine all ingredients except broccoli in slow cooker.

2. Cover. Cook on Low 8–10 hours.

3. Add broccoli 30 minutes before serving.

Chicken and Vegetables

Jeanne Heyerly,
Chenoa, IL

Makes 2 servings
Prep. Time: 10 minutes
Cooking Time: 8–9 hours
Ideal slow-cooker size: 4-qt.

2 medium potatoes, quartered

2–3 carrots, sliced

2 frozen chicken breasts, or 2 frozen drumstick/ thigh pieces

salt to taste

pepper to taste

1 medium onion, chopped

2 garlic cloves, minced

1–2 cups shredded cabbage

16-oz. can chicken broth

1. Place potatoes and carrots in slow cooker. Layer chicken on top. Sprinkle with salt, pepper, onion, and garlic. Top with cabbage. Carefully pour chicken broth around edges.

2. Cover. Cook on Low 8–9 hours.

Autumn Chicken and Veggies

Judy Govotsus,
Monrovia, MD

Makes 4-6 servings
Prep. Time: 10 minutes
Cooking Time: 5-10 hours
Ideal slow-cooker size: 6-qt.

4-6 potatoes, quartered

2-3 lbs. chicken pieces

2 large onions, quartered

1 whole bulb garlic, minced

¼ cup chopped fresh oregano

1 tsp. salt

½ tsp. pepper

1 Tbsp. olive oil

1. Place potatoes in bottom of slow cooker. Add chicken, onions, and garlic. Sprinkle with seasonings. Top with oil.

2. Cover. Cook on High 5–6 hours, or on Low 9–10 hours.

Braised Chicken with Summer Tomatoes

Karen Ceneviva,
Seymour, CT

Makes 6 servings
Prep. Time: 30 minutes
Cooking Time: 3–4 hours
Ideal slow-cooker size: 6-qt.

4½-lb. chicken, cut into 8 pieces (excluding back and wings; save them for making soup another day)

salt to taste

pepper to taste

4 Tbsp. extra-virgin olive oil, *divided*

1 large yellow onion, chopped

10 cloves garlic, peeled

½ cup wine vinegar

1½ cups chicken broth

4 fresh tarragon sprigs, or

6–8 medium (about 3½ lbs.) tomatoes, chopped

1. Season chicken to taste with salt and pepper.

2. Place 2 Tbsp. oil in large skillet. Brown chicken, a few pieces at a time, over medium-high heat in skillet. Turn once and brown underside.

3. When both sides of each piece of chicken are browned, remove from skillet and keep warm on platter.

4. Add 2 Tbsp. oil to skillet. Stir in chopped onion. Sauté over medium heat about 8 minutes.

5. Add garlic and sauté about 5 minutes. Add vinegar and broth and simmer 1 minute.

6. Carefully pour oil/vinegar/onion/garlic mixture into slow cooker. Place chicken on top.

7. Tuck tarragon sprigs around chicken pieces, or sprinkle with chopped tarragon. Spoon chopped tomatoes over top.

8. Cover. Cook on Low 3–4 hours, or until chicken is tender.

California Chicken

Shirley Sears,
Tiskilwa, IL

Makes 4-6 servings
Prep. Time: 10 minutes
Cooking Time: 8½–9½ hours
Ideal slow-cooker size: 4-qt.

3-lb. chicken, quartered

1 cup freshly squeezed orange juice

⅓ cup chili sauce

2 Tbsp. soy sauce

1 Tbsp. molasses

1 tsp. dry mustard

1 tsp. garlic salt

2 Tbsp. chopped green peppers

3 medium oranges, peeled and separated into slices

1. Arrange chicken in slow cooker.

2. In separate bowl, combine juice, chili sauce, soy sauce, molasses, dry mustard, and garlic salt. Pour over chicken.

3. Cover. Cook on Low 8–9 hours.

4. Stir in green peppers and oranges. Heat 30 minutes longer.

Variation:
Stir 1 tsp. curry powder in with sauces and seasonings. Stir 1 small can pineapple chunks and juice in with green peppers and oranges.

Chicken

Crusty Baked Chicken Breast

Eileen Eash,
Carlsbad, NM

Makes 8–10 servings
Prep. Time: 20–25 minutes
Baking Time: 20 minutes

2 cups dry bread crumbs

¾ cup grated Parmesan cheese

1 tsp. paprika

1 tsp. garlic salt

1 tsp. pepper

¼ cup fresh minced parsley

½ cup buttermilk

1 tsp. Worcestershire sauce

1 tsp. dry mustard

4 whole boneless, skinless chicken breasts, cut in strips

1. In a shallow bowl, combine bread crumbs, cheese, paprika, garlic salt, pepper, and parsley.

2. In another shallow bowl, combine buttermilk, Worcestershire sauce, and mustard.

3. Dip chicken pieces in buttermilk mixture and then roll in crumbs. Place coated chicken in a greased 9 × 13 baking dish in a single layer.

4. Pour remaining buttermilk over chicken.

5. Bake at 400° for 20 minutes.

Variation:
In Step 2, use 1 stick (½ cup) melted butter, instead of buttermilk. Use 2 tsp. prepared mustard instead of dry mustard.
—Erma Martin, East Earl, PA

Chicken

Chicken Sweet and Sour

Willard E. Roth,
Elkhart, IN

Makes 8 servings
Prep. Time: 10 minutes
Cooking Time: 6½ hours
Ideal slow-cooker size: 4- or 5-qt.

4 medium potatoes, sliced

3 boneless, skinless chicken breast halves

2 Tbsp. cider vinegar

¼ tsp. ground nutmeg

1 Tbsp. chopped fresh basil

2 Tbsp. brown sugar

1 cup freshly squeezed orange juice

¼ cup freshly minced parsley

2 cups peeled and sliced peaches

1. Place potatoes in greased slow cooker. Arrange chicken on top.

2. In separate bowl, combine vinegar, nutmeg, basil, brown sugar, and orange juice. Pour over chicken. Sprinkle with parsley.

3. Cover. Cook on Low 6 hours.

4. Remove chicken and potatoes from sauce and arrange on warm platter.

5. Turn cooker to High. Add peaches and heat until they are tender when poked with a fork.

Serving suggestion:
Spoon peaches and sauce over chicken and potatoes. Garnish with fresh parsley and orange slices.

Chicken

Almond Lemon Chicken

Judi Janzen,
Salem, OR

Makes 6 servings
Prep. Time: 35–40 minutes
Marinating Time: 1 hour
Cooking Time: 25–30 minutes

5 Tbsp. fresh lemon juice

3 Tbsp. prepared mustard

2 cloves garlic, finely chopped

6 Tbsp. olive oil, *divided*

6 boneless, skinless chicken breast halves

1 cup sliced almonds

2 cups chicken broth

1 tsp. cornstarch dissolved in 1 Tbsp. water

2 Tbsp. orange or lemon marmalade

2 Tbsp. chopped fresh parsley

¼ tsp. red pepper flakes

1. In a large bowl, combine first 3 ingredients. Stir in 5 tablespoons oil. Add chicken and marinate one hour at room temperature.

2. Meanwhile, in large skillet, sauté almonds in ½ Tbsp. oil until golden. Remove almonds from pan and set aside. Reserve drippings. Add remaining ½ Tbsp. oil.

3. Drain chicken, reserving marinade. Cook chicken over medium-high heat in skillet until brown on each side, about 6–10 minutes total, or until tender. Remove and keep warm.

4. Pour marinade into pan. Add chicken broth and cornstarch mixture. Cook over high heat, until it boils and is reduced by slightly more than half, about 5 minutes. Stir occasionally to loosen browned bits from skillet and to keep sauce smooth.

5. Add marmalade and stir over medium heat until melted. Stir in parsley and red pepper flakes.

6. Return chicken to pan and heat through.

7. Place chicken on serving platter. Spoon sauce over. Sprinkle with toasted almonds.

Chicken

Garlic Chicken Cutlets

Elaine Vigoda,
Rochester, NY

Makes 6 servings
Prep. Time: 10 minutes
Cooking Time: 20 minutes

4 chicken cutlets, approx. 1½ lbs.

2 Tbsp. matzo meal or flour

1 Tbsp. oil

6-8 garlic cloves, peeled and very lightly crushed

½ lb. fresh mushrooms, any combination of varieties, cut into pieces or slices

¼ cup balsamic vinegar

¾ cup chicken stock

1 bay leaf

3 sprigs fresh thyme, chopped

1 tsp. apricot jam

1. Dust chicken lightly with matzo meal or flour.

2. In large skillet, heat the oil over medium-high heat and add garlic. Sauté about 3 minutes, until browned.

3. Remove with a slotted spoon and reserve.

4. Add chicken to skillet and brown on one side for 3 minutes.

5. Turn chicken and top with reserved garlic and mushrooms. Cook 3 minutes.

6. While chicken is cooking, mix together vinegar, chicken stock, bay leaf, thyme, and jam in a small bowl. Pour over chicken and vegetables.

7. Reduce heat to low, cover the skillet, and cook approximately 10 minutes, or until chicken is done.

Chicken Casablanca

**Joyce Kaut,
Rochester, NY**

Makes 6–8 servings
Prep. Time: 30 minutes
Cooking Time: 4½–6½ hours
Ideal slow-cooker size: 4- or 5-qt.

2 large onions, sliced

¼ cup freshly grated ginger

3 garlic cloves, minced

2 Tbsp. oil

3 large carrots, diced

2 large potatoes, diced

3 lbs. skinless chicken pieces

½ tsp. ground cumin

½ tsp. salt

½ tsp. pepper

¼ tsp. cinnamon

2 Tbsp. raisins

14½-oz. can chopped tomatoes, or 5–6 whole
  tomatoes, peeled and chopped

3 small zucchini, sliced

15-oz. can garbanzo beans, drained

2 Tbsp. fresh chopped parsley

1. Sauté onions, ginger, and garlic in oil in skillet. (Reserve oil.) Transfer vegetables to slow cooker. Add carrots and potatoes.

2. Brown chicken over medium heat in reserved oil. Transfer to slow cooker. Mix gently with vegetables.

3. Combine seasonings in separate bowl. Sprinkle over chicken and vegetables. Add raisins and tomatoes.

4. Cover. Cook on High 4–6 hours.

5. Add sliced zucchini, beans, and parsley 30 minutes before serving.

Serving suggestion:
Serve over cooked rice or couscous.

Variation:
Add ½ tsp. turmeric and ¼ tsp. cayenne pepper to Step 3.

—Michelle Mann, Mt. Joy, PA

Chicken

Chicken Cacciatore

Donna Lantgen,
Arvada, CO

Makes 6 servings
Prep. Time: 10 minutes
Cooking/Baking Time: 65-90 minutes,
depending on thickness of chicken

6 boneless skinless chicken breast halves,
   each about 6 oz. in weight

1 medium green bell pepper, chopped

1 medium onion, chopped

2 cups fresh tomatoes, peeled and diced

1 Tbsp. Italian seasoning

mozzarella, or Parmesan cheese, shredded

1. Place chicken in well-greased
9 × 13 baking pan.

2. In mixing bowl, stir together green
pepper, onion, tomatoes, and seasoning.

3. Spoon vegetables evenly over chicken.

4. Cover. Bake at 350° for 45 minutes.

5. With a sharp knife make 2–3 vertical
slashes in thickest part of each chicken
breast. (Do not cut the whole way through.)
Baste with pan juices.

6. Cover. Return to oven and continue
baking 15 more minutes, or until
thermometer inserted in center of chicken
registers 165°.

7. Top chicken with cheese.

8. Return to oven for 5–10 minutes, or
until cheese melts.

Chicken Recuerdos de Tucson

**Joanna Harrison,
Lafayette, CO**

Makes 6 servings
Prep. Time: 15 minutes
Cooking Time: 30–40 minutes

1 whole chicken, cut up, or 6 chicken legs and
   thighs

1 Tbsp. olive oil

1 medium onion, chopped coarsely

3 cloves garlic, minced

1 tsp. ground cumin

2-3 green chilies, chopped, according to your
   taste preference

1 green bell pepper, chopped

1-2 zucchini, sliced

1 cup chopped tomatoes

2 cups corn

1½ Tbsp. fresh chopped oregano

2 tsp. fresh chopped basil

2 cups chicken broth

cilantro for garnish

1. Brown chicken in olive oil in Dutch oven or large stockpot. Remove chicken to platter. Reserve pan drippings.

2. Gently sauté onion and garlic in drippings until wilted.

3. Stir in cumin, green chilies, green pepper, and zucchini. Sauté until peppers wilt.

4. Add tomatoes, corn, oregano, basil, and broth.

5. Return chicken to pot.

6. Cover. Simmer 30–40 minutes, or until chicken is tender to the bone.

7. Garnish with cilantro and serve.

Chicken

Greek Chicken

Judy Govotsus,
Monrovia, MD

Makes 4-6 servings
Prep. Time: 10 minutes
Cooking Time: 5-10 hours
Ideal slow-cooker size: 6-qt.

4-6 potatoes, quartered

2-3 lbs. chicken pieces

2 large onions, quartered

1 whole bulb garlic, minced

½ cup chopped fresh oregano

1 tsp. salt

½ tsp. pepper

1 Tbsp. olive oil

1. Place potatoes in bottom of slow cooker. Add chicken, onions, and garlic. Sprinkle with seasonings. Top with oil.

2. Cover. Cook on High 5–6 hours, or on Low 9–10 hours.

Chicken

Lemon-Chicken Oven Bake

Judi Manos,
West Islip, NY

Makes 4 servings
Prep. Time: 10–15 minutes
Baking Time: 50 minutes

¼ cup zesty Italian dressing

½ cup chicken broth

1 Tbsp. honey

1½ lbs. bone-in chicken legs and thighs

1 lb. new potatoes, quartered

5 cloves garlic, peeled

1 lemon, cut in 8 wedges

1 Tbsp. fresh chopped rosemary, optional

1. In a mixing bowl, blend together dressing, broth, and honey.

2. Arrange chicken, potatoes, and garlic in well-greased 9 × 13 baking dish.

3. Drizzle with dressing mixture.

4. Situate lemons among the chicken and potatoes. Add rosemary if desired.

5. Bake at 400° for 45–50 minutes, or until chicken is done and potatoes are tender. (Temperature probe inserted into center of chicken should register 165°.)

6. Serve lemon wedges as garnish if you wish.

Chicken Angelo

Elaine Rineer,
Lancaster, PA

Makes 4 servings
Prep. Time: 20 minutes
Baking Time: 30–35 minutes

½ lb. fresh mushrooms, sliced, *divided*

2 eggs, beaten

1 cup dried bread crumbs

4 boneless, skinless chicken breast halves

2 Tbsp. butter or margarine

6 ozs. shredded mozzarella cheese

¾ cup chicken broth

1. Place half of mushrooms in greased 9 × 13 baking pan.

2. Beat eggs in a shallow bowl. Place bread crumbs in another shallow bowl. Dip chicken in egg. Then dip in bread crumbs, spooning bread crumbs over all sides of the chicken.

3. Melt butter in skillet. Brown chicken on both sides in batches; do not crowd the skillet. As you finish browning pieces, place them on top of the mushrooms.

4. Arrange remaining mushrooms over chicken. Top with cheese. Pour broth over top, being careful not to disturb the cheese.

5. Bake uncovered at 350° for 30–35 minutes.

6. Serve with angel-hair pasta. Garnish with parsley.

Brandied Peach Chicken

Shari Jensen,
Fountain, CO

Makes 6 servings
Prep. Time: 20 minutes
Baking Time: 45 minutes

6 boneless, skinless chicken breast halves

1¼ tsp. salt

½ cup finely chopped white onions

½ cup chopped cashews or pecans

½ tsp. ground ginger

5 fresh pitted peaches, sliced, *divided*

5⅓ Tbsp. (⅓ cup) butter, melted

½ cup light brown sugar

2 tsp. prepared mustard

1 cup sour cream

1 Tbsp. brandy

1. Cut a pocket in the side of each chicken breast, or pound chicken breasts to ¼" thickness between sheets of waxed paper. Sprinkle with salt.

2. Prepare filling in a mixing bowl by combining onions, chopped nuts, ginger, and 3 of the peaches cut into small pieces.

3. Divide peach mixture between the six chicken breasts by stuffing it into the created pockets or by placing it on top of each flat cutlet, rolling and securing the stuffed meat with a toothpick.

4. Pour melted butter into a foil-lined 9 × 13 baking dish. Place chicken on top of butter.

5. Bake uncovered at 350° for 25 minutes. Turn chicken over and bake 20 minutes longer.

6. While chicken bakes the last 20 minutes, combine the remaining 2 peaches (sliced), brown sugar, mustard, sour cream, and brandy in a saucepan.

7. Heat for 5 minutes over medium heat, making sure it doesn't boil. Serve over chicken breasts.

Chicken

Chicken Breasts with Fresh Fruit

**Robin Schrock,
Millersburg, OH**

Makes 4 servings
Prep. Time: 15-20 minutes
Cooking Time: 15 minutes

1½ Tbsp. olive oil

½ tsp. salt

½ tsp. pepper

1 clove garlic, minced

4 large boneless, skinless chicken breast
   halves

¼ cup butter

1 cup fresh pineapple chunks

1 cup fresh, quartered strawberries

1 kiwi, peeled, quartered, and sliced

¼ cup chopped red onions

half a 4-oz. can chopped green chilies

1 tsp. cornstarch

⅓ cup freshly squeezed orange juice

1. In a small bowl, combine oil, salt, pepper, and garlic. Spread over one side of each chicken breast.

2. In skillet, sauté chicken in butter, seasoned-side down, 4–6 minutes. Turn and cook another 4–6 minutes, or until chicken juices run clear.

3. While chicken is sautéing, cut up fruit and onions into mixing bowl. Stir in chilies.

4. In a small bowl, combine cornstarch and juice until smooth.

5. Remove cooked chicken from skillet to serving platter. Keep warm. Stir juice mixture into skillet and bring to a boil. Cook and stir for 1–2 minutes, or until thickened. Remove from heat and pour over fruit/onion/chilies mixture. Gently toss to coat.

6. Serve about ⅓ cup fruit sauce over each chicken breast.

Chicken Scaloppine

Betsy Chutchian,
Grand Prairie, TX

Makes 6-8 servings
Prep. Time: 5-10 minutes
Cooking Time: 25-30 minutes

6-8 boneless, skinless chicken breast halves

½ tsp. salt

¼ tsp. pepper

¼ cup flour

7 Tbsp. butter, *divided*

¼ lb. fresh mushrooms, sliced

2 tsp. fresh lemon juice

2 Tbsp. olive oil

¼ lb. ham, cut into thin strips

½ cup dry sherry

½ cup chicken broth

1. Place chicken breasts between 2 sheets of plastic wrap and pound with a mallet or rolling pin to flatten.

2. Place salt, pepper, and flour in shallow bowl. Dip each breast half into mixture, coating both sides well.

3. Melt 3 tablespoons butter in skillet. Add mushrooms and sauté about 5 minutes.

4. Remove mushrooms and sprinkle with lemon juice. Set aside.

5. Heat remaining butter and oil in skillet. Add several chicken breasts to the skillet (do not crowd them), and sauté until lightly browned on both sides. Remove chicken pieces as they brown and keep them warm on a platter covered with foil.

6. Add ham to skillet and brown. Remove and keep warm in a separate bowl.

7. Add sherry and broth to skillet, bringing to a boil and cooking for 2 minutes.

8. Stir up any brown particles in the skillet so that they flavor the sauce. Return chicken and mushrooms to skillet. Bring sauce to a boil again, then simmer uncovered for 3–5 minutes, until reduced by one-third.

9. Place chicken on a serving platter.

10. Spoon ham and mushrooms on top of chicken.

11. Pour sauce over chicken and serve.

Chicken

Chicken in Alfredo Sauce

Joyce Clark,
East Amherst, NY

Makes 4-6 servings
Prep. Time: 20-30 minutes
Cooking/Baking Time: 30-35 minutes

½ cup cooked spinach, stems removed

4 boneless, skinless chicken breast halves,
    slightly flattened

2 thin slices ham, each cut in half

¼ red bell pepper, cut in thin strips

Alfredo sauce:
1 Tbsp. butter

2 Tbsp. flour

1 clove garlic, minced

¾ cup whipping cream

1¼ cups milk

1 tsp. grated lemon peel

pinch of ground nutmeg

¼ tsp. salt

¼ cup grated Parmesan cheese

1 Tbsp. chopped fresh parsley

cooked rice or pasta

1. Squeeze spinach until dry. Divide evenly over chicken breasts. Top each breast with a half slice of ham and a few red pepper strips.

2. Roll breasts up firmly, beginning at thinnest end of breast. Secure each with a toothpick and place, seam-side down, in a single layer in a greased baking pan. Set aside.

3. In a small saucepan, melt butter. Add flour, garlic, cream, milk, lemon peel, nutmeg, salt, Parmesan cheese, and parsley. Stir and blend well. Cook over low heat, stirring occasionally until sauce begins to gently boil. Then stir continuously until smooth and thickened. Pour over chicken rolls.

4. Cover and bake at 350° for 20 minutes, turning after 10 minutes. Baste rolls with sauce.

5. Uncover and stir sauce as well as you can. Spoon up over chicken. Bake 5–7 minutes more.

6. To serve, cut meat rolls in half and serve over rice or pasta. Whisk sauce smooth and ladle over top.

Chicken

Chicken Broccoli Lo Mein

Pamela Pierce,
Annville, PA

Makes 4–6 servings
Prep. Time: 10 minutes
Cooking Time: 15 minutes

¼ cup peanut butter

¼ cup soy sauce

1½ Tbsp. brown sugar

1 Tbsp. fresh lemon juice

⅓ cup hot water

2 cloves garlic, minced

2 Tbsp. oil

1 lb. uncooked boneless, skinless chicken breasts, cubed

1 medium bunch broccoli, cut in bite-sized pieces

½ lb. fettucine or lo mein noodles, cooked and set aside

1. In a jar with a tight lid, mix peanut butter, soy sauce, brown sugar, lemon juice, hot water, and garlic. Shake well until blended.

2. In skillet, stir-fry chicken in oil for 5–6 minutes. Add broccoli. Cook an additional 3–4 minutes.

3. Add sauce to skillet. Stir in noodles. Cook 2 more minutes and then serve.

Chicken

Yogurt Chicken Curry

Laverne Nafziger,
Goshen, IN

Makes 10 servings
Prep. Time: 15 minutes
Cooking Time: 4–5 hours
Ideal slow-cooker size: 6-qt.

2 lbs. (1 quart) plain yogurt

4 heaping tsp. curry powder

2 heaping tsp. turmeric

1 heaping tsp. ground coriander

8 boneless, skinless chicken thighs

1 large onion, chopped

5 garlic cloves, chopped

1" ginger root, grated or finely chopped

½ tsp. salt

1 medium raw potato, grated

1 cup sour cream

1 cup chopped fresh cilantro, optional

1. Mix yogurt, curry powder, turmeric, and coriander in large nonmetallic bowl.

2. Submerge chicken thighs in mixture. Cover and place in refrigerator to marinate 8 hours or overnight.

3. Grease interior of slow-cooker crock.

4. When ready to cook, remove chicken from sauce and set aside.

5. Put sauce into cooker. Add onion, garlic, ginger, salt, and raw potato. Mix together well.

6. Push thighs down into sauce. If you need to make a second layer, stagger the pieces so they don't directly overlap each other. Spoon sauce over thighs on both layers.

7. Cover. Cook on Low 4 hours. Check to see if chicken is fully cooked by inserting an instant-read meat thermometer into the thighs. If it registers 160°–165°, the chicken's finished. If not, continue cooking another hour on Low. Check again to see if it's reached the safe temperature. If not, continue cooking for 30-minute intervals, checking the temperature at the end of each.

8. When chicken is cooked, remove it to a platter.

9. Stir sour cream into sauce in cooker. Put chicken back into sauce in cooker. Cover and cook 30 more minutes on Low.

10. To serve, put chicken on platter. Pour sauce over. Top with cilantro just before serving. Pass a bowl of cooked rice, followed by the Yogurt Chicken Curry.

Chicken

Chicken Vegetable Strudel

**Ruth C Hancock,
Earlsboro, OK**

Makes 4 servings
Prep. Time: 25 minutes
Baking Time: 30–35 minutes

2 cups diced cooked chicken

½ cup shredded carrots

½ cup finely chopped broccoli

⅓ cup finely chopped red bell pepper

1 cup shredded sharp cheddar cheese

½ cup mayonnaise

2 cloves garlic, minced

1½ tsp. fresh chopped dill

¼ tsp. salt

¼ tsp. pepper

2 tubes crescent rolls

1 egg white, beaten

2 Tbsp. slivered almonds

1. In a large bowl, combine chicken, carrots, broccoli, bell pepper, cheese, mayonnaise, garlic, dill weed, salt, and pepper. Mix well.

2. Unroll crescent rolls, placing squares against each other in a greased 10 × 15 jelly-roll pan. Dough will hang over the sides of the pan. Pinch the center seam together.

3. Place chicken mixture down the center of the dough.

4. Cut dough in 1½"-wide strips, cutting in 3½" toward the center.

5. Starting at one end, pick up alternate strips from each side, twist each one twice, and then lay each at an angle across the filling. Seal the ends against the dough when attaching them.

6. In a small mixing bowl, beat the egg white until foamy. Brush over dough. Sprinkle with almonds.

7. Bake at 375° for 30–35 minutes.

Stuffed Quesadillas

Stacy Schmucker Stoltzfus,
Enola, PA

Makes 2-4 servings
Prep. Time: 20-25 minutes
Cooking Time: 6-10 minutes

8 6" corn tortillas

2 cups shredded Monterey Jack cheese

1 cup canned black beans, drained

¼ cup diced onions

½ cup chopped fresh cilantro

2 plum tomatoes, chopped

1 red or green bell pepper, chopped

2 cups shredded, cooked chicken

1 lime, cut into wedges

sour cream and salsa

1. Place 4 tortillas onto workspace. Sprinkle ¼ cup cheese over each tortilla.

2. Dividing each ingredient into 4 parts, continue layering on each tortilla in this order: black beans, onions, cilantro, tomatoes, pepper, and chicken. Top each with ¼ cup cheese.

3. Squeeze lime juice over all. Cover with remaining tortillas.

4. Heat large skillet on medium-high heat. Place 2 tortilla stacks in hot skillet and cook 3–5 minutes, or until tortilla is browned.

5. Carefully flip onto other side and cook until cheese is melted.

6. Remove from pan and cut with a pizza cutter into fourths. Keep warm.

7. Continue with the remaining 2 tortilla stacks, browning and flipping until done. Cut into fourths, also.

8. Serve with sour cream and salsa on the side.

TIP

The ingredient amounts for filling are approximate. Use what you like.

Chicken

Chicken and Broccoli Pita Sandwiches

**Vonnie Oyer,
Hubbard, OR**

Makes 4–6 servings
Prep. Time: 15 minutes

2 cups chopped cooked chicken

2 tomatoes, chopped

1½ cups chopped raw broccoli

1 hard-cooked egg, chopped

⅓ cup cooked rice

½ cup grated cheese

1 avocado, chopped, optional

2 Tbsp. honey

2 Tbsp. prepared mustard

¾ cup mayonnaise

4 pita breads

1. Mix chicken, tomatoes, broccoli, egg, rice, cheese, and avocado together in a large bowl.

2. Mix honey, mustard, and mayonnaise in a small bowl.

3. Pour dressing over chicken mixture and stir gently.

4. Cut pita breads in half. Fill with chicken mixture.

Edie's Paella

Joy Sutter,
Perkasie, PA

Makes 4–6 servings
Prep. Time: 15 minutes
Cooking Time: 25 minutes
Standing Time: 10 minutes

¼ cup olive oil

1½ lbs. boneless, skinless chicken breasts, diced

1 lb. Italian sausage, cut in pieces

1 large onion, chopped

3-4 tomatoes, chopped

5 cups chicken broth

15-oz. can black beans, drained and rinsed

15.5-oz. can pinto beans, drained and rinsed

15.5-oz. can great northern beans, drained and rinsed

1 tsp. fresh rosemary leaves

salt and pepper to taste

1 lb. small-grained rice

1. In a large stockpot, heat olive oil. Add chicken and brown.

2. Remove chicken, but reserve drippings. Brown sausage and onion in stockpot. Drain off drippings.

3. Stir in tomatoes.

4. Add chicken broth and simmer 10 minutes.

5. Add beans, rosemary, salt, and pepper. Stir well.

6. Add rice. Stir and then cook for 20–25 minutes, until rice is soft and liquid evaporates.

7. Let stand 10 minutes before serving.

Chicken

Sunday Chicken Stew with Dumplings

Kathy Hertzler,
Lancaster, PA

Makes 6 servings
Prep. Time: 1 hour
Cooking Time: 6½–7½ hours
Ideal slow-cooker size: 5-qt.

½ cup flour

1 tsp. salt

½ tsp. white pepper

3-lb. broiler/fryer chicken, cut up and skin removed

2 Tbsp. olive oil

3 cups chicken broth

6 large carrots, cut in 1-inch-thick pieces

2 celery ribs, cut into ½-inch-thick slices

1 large sweet onion, chopped into ½-inch thick slices

1 Tbsp. fresh chopped rosemary

1½ cups peas

Dumplings:
1 cup flour

½ Tbsp. fresh minced rosemary

2 tsp. baking powder

½ tsp. salt

1 egg, beaten

½ cup milk

1. To prepare chicken, combine flour, salt, and pepper in a large resealable plastic bag.

2. Add chicken, a few pieces at a time. Shake to coat.

3. In a large skillet, brown chicken in olive oil, a few pieces at a time.

4. As the pieces brown, remove to a platter and keep warm.

5. When all the chicken is brown, gradually add broth to skillet while bringing to a boil. Stir up the browned, flavorful bits sticking to the skillet.

6. In a 5-quart slow cooker, layer in carrots, celery, and onion.

7. Sprinkle with rosemary.

8. Add chicken. Carefully add hot broth.

9. Cover. Cook 6–7 hours on Low, or until chicken juice runs clear, vegetables are tender, and stew is bubbling.

10. Stir in peas.

11. To make the dumplings, combine flour, minced rosemary, baking powder, and salt in a small bowl.

12. In a separate bowl combine egg and milk.

13. Stir wet ingredients into dry ingredients until just combined.

14. Drop by spoonfuls into simmering chicken mixture.

15. Cover. Cook on High 25–30 minutes, or until a toothpick inserted in dumpling comes out clean. (Try this after 25 minutes; otherwise, do not lift the cover while simmering).

Serving suggestion:
Serve each person with a "scoop" of dumpling topped with vegetables and broth, with a piece of chicken on the side.

TIP

The dumplings cook best if you use an oval, or wide, more shallow slow cooker.

Turkey

Turkey in a Pot

Dorothy M. Pittman,
Pickens, SC

Makes 10–12 servings
Prep. Time: 5–10 minutes
Cooking Time: 6 hours
Ideal slow-cooker size: 5-qt.

4–5 lb. turkey breast

1 medium onion, chopped

1 rib celery, chopped

¼ cup melted margarine

salt to taste

lemon-pepper seasoning to taste

1½ cups chicken broth

1. Wash turkey breast. Pat dry. Place in greased slow cooker. Put onion and celery in cavity.

2. Pour margarine over turkey. Sprinkle with seasonings. Pour broth around turkey.

3. Cover. Cook on High 6 hours. Let stand 10 minutes before carving.

Savory Turkey and Mushrooms

Clara Newswanger, Gordonville, PA

Makes 6–8 servings
Prep. Time: 20 minutes
Cooking Time: 4–4½ hours
Ideal slow-cooker size: 5-qt.

1 medium onion, chopped

½ stick (¼ cup) butter

3 cups fresh mushrooms, sliced

4 Tbsp. cornstarch

1 cup beef broth

2 Tbsp. soy sauce

2½ lbs. boneless, skinless turkey thighs, cut in 4" cubes

salt and pepper, optional

Cooked rice or noodles

1. Sauté chopped onion in butter in saucepan.

2. Stir in mushrooms and cornstarch until well mixed.

3. Stir in beef broth and soy sauce. Bring to a boil, stirring continuously so mixture thickens but doesn't stick.

4. Grease interior of slow-cooker crock.

5. Place cut-up turkey evenly over bottom of crock. Pour sauce over meat.

6. Cover. Cook on Low 4–4½ hours, or until turkey is tender when pierced with a fork.

7. Taste broth and season with salt and pepper if you wish.

8. Serve over cooked rice or noodles.

Turkey

Turkey Stir-Fry

Arianne Hochstetler,
Goshen, IN

Makes 6 servings
Prep. Time: 15–20 minutes
Cooking Time: 20 minutes

1½ lbs. boneless turkey, cut into strips

1 Tbsp. cooking oil

1 large onion, chopped

1 carrot, julienned

half a green pepper, sliced

2 cups fresh, sliced mushrooms

1 cup chicken broth

3 Tbsp. cornstarch

3 Tbsp. soy sauce

½ tsp. ginger

1 tsp. curry powder

2 cups pea pods, trimmed

⅓ cup cashews, optional

1. In a large skillet or wok, stir-fry turkey in oil over medium-high heat until no longer pink, about 5–6 minutes. Remove turkey from pan and keep warm.

2. Stir-fry the onion, carrot, green pepper, and mushrooms until crisp-tender, about 5 minutes.

3. In a small bowl, combine chicken broth, cornstarch, soy sauce, ginger, and curry powder until smooth.

4. Add to the skillet. Cook and stir until thickened and bubbly.

5. Return turkey to skillet with pea pods. Cook and stir until heated through.

6. Serve over cooked rice. Top with cashews, if desired.

Variation:
You can use sliced beef, pork, or chicken instead of turkey.

TIPS

1. Chop all the vegetables before you cut the turkey into strips. Then all ingredients are ready to go as you need them.
2. Cook the rice at the same time as you are preparing and cooking the stir-fry.

Turkey

Turkey or Chicken Curry

Angie Clemens,
Dayton, VA

Makes 8–10 servings
Prep. Time: 30 minutes
Cooking Time: 75 minutes

⅔ cup minced onions

1 cup chopped apples

¼ cup vegetable oil

¼ cup flour

1 Tbsp. curry powder

hot sauce to taste

1 qt. chicken broth

2 cloves garlic, crushed

2 Tbsp. freshly grated ginger

1 large tomato, sliced, *optional*

2 cups diced cooked turkey or chicken

1. In a large skillet, heat onions and apples in oil. Cook, covered, until clear, stirring several times.

2. Add flour and curry powder.

3. Slowly stir in hot sauce, if you wish, and the broth until well blended. Add garlic, ginger, and tomato, if you wish.

4. Bring to a boil. Cover and simmer 1 hour, stirring occasionally.

5. Add meat and cook long enough to heat through.

Serving suggestions:
Serve over rice along with serving dishes of chutney, sliced scallions, shredded coconut, peanuts, pineapple chunks, and raisins or craisins.

Seafood

Shrimp Primavera

Elaine Rineer,
Lancaster, PA

Makes 4 servings
Prep. Time: 20 minutes
Cooking Time: 10 minutes

1½ cups chopped broccoli

½ cup thinly sliced carrots

1 Tbsp., plus 1 tsp., vegetable or olive oil

1 cup sliced mushrooms

2 garlic cloves, minced

1 cup chicken broth

1 Tbsp. cornstarch

1 lb. shrimp, peeled and deveined

2 Tbsp. grated Parmesan cheese

2 Tbsp. parsley

1. In large skillet or wok, sauté broccoli and carrots in oil. Stir-fry until carrots are crisp-tender.

2. Stir in mushrooms and garlic. Stir-fry 1 minute.

3. In a small bowl, whisk together broth and cornstarch. Pour over vegetables.

4. Add shrimp. Cook until shrimp turns pink and sauce thickens.

5. Stir in remaining ingredients.

Shrimp Jambalaya

Karen Ashworth,
Duenweg, MO

Makes 6–8 servings
Prep. Time: 15 minutes
Cooking Time: 2¼ hours
Ideal slow-cooker size: 6-qt.

2 Tbsp. margarine

2 medium onions, chopped

2 green bell peppers, chopped

3 ribs celery, chopped

1 cup chopped cooked ham

2 garlic cloves, chopped

1½ cups instant rice

1½ cups beef broth

28-oz. can chopped tomatoes, or 10–12 whole tomatoes, peeled and chopped

2 Tbsp. chopped fresh parsley

2 tsp. fresh chopped basil

1½ tsp. fresh chopped thyme

¼ tsp. pepper

⅛ tsp. cayenne pepper

1 lb. shelled, deveined, medium-size shrimp

1. Melt margarine in slow cooker set on High. Add onions, peppers, celery, ham, and garlic. Cook 30 minutes.

2. Add rice. Cover and cook 15 minutes.

3. Add broth, tomatoes, 2 Tbsp. parsley, and remaining seasonings. Cover and cook on High 1 hour.

4. Add shrimp. Cook on High 30 minutes, or until liquid is absorbed.

Serving suggestion:
Garnish with 1 Tbsp. parsley.

Shrimp with Ginger and Lime

**Joy Uhler,
Richardson, TX**

Makes 2–4 servings
Prep. Time: 15–20 minutes
Cooking Time: 10 minutes

3 Tbsp. fresh lime juice

4 Tbsp. olive oil, *divided*

1 Tbsp. fresh minced ginger

1 Tbsp. brown sugar

1 tsp. grated lime zest

1 tsp. sesame seed oil

1 large garlic clove, minced

1 lb. cooked shrimp, peeled and deveined

cooked rice

2 Tbsp. fresh chopped cilantro

1. In a large mixing bowl, stir together lime juice, 3 Tbsp. olive oil, ginger, brown sugar, lime zest, sesame seed oil, and garlic clove.

2. Stir in shrimp and mix well so that they're covered with the marinade. Allow shrimp to marinate for 15 minutes.

3. Pour 1 Tbsp. olive oil into large skillet or wok. Spoon in shrimp mixture and stir-fry until heated through.

4. Serve over prepared rice. Sprinkle with chopped cilantro.

Cajun Shrimp

**Mary Ann Potenta,
Bridgewater, NJ**

Makes 4–5 servings
Prep. Time: just minutes!
Cooking Time: 10–12 minutes

1½ sticks (12 Tbsp.) butter, *divided*

½ cup chopped scallions

1 tsp. minced garlic

1 tsp. cayenne pepper

½ tsp. white pepper

½ tsp. black pepper

¼ tsp. dry mustard

½ tsp. salt

1 tsp. Tabasco sauce

2 lbs. shrimp, peeled and cleaned

cooked rice

1. Melt 1 stick of butter in large skillet. Add scallions and garlic and sauté till clear, but not brown, about 1 minute.

2. Add peppers, mustard, and salt. Cook and stir for 3 minutes.

3. Mix in half-stick of butter and Tabasco sauce until blended.

4. Add shrimp. Cook just until pink. Do not overcook.

5. Serve over cooked rice

NOTE

This is hot! You can tone things down by reducing the amounts of the 3 peppers and the Tabasco sauce.

Seafood

Sesame Shrimp and Asparagus

Karen Kay Tucker,
Manteca, CA

Makes 6 servings
Prep. Time: 30 minutes
Cooking Time: 10 minutes

1½ lbs. fresh asparagus

1 Tbsp. sesame seeds

⅓ cup vegetable oil or olive oil

2 small red onions, sliced in rings

1½ lbs. large shrimp, peeled and deveined

4 tsp. soy sauce

1¼ tsp. salt

1. About 30 minutes before serving, prepare asparagus. Hold base of each stalk firmly and bend. The end will break off at the spot where it becomes too tough to eat. Discard ends or freeze and use when making stock.

2. Wash and trim asparagus. Then cut into 2" pieces and steam in ½" water in saucepan until crisp-tender. Plunge asparagus into cold water to stop cooking. Set aside.

3. In a large skillet or wok, over medium heat, toast sesame seeds until golden brown, stirring seeds and shaking skillet often. Remove seeds to small bowl.

4. In same skillet or wok, over medium-high heat, heat oil until hot. Add onions and shrimp. Cook until shrimp are pink, about 5 minutes.

5. Drain asparagus. Add to skillet with shrimp. Stir in sesame seeds, soy sauce, and salt. Heat until asparagus is warm.

Seafood Gumbo

**Barbara Katrine Rose,
Woodbridge, VA**

Makes 10 servings
Prep. Time: 45 minutes
Cooking Time: 3–4 hours
Ideal slow-cooker size: 4- or 5-qt.

1 lb. okra, sliced

2 Tbsp. butter

¼ cup butter, melted

¼ cup flour

1 bunch scallions, sliced

½ cup chopped celery

2 garlic cloves, minced

16-oz. can chopped tomatoes and juice, or
    5–6 whole tomatoes, peeled and chopped

1 bay leaf

1 Tbsp. chopped fresh parsley

1 fresh thyme sprig, chopped

1½ tsp. salt

½–1 tsp. red pepper

3–5 cups water, depending upon the
    consistency you like

1 lb. peeled and deveined fresh shrimp

½ lb. fresh crabmeat

1. Sauté okra in 2 Tbsp. butter until okra is lightly browned. Transfer to slow cooker.

2. Combine ¼ cup melted butter and flour in skillet. Cook over medium heat, stirring constantly until roux is the color of chocolate, 20–25 minutes. Stir in scallions, celery, and garlic. Cook until vegetables are tender. Add to slow cooker. Gently stir in remaining ingredients.

3. Cover. Cook on High 3–4 hours.

Seafood

Flounder Zucchini Bundles

Betty L. Moore,
Plano, IL

Makes 4 servings
Prep. Time: 15 minutes
Baking Time: 20 minutes

4 6-oz. flounder fillets

¼ tsp. lemon pepper, *divided*

1 medium lemon, thinly sliced, *divided*

1 medium zucchini, cut into ¼"-thick slices, *divided*

12 cherry tomatoes, sliced, *divided*

1 tsp. fresh chopped dill weed, *divided*

½ tsp. fresh chopped basil, *divided*

1. Place 1 fillet on double thickness of 15 × 18 piece of heavy-duty aluminum foil.

2. Sprinkle with ¼ of lemon pepper.

3. Top with ¼ of lemon slices, zucchini, and tomatoes.

4. Sprinkle with ¼ of dill and basil.

5. Fold foil around fish and seal tightly. Place on baking sheet.

6. Repeat with other fillets.

7. Bake at 425° for 15–20 minutes, or until fish flakes easily.

Meatless

Black Bean and Butternut Burritos

Janelle Myers-Benner,
Harrisonburg, VA

Makes 8 burritos
Prep. Time: 45 minutes
Baking Time: 15–20 minutes

1 Tbsp. oil

1 small or medium-sized onion, chopped

3–4 cups butternut squash, cut into ½" cubes

½ tsp. cumin

¼ tsp. cinnamon

½ tsp. salt

2 cups cooked, or a 15-oz. can, black beans, drained

8 tortillas

1½ cups grated cheese

sour cream

salsa

cilantro, if you wish

1. In a large skillet or saucepan, heat oil. Sauté onions until tender.

2. Add squash. Cover and cook over medium heat until tender.

3. Add cumin, cinnamon, and salt. Add beans. Cover, and heat through.

4. Put ⅛ of mixture in each tortilla, top with 3 Tbsp. cheese, and roll up. Place seam-side down in a greased 9 × 13 baking pan.

5. Bake uncovered in 350° oven for about 15–20 minutes, until heated through.

6. Serve with sour cream and salsa, and cilantro if you wish.

TIP

Tortillas freeze well with the mixture inside so I often make a double or triple batch. You can also freeze just the filling.

Black Bean and Kale or Spinach Tostata

Peg Zannotti,
Tulsa, OK

Makes 4–6 servings
Prep. Time: 15 minutes
Baking Time: 25 minutes

1 bunch scallions, chopped

3 garlic cloves, minced

1½ tsp. cumin

1½ tsp. coriander

1 Tbsp. poblano pepper, minced

3 Tbsp. olive oil

15-oz. can black beans, drained and rinsed

½ cup fresh orange juice

1 bunch kale, or 3 cups fresh spinach, chopped

salt to taste

8 6" corn tortillas

⅓–½ cup grated cheese of your choice

⅓–½ cup sour cream, optional

1. In a large skillet, sauté scallions, garlic, cumin, coriander, and poblano in olive oil for 8 minutes. (Wear gloves when you deseed the pepper, and do not allow the pepper to touch your eyes or skin.)

2. Add black beans and cook for 3 minutes, stirring and mashing the beans with the back of a spoon.

3. Add orange juice and kale or spinach. Cover and simmer for about 10 minutes, stirring frequently.

4. Add salt to taste.

5. Heat tortillas by lightly frying them, microwaving them, or heating them in the oven for several minutes.

6. For each serving, start with a heated tortilla, cover it generously with the black bean mixture, 1–2 Tbsp. cheese, and 1–2 Tbsp. sour cream if you wish.

TIP

The filling in this recipe also works well as a dip for chips.

Meatless

Exceptional Eggplant Casserole

Lisa Good,
Harrisonburg, VA

Makes 6–8 servings
Prep. Time: 15–20 minutes
Baking Time: 45–50 minutes

½ cup chopped onions

½ cup chopped green peppers

½ cup chopped celery

1 tsp. oil

2 8-oz. cans tomato sauce

⅓ cup brown sugar

¼ fresh chopped oregano

1 clove garlic, minced

1 medium-sized eggplant, peeled or unpeeled, sliced in ⅛"-thick slices

1½ cups mozzarella cheese

1. In a large skillet or saucepan, sauté the onions, green peppers, and celery in the oil.

2. Add the tomato sauce, brown sugar, oregano, and garlic to the sautéed vegetables. Mix well.

3. Layer one-third of the sauce mixture, one-third of the eggplant, and one-third of the cheese into a greased 2-qt. baking dish. Repeat the layers twice.

4. Bake uncovered at 350° for 45–50 minutes.

Double-Cheese Zucchini Bake

Janet Schaeffer,
Lansing, IL

Makes 12–15 servings
Prep. Time: 15–20 minutes
Baking Time: 35–40 minutes

½ cup butter

1 clove garlic, chopped

8 medium-sized, peeled or unpeeled, zucchini, sliced

1 cup Italian-seasoned bread crumbs, *divided*

3 cups shredded Monterey Jack cheese, *divided*

2 cups grated Parmesan cheese, *divided*

1 Tbsp. Italian seasoning

3 eggs

2 cups half-and-half, or 2 cups whipping cream

1. In large saucepan, melt butter. Add garlic and cook about 3 minutes.

2. Add zucchini to garlic and butter. Sauté until soft, about 10 minutes.

3. Stir in ½ cup bread crumbs, 2 cups Monterey Jack cheese, 1 cup Parmesan cheese, and Italian seasoning. Blend well.

4. Spoon mixture into a greased 9 × 13, or larger, baking dish.

5. In a mixing bowl, beat eggs. Mix in half-and-half. Pour over baking dish contents and let it settle into the zucchini mixture.

6. Top with remaining 1 cup Monterey Jack cheese, 1 cup Parmesan cheese, and ½ cup bread crumbs.

7. Bake at 350°, uncovered, for 35–40 minutes, or until knife inserted in center comes out clean.

TIP

You can make the dish the day before serving it and refrigerate it unbaked. If you put it in the oven cold, increase the baking time to 50–60 minutes

Meatless

Zucchini Babka

Esther J. Mast,
Lancaster, PA

Makes 6-8 servings
Prep. Time: 20 minutes
Baking Time: 30-45 minutes

3 eggs

½ cup vegetable oil

4 cups diced zucchini, peeled or unpeeled

1 medium-sized onion, chopped

1 cup all-purpose baking mix

½ cup grated cheddar cheese

1 tsp. salt

1 Tbsp. fresh chopped oregano

dash of pepper

Parmesan cheese

1. In a large mixing bowl, beat eggs. Blend in oil.

2. Add zucchini, onion, baking mix, cheese, salt, oregano, and pepper. Mix well.

3. Pour into greased 1½–2-qt. baking dish. Sprinkle with Parmesan cheese.

4. Bake at 350° for 30–45 minutes, or until nicely browned.

Variations:

1. Use 3 cups zucchini and 1 cup cheese in the batter.
2. Use 1 clove minced garlic instead of onions.

   —Evie Hershey, Atglen, PA

3. Use 3 cups zucchini and 4 eggs.
4. Use 2 Tbsp. parsley, ½ tsp. salt, and ½ tsp. dried oregano.

   —Joyce Kreiser, Manheim, PA
   —Virginia Martin, Harrisonburg, VA
   —Joanne Kennedy, Plattsburgh, NY

5. Use 4 eggs.
6. Add ½ cup shredded Swiss cheese to the batter, and sprinkle the Parmesan cheese on top.

   —Becky Frey, Lebanon, PA

Taco-Rito

Marlene Fonken,
Upland, CA

Makes 4 servings
Prep. Time: 20–25 minutes
Cooking Time: 5 minutes

1 Tbsp., plus 1 tsp., vegetable oil

1½ cups broccoli florets

1 cup sliced fresh mushrooms

½ cup chopped green peppers

½ cup sliced onions

½ cup diced tomatoes

4 ozs. shredded cheddar, or pepper, cheese

4 1-oz. flour tortillas, warmed

1. In a skillet, heat oil over medium-high heat. Add broccoli, mushrooms, green peppers, and onions. Stir-fry until tender-crisp, about 2–5 minutes.

2. Remove from heat and stir in tomatoes and cheese. Stir until cheese is partially melted.

3. Divide among the 4 tortillas. Roll up to eat!

TIP

Add some taco sauce to Step 2 if you wish.

Meatless

Lentil and Rice with Tomato Cucumber Salad

**Mary Longenecker,
Bethel, PA**

Makes 4-6 servings
Prep. Time: 20 minutes
Cooking Time: 45 minutes

¾ cup brown lentils, rinsed

3½ cups water

1 cup long-grain rice

2 tsp. salt

½-1 tsp. cumin, according to your taste
  preference

3 Tbsp. oil

1-2 sliced onions, whichever you prefer

Salad:

2 small cucumbers, diced

2 medium-sized tomatoes, diced

½-1 small onion, diced

2 Tbsp. lemon juice

2 Tbsp. oil

1 garlic clove, minced or crushed

2 tsp. salt

1. In a large saucepan, combine lentils and water. Cover and bring to a boil. Cook on medium heat for 10 minutes.

2. Add rice, salt, and cumin. Cover and bring to a boil. Cook on low for 20–25 minutes, or until rice is cooked.

3. While rice and lentils cook, place oil in skillet. Sauté sliced onions in 3 Tbsp. oil until brown and limp. Set sautéed onions aside until time to serve.

4. In a mixing bowl, combine cucumbers, tomatoes, and diced onion.

5. In a small bowl, stir together lemon juice, 2 Tbsp. oil, garlic, and salt. Pour over cucumber mixture. Stir gently together.

6. To serve, press lentil/rice mixture into a cup or small bowl. Unmold in center of a large plate or platter. Top with sautéed onions. Place spoonfuls of salad around the lentil mixture. Sprinkle extra juice from salad over all.

Meatless

Tempeh Stuffed Peppers

Sara Harter Fredette,
Williamsburg, MA

Makes 4 servings
Prep. Time: 20 minutes
Cooking Time: 3–8 hours
Ideal slow-cooker size: 5-qt.

4 oz. tempeh, cubed

1 garlic clove, minced

28-oz. can crushed tomatoes, *divided*, or
    10–12 whole tomatoes, peeled and crushed

2 tsp. soy sauce

¼ cup chopped onions

1½ cups cooked rice

1½ cups and 1/4 cup shredded cheese,
    divided

Tabasco sauce, optional

4 green, red, or yellow, bell peppers, tops
    removed and seeded

1. Steam tempeh 10 minutes in saucepan. Mash in bowl with the garlic, half the tomatoes, and soy sauce.

2. Stir in onions, rice, 1½ cups cheese, and Tabasco sauce. Stuff into peppers.

3. Place peppers in slow cooker, 3 on the bottom and one on top. Pour remaining half of tomatoes over peppers.

4. Cover. Cook on Low 6–8 hours, or on High 3–4 hours. Top with remaining cheese in last 30 minutes.

Meatless

Tomato Spaghetti Sauce

Jean Butzer,
Batavia, NY

Makes 6 servings
Prep. Time: 10 minutes
Cooking Time: 10½–12½ hours
Ideal slow-cooker size: 2½-qt.

1 cup finely chopped onions

2 garlic cloves, minced

2 lbs. fresh tomatoes, peeled and chopped, or
    28-oz. can tomatoes, cut up, with juice

6-oz. can tomato paste

1 Tbsp. sugar

2 tsp. instant beef bouillon granules

1 Tbsp. fresh chopped oregano

1 tsp. fresh chopped basil

1 large bay leaf

salt to taste

pepper to taste

¾ cup sliced mushrooms

2 Tbsp. cornstarch

2 Tbsp. cold water

1. Combine all ingredients except mushrooms, cornstarch, and water in slow cooker.

2. Cover. Cook on Low 10–12 hours.

3. Remove bay leaf. Stir in mushrooms.

4. Combine cornstarch and water. Stir into sauce.

5. Cover. Cook on High until thickened and bubbly, about 25 minutes.

Italian Vegetable Pasta Sauce

Sherril Bieberly,
Salina, KS

Makes 2½ quarts sauce
Prep. Time: 25 minutes
Cooking Time: 5–18 hours
Ideal slow-cooker size: 4- or 5-qt.

3 Tbsp. olive oil

1 cup packed chopped fresh parsley

3 ribs celery, chopped

1 medium onion, chopped

2 garlic cloves, minced

2-inch sprig fresh rosemary

2 small fresh sage leaves

32-oz. can tomato sauce

32-oz. can chopped tomatoes, or 10–12 whole
tomatoes, peeled and chopped

1 small dried hot chili pepper

¼ lb. fresh mushrooms, sliced

1½ tsp. salt

1. Heat oil in skillet. Add parsley, celery, onion, garlic, rosemary, and sage. Sauté until vegetables are tender. Place in slow cooker.

2. Add tomatoes, chili pepper, mushrooms, and salt.

3. Cover. Cook on Low 12–18 hours, or on High 5–6 hours.

Variation:
Add 2 lbs. browned ground beef to olive oil and sautéed vegetables. Continue with recipe.

Meatless

Classic Pesto

**Leona Yoder,
Hartville, OH**

Makes about 1½ cups
Prep. Time: 10 minutes

2 cups lightly packed fresh basil

1 cup (about 5 ozs.) grated Parmesan cheese

½–⅔ cup extra-virgin olive oil

1-2 cloves garlic, minced, *optional*

1. Whirl basil, Parmesan, half the oil, and, if desired, garlic in a blender or food processor until smooth. Add more oil, if needed.

2. If you're not ready to use the pesto immediately, cover and refrigerate it for up to 5 days. Or freeze it if you want to store it longer.

3. Serve over your favorite cooked pasta, or on bruschetta.

Spinach Pesto

**Vic and Christina Buckwalter,
Keezletown, VA**

Makes 1½ cups pesto
Prep. Time: 15 minutes
Cooking Time: 12 minutes

Pesto:
4 packed cups fresh spinach leaves

3 garlic cloves

2 Tbsp. pine nuts

¼ packed cup fresh basil

½ cup extra-virgin olive oil

⅛ tsp. salt

Pasta for 4-5 servings:
1 lb. linguine, or pasta of your choice

¼–½ cup pesto

2 Tbsp. Parmesan cheese, freshly grated

2 Tbsp. pasta water

1. Process pesto ingredients in blender until smooth. Store in refrigerator or freeze for later use.

2. When ready to use, cook 1 lb. linguine according to package directions. Drain, saving 2 Tbsp. of pasta water.

3. Mix together ¼–½ cup of pesto, Parmesan cheese, and reserved pasta water. Stir mixture into pasta.

Variations:
1. Sometimes we toss chopped fresh tomatoes from the garden into Step 3.
2. This pesto makes an excellent pizza topping, along with your favorite cheeses.

Southwestern Pesto Pasta

**Carrie Wood,
Paxton, MA**

Makes 4–6 servings
Prep. Time: 10 minutes
Cooking Time: 10–12 minutes

1 cup loosely packed cilantro leaves

1 cup loosely packed flat parsley

⅓ cup toasted pepitas (pumpkin seeds)

1 clove garlic, peeled

½ cup crumbled feta cheese

½ cup extra-virgin olive oil

salt to taste

1 lb. spaghetti or linguine

1. Process all ingredients except pasta in a food processor until a rough paste is formed, adding additional olive oil if the paste seems too dry.

2. Cook spaghetti or linguine according to package directions. Drain.

3. Toss pesto thoroughly with hot pasta and then serve.

Homemade Spaghetti Sauce

**Beverly Hummel,
Fleetwood, PA**

Makes 12 cups
Prep. Time: 20 minutes
Cooking Time: 4–5 hours
Ideal slow-cooker size: 6-qt.

4 qts. cherry tomatoes

1 onion, minced

2 cloves garlic, minced

1 Tbsp. oil

3 tsp. sugar

3 tsp. fresh chopped rosemary

2 Tbsp. fresh chopped thyme and/or basil

2 tsp. Italian seasoning

1 tsp. salt

½ tsp. pepper

hot cooked spaghetti

1. Stem tomatoes, leaving the skins on. Blend until smooth in blender.

2. In a skillet, sauté onions and garlic in oil.

3. Add sauté to slow cooker. Add tomatoes, sugar, rosemary, thyme, Italian seasoning, salt and pepper.

4. Simmer on low in slow cooker until thickened, about 4–5 hours. Remove the lid for the final 30–60 minutes of cooking time if you'd like a thicker sauce.

5. Serve over spaghetti.

Vegetable Alfredo Sauce

Judy Buller,
Bluffton, OH

Makes 10-12 servings
Prep. Time: 30-45 minutes
Baking Time: 55-60 minutes
Standing Time: 15 minutes

9 lasagna noodles

½ cup chopped onion

1 clove garlic, minced

1 Tbsp. olive oil

1 carrot, shredded

4 cups fresh, chopped spinach

1 cup chopped broccoli

¼ tsp. salt

¼ tsp. pepper

Alfredo sauce (double recipe from page 272)

15-oz. carton ricotta cheese

½ cup Parmesan cheese

1 egg

2 cups shredded Colby, or Monterey Jack, cheese

1 cup shredded mozzarella cheese

1. Soak noodles in hot water for 15 minutes. Rinse, drain, and set aside.

2. In large skillet, cook onion and garlic in 1 Tbsp. oil until crisp-tender. Add carrot, spinach, broccoli, salt, and pepper.

3. Remove ½ cup Alfredo sauce and set aside.

4. Stir remaining Alfredo sauce into skillet. Mix well and heat thoroughly. Set aside.

5. Combine ricotta and Parmesan cheeses, egg, and Colby or Monterey Jack cheese in a large bowl. Mix well.

6. In a greased 9 × 13 baking pan, spread ½ cup Alfredo sauce on bottom. Layer in this order: 3 noodles, one-third of the cheese mixture, one-third of the Alfredo sauce mixture.

7. Repeat layers two more times. Top with mozzarella cheese.

8. Cover and bake at 350° for 45 minutes. Uncover and bake 10–15 minutes more.

9. Let stand 15 minutes before serving.

Fettuccine with Butter-Herb Sauce

Stacy Stoltzfus,
Grantham, PA

Makes 3-4 servings
Prep. Time: 5 minutes
Cooking/Baking Time: 8-10 minutes

⅓ lb. uncooked fettuccini noodles

half a stick (4 Tbsp.) butter, melted

1 Tbsp., or more, fresh basil

¾ tsp. fresh chopped thyme

¼ cup fresh parsley

1 Tbsp. chives, optional

1. Cook fettuccini noodles according to package directions.

2. Meanwhile blend remaining ingredients in a small pitcher.

3. Drain noodles very well when done and transfer to a serving bowl.

4. Pour melted butter with herbs over noodles. Toss and serve immediately.

Penne with Herb, Cheese, and Spinach

**Barbara A. Nolan,
Pleasant Valley, NY**

Makes 4 servings
Prep. Time: 10 minutes
Cooking/Baking Time: 25–30 minutes

½ lb. penne pasta

2 Tbsp. olive oil

2 Tbsp. minced garlic

10-oz. fresh baby spinach, washed

5–6-oz. container garlic/herb cheese spread

½ cup pasta cooking water

salt and pepper to taste, optional

1. Cook pasta according to directions on box. Set aside ½ cup cooking water. Drain the rest of the water off, and keep pasta warm.

2. Heat olive oil in large stockpot.

3. Cook minced garlic until soft, 5–6 minutes. Do not brown.

4. Add spinach and cook until wilted, about 3–4 minutes.

5. Coarsely chop spinach.

6. Add cheese spread and ½ cup water from pasta to spinach in pan. Cook over medium-low heat, stirring to melt cheese.

7. Add cooked pasta to spinach/cheese mixture.

8. Season with salt and pepper if you wish.

9. Toss gently. Serve immediately.

Pasta with Fresh Tomatoes and Basil

Naomi Cunningham,
Arlington, KS

Makes 2 servings
Prep. Time: 5 minutes
Standing Time: 2-3 hours
Cooking/Baking Time: 15 minutes

2 large fresh tomatoes, chopped

2 Tbsp. snipped fresh basil

1 garlic clove, minced

¼ tsp. pepper

4 ozs. dry bow tie, or other, pasta, cooked and drained additional fresh basil, optional

1. Combine the tomatoes, basil, garlic, and pepper in a mixing bowl.

2. Set aside at room temperature for several hours.

3. Serve over hot cooked pasta.

4. Garnish with additional basil if you wish.

Minestra Di Cesi

**Jeanette Oberholtzer,
Manheim, PA**

Makes 4–6 servings
Prep. Time: 25 minutes
Soaking Time: 8 hours, or overnight
Cooking Time: 5½–6 hours
Ideal slow-cooker size: 4-qt.

1 lb. dry garbanzo beans

1 sprig fresh rosemary

10 leaves fresh sage

2 Tbsp. salt

1–2 large garlic cloves, minced

olive oil

1 cup uncooked small pasta, your choice of
shape, or uncooked penne

1. Grease interior of slow-cooker crock.

2. Wash garbanzo beans. Place in slow cooker. Cover with water. Stir in rosemary, sage, and salt. Soak 8 hours, or overnight.

3. Drain water. Remove herbs.

4. Refill slow cooker with garbanzo beans and fresh water to 1 inch above the garbanzo beans.

5. Cover. Cook on Low 5 hours.

6. Sauté garlic in olive oil in skillet until clear.

7. Puree half of the garbanzo beans, along with several cups of broth from cooker, in blender. Return puree to slow cooker.

8. Add garlic and oil.

9. Boil pasta in saucepan until al dente, about 5 minutes. Drain. Add to beans.

10. Cover. Cook on High 30–60 minutes, or until pasta is tender and heated through, but not mushy.

Florentine Roll-Ups

Elaine Rineer,
Lancaster, PA

Makes 12 servings
Prep. Time: 35–45 minutes
Baking Time: 45 minutes

16-oz. pkg. lasagna noodles

4 cups (2 lbs.) ricotta, or cottage cheese

2 cups (8 oz.) grated cheddar cheese

1 cup cleaned, well drained, and chopped
fresh spinach

1/2 cup chopped scallions

1 egg, beaten

1/4 tsp. black pepper

1/4 tsp. salt

3 cups of spaghetti sauce, your favorite flavor,
divided

Parmesan cheese

1. Cook pasta according to package directions. Drain. Lay flat on waxed paper to cool.

2. In large mixing bowl, stir together ricotta or cottage cheese, cheddar cheese, spinach, scallions, egg, pepper, and salt.

3. Spread ⅓ cup mixture on each lasagna noodle. Roll up. Secure with toothpick if needed to keep from unrolling.

4. Spread ⅔ cup spaghetti sauce on bottom of well-greased 9 × 13 baking pan.

5. Place rolls seam-side down in pan.

6. Top with remaining sauce. Sprinkle with Parmesan cheese.

7. Cover. Bake at 350° for 45 minutes.

Ricotta Gnocchi with Spinach Sauce

**Judy Hershberger,
Millersburg, OH**

Makes 4 servings
Prep. Time: 35 minutes
Cooking/Baking Time: 40 minutes

2 Tbsp. butter

1 large onion, halved and thinly sliced

1½ cups, plus 1 Tbsp., all-purpose flour, *divided*

2 cups half-and-half

½ tsp. ground nutmeg

5 oz. baby spinach, rinsed and dried

15-oz. ricotta cheese

3 large eggs

1 cup grated Parmesan cheese, *divided*

1 tsp. salt

½ tsp. pepper

1. Bring a large Dutch oven of salted water to a boil.

2. Meanwhile, in a large, ovenproof skillet, melt the butter over medium-low heat.

3. Add the onion and cook, stirring occasionally, until softened and golden, 10–12 minutes.

4. Add 1 Tbsp. flour and cook, stirring constantly, 2 minutes.

5. Add the half-and-half and simmer, stirring constantly, until slightly thickened, about 3 minutes.

6. Add the nutmeg. Season with salt and pepper.

7. Working in batches, stir in the spinach and cook over low heat until just wilted, 3–5 minutes. Cover and set sauce aside.

8. In a medium bowl, lightly beat together the ricotta, eggs, ½ cup Parmesan, the remaining 1½ cups flour, and salt and pepper. Stir until well combined.

9. Using a soup spoon, drop 10–12 generous spoonfuls of dough (about half the dough) into the boiling water. Cook for 3 minutes. Gently stir the gnocchi to keep them from clumping together.

10. When the gnocchi rise to the surface, cook for about 3 minutes more.

11. Using a slotted spoon, transfer gnocchi to a towel-lined plate to drain. Repeat process with the remaining dough.

12. Add the cooked gnocchi to the spinach sauce and stir gently to coat.

13. Transfer mixture to a baking dish. Sprinkle with the remaining ½ cup Parmesan.

14. Broil until golden, about 3 minutes.

Pasta Vanesa

**Barry Coggin,
Jacksonville, FL**

Makes 6 servings
Prep. Time: 30 minutes
Cooking Time: 1 hour and 45 minutes

2 medium-sized onions, chopped

1 yellow bell pepper, chopped

1 orange bell pepper, chopped

3 cloves garlic, thinly sliced

10.75-oz. can tomato puree

3 8-oz. cans tomato sauce

6-oz. can tomato paste

1 pkg. (5 links) sweet Italian sausage, chopped

3 links hot Italian sausage, chopped

salt to taste

pepper to taste

1½ tsp. Italian seasoning

2 large Tbsp. honey

1 cup water

1 cup whipping cream

1 lb. spaghetti, uncooked

¼ cup fresh chopped parsley

1. In a large nonstick skillet, sauté onions, bell peppers, and garlic until just tender.

2. Add tomato puree, sauce, and paste. Blend well. Simmer covered for 1 hour.

3. Meanwhile, in a separate skillet, brown sausages. Add to tomato mixture.

4. Season with salt, pepper, and Italian seasoning. Then stir in honey and water.

5. Simmer covered for 30 minutes.

6. Just before serving, add whipping cream to tomato mixture. Cook until heated through, but do not boil.

7. As you begin Step 5, begin to cook the spaghetti according to the package directions. Drain.

8. Serve tomato sauce over cooked spaghetti. Sprinkle with fresh parsley.

TIP

You can prepare the sauce ahead of time—all but the whipping cream—and warm it when you are ready to serve. Add the whipping cream when the sauce is fully heated, and do not allow the sauce to boil after you've stirred in the whipping cream.

Zesty Macaroni and Cheese

Rosemarie Fitzgerald,
Gibsonia, PA

Makes 4 servings
Prep. Time: 15 minutes
Cooking/Baking Time: 40 minutes

¼ lb. uncooked whole wheat elbow macaroni

1¼ cups hot milk

½ lb. cheddar cheese, shredded

6 Tbsp. dry bread crumbs or ¾ cup fresh crumbs

2 Tbsp. chopped fresh parsley

1 medium onion, chopped

1 green bell pepper, finely chopped

3-4 scallions, chopped, or more to taste

1 tsp. salt, optional

2 eggs, beaten

sprinkle of paprika

1. Cook macaroni until tender-firm. Drain and set aside.

2. In a large bowl, pour hot milk over cheese and crumbs.

3. Add parsley, onion, pepper, scallions, and salt if you wish.

4. Stir in eggs and cooked macaroni.

5. Pour into lightly greased 3-quart casserole dish. Sprinkle with paprika.

6. Bake at 350° for 30 minutes, or until the top of the casserole is firm and golden brown.

Summer Squash Lasagna

**Natalia Showalter,
Mt. Solon, VA**

Makes 12 servings
Prep. Time: 30–45 minutes
Cooking Time: 4–5 hours
Ideal slow-cooker size: 6- or 7-qt.

2 medium zucchini squash, unpeeled and sliced thinly

2 medium yellow squash, unpeeled and sliced thinly

8 oz. portobello mushrooms, sliced

1 large onion, diced

1 red bell pepper, chopped

4 cups fresh tomatoes, chopped

6-oz. can tomato paste

2 large cloves garlic, minced

1 tsp. finely chopped basil

1 Tbsp. brown sugar

½ tsp. salt

1½ tsp. chopped oregano

½ tsp. coarsely ground black pepper

15 oz. ricotta cheese or 12 oz. cottage cheese

8-oz. pkg. cream cheese, softened

2 large eggs, beaten

2 tsp. fresh chopped parsley

6 uncooked lasagna noodles, *divided*

2–4 cups shredded mozzarella cheese

2 cups shredded Colby cheese or Italian cheese blend, *divided*

1. Grease interior of slow-cooker crock.

2. Place zucchini and yellow squash, mushrooms, onions, red bell pepper, tomatoes, tomato paste, garlic, basil, brown sugar, salt, oregano, and pepper into large bowl. Mix together gently but well.

3. In a separate bowl, combine ricotta, cream cheese, eggs, and parsley until well blended. Set aside.

4. Spread half of vegetable mixture in bottom of crock.

5. Top with 3 noodles, breaking them to fit and cover the vegetables.

6. Spread with half the ricotta mixture.

7. Sprinkle with half the mozzarella and Colby cheeses.

8. Repeat layers.

9. Cover. Cook on Low 4–5 hours, or until vegetables are as tender as you like them and noodles are fully cooked.

10. Let stand 10–15 minutes to allow lasagna to firm up before serving.

Veggie Macaroni and Cheese

**Dorothy Lingerfelt,
Stonyford, CA**

Makes 12 servings
Prep. Time: 30 minutes
Cooking/Baking Time: 30 minutes

1½ cups uncooked elbow macaroni

3 cups chopped broccoli

2 cups chopped cauliflower

3 carrots, thinly sliced

2 celery ribs, sliced

1 medium onion, diced

1 Tbsp. butter

¼ cup all-purpose flour

1 cup milk

3 cups shredded cheddar cheese

1 Tbsp. Dijon mustard

¼ tsp. pepper

¼ tsp. paprika

1. In a large pot of salted boiling water, cook macaroni 1–2 minutes.

2. Add broccoli, cauliflower, carrots, and celery and cook 5 more minutes.

3. Drain, but reserve 1 cup cooking water.

4. Pour vegetables and macaroni into lightly greased 9 × 13 baking pan. Set aside.

5. Meanwhile, in a saucepan, sauté onions in butter until tender.

6. Sprinkle with flour and stir until blended.

7. Over low heat, gradually stir in milk and reserved 1 cup cooking water.

8. Bring to boil over medium heat, stirring. Cook and stir for 2 minutes, or until thickened.

9. Turn off heat. Stir in cheese, mustard, and pepper.

10. Pour sauce over macaroni mixture in pan. Stir to coat. Spread evenly in pan.

11. Sprinkle with paprika.

12. Bake uncovered at 350° for 15–20 minutes or until heated through.

Pork Tenderloin with Pasta in Tomato and Red Pepper Sauce

Joyce Clark,
East Amherst, NY

Makes 4–6 servings
Prep. Time: 15 minutes
Cooking Time: 30 minutes

1 Tbsp. butter

1 Tbsp. vegetable oil

2 cups sliced mushrooms

2 onions, chopped

2 garlic cloves, crushed

1 red bell pepper, chopped

3 tsp. fresh chopped oregano

2 Tbsp. flour

1 tsp. chili powder

½ tsp. salt

½ tsp. black pepper

1 lb. pork tenderloin, cut into 1" cubes

3 cups milk

9 ozs. dry penne pasta

14-oz. can tomato sauce

1. Melt butter in a large skillet. Add vegetable oil, mushrooms, onions, garlic, red pepper, and oregano. Cook over medium heat until onion is softened.

2. Place flour, chili powder, salt, and pepper in a ziplock plastic bag. Add pork pieces and shake to coat.

3. Add floured pork and any remaining flour mixture to skillet. Cook, stirring occasionally, until pork is browned on all sides.

4. Add milk, pasta, and tomato sauce. Bring mixture to a boil, stirring constantly.

5. Reduce heat, cover, and simmer 15 minutes until pasta is tender.

Baked Pasta with Chicken Sausage

**Kim Rapp,
Longmont, CO**

Makes 8 servings
Prep. Time: 40 minutes
Baking Time: 20–30 minutes

1 lb. uncooked rigatoni

10-oz. pkg. fresh baby spinach

1 Tbsp. olive oil

1 medium red onion, chopped

4 cloves garlic, minced

¼ cup vodka, optional

28-oz. can whole tomatoes with juice,
lightly crushed with hands or 2 lbs. whole
tomatoes, peeled

1½ tsp. fresh chopped oregano

½ cup heavy cream

12-oz. smoked chicken sausage, halved
lengthwise then cut into ¼"-thick slices

6 oz. fontina cheese: 4 oz. cubed; 2 oz.
shredded

¼ cup grated Parmesan cheese

1. Cook rigatoni according to package
directions for 4 minutes.

2. Stir in baby spinach. Continue cooking
3 minutes. Drain pasta and spinach well.
Return to cooking pot and keep warm.

3. Heat oil in large skillet over medium
heat. Add onion. Cook about 3 minutes.

4. Stir in garlic. Remove from heat.

5. Add vodka if you wish. Return to fairly
high heat and cook until liquid is almost
evaporated, about 1 minute.

6. Stir in tomatoes and oregano. Cook
10–15 minutes.

7. Add cream and warm, cooking gently
about 5 minutes.

8. Add sausage and cubed fontina to pot.
Toss to coat.

9. Season with several grinds of salt and
pepper.

TIP

Add ¼ cup water or broth if
mixture seems dry before baking.

10. Divide evenly between 2 greased 1½-quart baking dishes, or spoon into 1 greased 9 × 13 baking dish.

11. Top with grated fontina and Parmesan cheeses.

12. Bake at 400° until browned, about 20–30 minutes.

Gnocchi with Chicken

Janie Steele,
Moore, OK

Makes 8 servings
Prep. Time: 30 minutes
Cooking Time: 7 hours
Ideal slow-cooker size: 5-qt.

1 lb. gnocchi, store-bought or homemade

2 cups cooked chicken, cut into cubes

1 onion, chopped

1 cup chopped or shredded carrots

2 cloves garlic

Salt and pepper, to taste

2 cups heavy cream

1½ cups grated Parmesan cheese

¼ tsp. nutmeg

1½ cups fresh chopped spinach

1. Cook gnocchi according to directions. Drain and add other ingredients to slow cooker except for spinach.

2. Cover and cook on Low for 7 hours. Add spinach during the last 30 minutes and serve.

Quick Shrimp Pasta

Sandra Chang,
Derwood, MD

Makes 4–6 servings
Prep. Time: 30 minutes
Cooking Time: 20 minutes

1 lb. spaghetti

1 Tbsp. vegetable oil

1 lb. raw shrimp, peeled and deveined

kosher salt

ground black pepper

1 medium-sized zucchini, unpeeled and cut
    into ½" pieces

3 cloves garlic, minced

½ cup extra-virgin olive oil

⅓ cup fresh flat-leaf parsley

½ tsp. cracked black pepper

1 cup grated Parmesan cheese, *divided*

1. Cook spaghetti according to package directions. When finished cooking, drain, return to cooking pot, and keep warm.

2. Meanwhile, in a large skillet, heat vegetable oil over high heat until smoking hot.

3. Place shrimp in pan and sear for 1 to 2 minutes per side, or until just cooked through. Stir in a dash of kosher salt and a dash of pepper. Remove seasoned shrimp to a large serving bowl and keep warm.

4. Sauté zucchini pieces and minced garlic briefly in skillet until crisp-tender.

5. Add zucchini and garlic to shrimp.

6. Mix in olive oil, garlic, parsley, pepper, and ½ cup Parmesan cheese.

7. Add cooked pasta and remaining cheese. Toss well and serve.

Variation:
Substitute 1½ lbs. scallops for the shrimp for a different quick meal.

Shrimp and Mushroom Linguine

**Cyndie Marrara,
Port Matilda, PA**

Makes 4 servings
Preparation Time: 10 minutes
Cooking Time: 30 minutes

2 cups fresh mushroom slices

1 stick (½ cup) butter

¼ cup flour

⅛ tsp. pepper

3 cups milk

2 cups peeled and cooked shrimp

¼ cup Parmesan cheese

8 ozs. linguine

Parmesan cheese

1. Cook linguine according to package directions. Drain.

2. In a large skillet, sauté mushrooms in butter. Blend in flour and pepper.

3. Add milk, and stir constantly until thickened.

4. Add shrimp and Parmesan cheese. Heat thoroughly.

5. Combine shrimp sauce with linguine. Toss lightly and sprinkle with additional Parmesan cheese.

Grill Pack Dinner

Shelia Heil,
Lancaster, PA

Makes 1 serving
Prep. Time: 10 minutes
Grilling Time: 45 minutes

¼-lb. burger

1 potato, sliced thin

1 carrot, sliced thin

¼ onion, diced

½ tsp. salt

1. Layer ingredients onto large sheet of double-strength aluminum foil. Wrap up and seal well.

2. Place on baking sheet with sealed edge up.

3. Grill for 45 minutes, or until meat and veggies are done to your liking.

TIP

Make as many packets as the number of people you plan to feed. In fact, it's fun to make an assembly line and have everyone create her/his own package.

Flank Steak

**Sharon Swartz Lambert,
Harrisonburg, VA**

Makes 2-4 servings
Prep. Time: 10 minutes
Marinating Time: 5-24 hours
Grilling Time: 15 minutes

½-2-lb. flank steak

1 Tbsp. cooking sherry

2 Tbsp. soy sauce

1 tsp. fresh minced garlic

1 tsp. honey

1. Diamond-cut ¼"-wide slashes on both sides of flank steak.

2. Mix marinade ingredients together in a small bowl.

3. Place steak in a long dish. Pour marinade over top. Cover and refrigerate 5–24 hours, or overnight.

4. Grill 5 minutes per side over high heat. (You may need a bit more time, depending on thickness of the meat.)

5. Cut into thin slices on the diagonal.

Serving suggestion:
Garnish with chopped fresh herbs of choice.

Grilled Pork Chops

**Laura R. Showalter,
Dayton, VA**

Makes 4 servings
Prep. Time: 10 minutes
Marinating Time: 2 hours
Grilling Time: 20 minutes

1 large onion, sliced

¾ cup fresh lime, or lemon, juice

½ tsp. cayenne pepper

1 clove garlic, minced

½ tsp. salt, optional

4 pork chops

1. Combine all ingredients except the pork chops in a large resealable bag or container with tight-fitting lid. Combine well.

2. Submerge chops in marinade.

3. Seal bag or container and refrigerate at least 2 hours.

4. Remove chops from marinade and grill, covered, over medium-hot heat 8–10 minutes on each side.

5. Bring the marinade to a boil in a small saucepan. Use it to baste the chops if you wish while they grill.

Marinated Chicken Breasts

**Mary Longenecker,
Bethel, PA**

Makes ¼–1 cup marinade, enough for
4–12 servings of chicken
Prep. Time: 10 minutes
Marinating Time: 3–8 hours
Grilling Time: 10–12 minutes
Standing Time: 10 minutes

1-3 lbs. boneless, skinless, chicken breast
  halves

2 Tbsp. olive oil

3 Tbsp. red wine vinegar

¼ cup honey

¼ cup soy sauce

1 garlic clove, crushed

2 Tbsp. chopped fresh parsley

½ tsp. pepper

1. Pound chicken between sheets of plastic wrap until it is ½" thick. Place flattened chicken in a shallow glass or plastic bowl(s) in a single layer.

2. In a small bowl, combine oil, vinegar, honey, soy sauce, garlic, parsley, and pepper.

3. Pour over chicken. Marinate for 3–8 hours.

4. Grill until tender, about 5 minutes per side.

5. After removing from grill, allow to stand for 10 minutes before slicing.

6. Serve with hot vegetables, or to top a salad, or as sandwich filling.

Barbecued Chicken

Dawn Ranck,
Lansdale, PA

Makes 8 servings
Prep. Time: 10 minutes
Grilling Time: 25–30 minutes

½ cup vinegar

½ Tbsp. salt

1 stick (½ cup) butter

8 legs and thighs, or 8 whole breasts

Topping:

¼ cup lemon juice

1 Tbsp. brown sugar

1 Tbsp. Worcestershire sauce

1 tsp. salt

½ tsp. dry mustard

1 stick (½ cup) butter

¼ cup ketchup

2 Tbsp. fresh parsley, chopped

2 Tbsp. fresh chopped lemon thyme

2 Tbsp. chives, chopped

1. In a small saucepan, combine vinegar, salt, and 1 stick butter. Heat until butter is melted.

2. Grill chicken, brushing frequently with vinegar mixture, until chicken is almost fully cooked.

3. In another saucepan, combine all topping ingredients. Heat until butter is melted. Stir to blend well.

4. Brush topping on chicken. Grill 5 minutes. Turn chicken over. Brush topping on other side and grill an additional 5 minutes.

Lemon Grilled Chicken Breasts

**Wilma Haberkamp,
Fairbank, IA**

Makes 4 servings
Prep. Time: 15 minutes
Grilling Time: 4-5 minutes

1¼ lbs. boneless, skinless chicken breasts

2 lemons

2 Tbsp. olive oil

½ tsp. salt

½ tsp. coarsely ground pepper

1. Prepare grill for direct grilling over medium heat.

2. Pound chicken to uniform ¼" thickness.

3. Grate 1½ Tbsp. lemon peel and squeeze 3 Tbsp. lemon juice into a small bowl.

4. Add oil, salt, and pepper. Whisk until well blended.

5. In large bowl, toss chicken with marinade.

6. Place on grill. Cook 2–2½ minutes.

7. Turn over. Cook 2–2½ minutes more, or until juices run clear.

Curried Coconut Chicken

**Dawn Ranck,
Lansdale, PA**

Makes 4 servings
Prep. Time: 10 minutes
Marinating Time: 30 minutes–6 hours
Grilling Time: 10 minutes

3 boneless, skinless chicken thighs or breast
   halves
bamboo skewers, presoaked
4 garlic cloves, crushed
1 Tbsp. grated fresh ginger
1 onion, chopped
1 handful cilantro, chopped
3 Tbsp. fish sauce
1 Tbsp. garam masala
⅓ cup coconut milk
salt to taste
pepper to taste

1. Spread chicken thighs or breasts flat. Thread 2 skewers diagonally through each thigh or breast to form a cross. Place in baking pan with sides.

2. In blender, combine garlic, ginger, onion, cilantro, fish sauce, garam masala, and coconut milk. Add salt and pepper to taste. Pulse until smooth. Pour over chicken. Cover and refrigerate for 30 minutes–6 hours.

3. Grill over medium-hot coals for 5 minutes per side, or until chicken is cooked (opaque with no trace of pink). Or do the chicken in the broiler for 5 minutes per side.

Zesty Grilled Fish

Julie McKenzie,
Punxsutawney, PA

Makes 6 servings
Prep. Time: 5 minutes
Marinating Time: 1–2 hours
Grilling Time: 10–11 minutes

2 lbs. fresh fish steaks or thick fillets

¼ cup soy sauce

¼ cup orange juice

2 Tbsp. ketchup

2 Tbsp. vegetable oil

1 Tbsp. fresh lemon juice

1½ tsp. fresh chopped oregano

½ tsp. pepper

1 garlic clove, finely chopped

1. Arrange fish in a single layer in a glass or plastic dish. In a small bowl, combine remaining ingredients and pour over fish. Marinate 1–2 hours.

2. Grill fish over a hot fire, using foil with holes punched in it, or a fish basket. Cook approximately 6 minutes on first side; then turn over and cook another 4–5 minutes, checking to see if fish flakes easily. Do not overcook!

NOTE

You can baste the fish with the marinade while grilling the first side, if you wish.

Grilled Barbecue Shrimp

Denise Martin,
Lancaster, PA

Makes 6 servings
Prep. Time: 10 minutes
Marinating Time: 1–2 hours
Grilling Time: 6 minutes

1 Tbsp. Worcestershire sauce

½ cup olive oil

1 tsp. seasoning salt

½ tsp. Tabasco sauce

2 cloves garlic, minced

2 Tbsp. fresh lemon juice

1 Tbsp. fresh chopped oregano

¼ cup ketchup

2 lbs. large raw shrimp, peeled and deveined

1. Combine all ingredients except raw shrimp. Blend well.

2. Add shrimp to marinade. Cover and let stand 1–2 hours in the refrigerator.

3. To grill, place shrimp on a screen or grate with small holes. Grill about 3 minutes per side over medium heat, or until shrimp are bright pink, basting often.

TIP

You can also broil the shrimp, following the directions above.

Vegetable Shish Kebabs

Rosemarie Fitzgerald,
Gibsonia, PA

Makes 4 servings
Prep. Time: 15–20 minutes
Grilling Time: 10–15 minutes

Wooden skewers, presoaked

1 pint cherry tomatoes

2–3 small zucchini, unpeeled, cubed for skewers

1 medium red onion, cut for skewers

1 lb. fresh mushrooms, whole or if large, cut for skewers

16-oz. bottle Catalina salad dressing

1. Thread vegetables onto skewers. Thread zucchini through its outside edges and not through the centers of the cubes.

2. Grill, basting with dressing, until vegetables are done to your liking.

3. Serve over cooked rice.

Grilled Asparagus

Kelly Amos,
Pittsboro, NC

Makes 4 servings
Prep. Time: 10 minutes
Marinating Time: 30 minutes
Grilling Time: 5–10 minutes

1 lb. (about 3½ cups) asparagus

Dressing:

3 Tbsp. balsamic vinegar

2 Tbsp. fresh lemon juice

1 Tbsp. olive oil

2 tsp. low-sodium soy sauce

black pepper to taste

1. Snap off rough ends of cleaned asparagus.

2. Combine dressing ingredients together in a good-sized mixing bowl.

3. Add asparagus to dressing. Let marinate for approximately 30 minutes.

4. Brush grill grates with some oil. Turn grill onto low.

5. Cook asparagus on grill 5–10 minutes, turning every few minutes until lightly browned.

Grilled Vegetables

Deborah Heatwole,
Waynesboro, GA

Makes 4 servings
Prep. Time: 15–30 minutes, depending on
how fast you slice veggies
Grilling Time: 15–25 minutes

4 cups sliced fresh summer squash and/or
  zucchini

4 cups sliced sweet onions, such as Vidalia

3-4 Tbsp. olive, or canola, oil

1-2 Tbsp. red wine vinegar

salt and pepper to taste

1. Toss all ingredients in a large bowl until
vegetables are evenly coated with oil and
vinegar.

2. Spray a grill basket with nonstick
cooking spray. Place on grill rack over hot
coals.

3. Pour vegetables into basket, replace grill
lid, and cook 15–25 minutes, until vegetables
reach desired doneness, stirring every
4–5 minutes.

TIP

This is a versatile dish. Add or
substitute your favorite garden
vegetables, especially those that
are in season.

Grilled Asparagus Spears

**Dale and Shari Mast,
Harrisonburg, VA**

Makes 6–8 servings
Prep. Time: 7 minutes
Grilling Time: 12 minutes

2 lbs. fresh asparagus spears

1 Tbsp. olive oil

seasoned salt

1. Break woody ends off washed asparagus.

2. In a large bowl or Ziploc bag, toss asparagus spears with oil and salt to taste.

3. Place spears directly onto preheated grill on low heat.

4. Grill for 12 minutes, turning spears 2–3 times.

5. Serve hot or at room temperature.

Chili Lime Grilled Corn

Betty Moore,
Plano, IL

Makes 8 servings
Prep. Time: 15 minutes
Soaking Time: 3–4 hours
Grilling Time: 25 minutes

8 ears fresh corn with husks

1 stick (½ cup) butter, softened

1 tsp. grated lime rind

1 tsp. fresh lime juice

chili powder

1. Remove outer husks from corn. Pull back inner husks. Remove and discard silks. Pull husks back up on corn. Soak in cool water for 3 or 4 hours, putting a plate on top of corn to keep under water.

2. Mix butter, lime juice and grated lime rind in a small bowl.

3. Remove corn from water. Grill corn in its husks over medium heat on grill for 25 minutes. Turn often.

4. Carefully remove husks.

5. Spread corn with butter mixture. Sprinkle with chili powder if you wish. Or add ½ tsp. chili powder to butter mixture before spreading on corn.

Grilled Cabbage

Jenelle Miller,
Marion, SD

Makes 4 servings
Prep. Time: 5-10 minutes
Grilling Time: 40-45 minutes

small head of cabbage
half a stick (4 Tbsp.) butter
seasoned salt
4 slices bacon, uncooked

1. Remove outer leaves of cabbage head. Cut cabbage into 4 wedges.

2. Lay each wedge on a square of aluminum foil.

3. Spread 1 Tbsp. of butter over side of wedge.

4. Sprinkle each generously with seasoned salt.

5. Wrap a piece of bacon around each wedge.

6. Wrap tightly in foil.

7. Lay over hot coals. Grill 40–45 minutes, or until tender when jabbed with a fork.

Zucchini on the Grill

Judy Buller,
Bluffton, OH

Makes as many servings as you wish
Prep. Time: 5 minutes
Grilling Time: 5–6 minutes

medium-sized zucchini

olive oil

pepper

seasoning salt

garlic powder

1. Wash, but do not peel, zucchini. Slice into long strips about ¼" thick.

2. Brush both sides with olive oil. Gently sprinkle both sides with pepper, seasoning salt, and garlic powder.

3. Place on grill, turning frequently. Each side takes about 3 minutes, but watch carefully so as not to overdo or burn the slices.

Grilled Parmesan Potatoes

Joanna Bear,
Salisbury, MD

Makes 4 servings
Prep. Time: 10 minutes
Grilling Time: 18–20 minutes

1 lb. small red potatoes

¼ cup chopped scallions, optional

2 tsp. cooking oil

1 Tbsp. fresh chopped oregano

1 clove garlic, minced

¼ tsp. salt

1 Tbsp. Parmesan cheese

1. Cut potatoes in ½" cubes. Place in medium bowl.

2. Add scallions, if you wish, and oil. Toss to coat.

3. Place potatoes in center of 12 × 12 sheet of heavy-duty aluminum foil.

4. Combine spices and cheese in a small bowl. Sprinkle over potatoes.

5. Fold foil into pouch, sealing tightly to prevent leaks.

6. Place pouch on a grill over medium hot coals for 18–20 minutes, or until potatoes are tender.

Potato Packets

Barb Harvey,
Quarryville, PA

Makes 4 servings
Prep. Time: 20 minutes
Grilling Time: 20–30 minutes

4 medium-sized potatoes, julienned

3 carrots, julienned

⅓ cup chopped onion

2 Tbsp. butter

salt and pepper, optional

½ cup shredded Parmesan, or cheddar, cheese

1. Divide potatoes, carrots, and onion equally between four pieces of heavy-duty aluminum foil.

2. Top with butter. Sprinkle with salt and pepper if you wish.

3. Bring opposite short ends of foil together over vegetables and fold down several times. Fold unsealed ends toward vegetables and crimp tightly.

4. Grill, covered, over medium coals for 20–30 minutes, or until potatoes are tender.

5. Remove from grill.

6. Open foil and sprinkle with cheese. Reseal for 5 minutes, or until cheese melts.

Grilled Apple Crisp

Charlotte Shaffer,
East Earl, PA

Makes 6–8 servings
Prep. Time: 30 minutes
Grilling Time: 20–25 minutes

10 cups thinly sliced apples (about 8 medium-sized)

1 cup dry old-fashioned oats

1 cup packed brown sugar

¼ cup flour

3 tsp. cinnamon

1 tsp. nutmeg

half a stick (¼ cup) butter, cold

1. Spread apple slices over a double thickness of heavy-duty aluminum foil, approximately 12 × 24" in size.

2. In small bowl, combine oats, brown sugar, flour, cinnamon, and nutmeg. Cut in butter until mixture is crumbly. Sprinkle over apples.

3. Fold foil around apple mixture and seal tightly.

4. Grill over medium heat for 20–25 minutes, or until apples are tender.

TIP

Put this package of apples on the grill after you've finished grilling your meat. The apples will bake while you eat your main course and be ready in time for dessert.

Grilled Peach Melba

Stacy Schmucker Stoltzfus,
Enola, PA

Makes 4 servings
Prep. Time: 10 minutes
Grilling Time: 5–10 minutes

4 large, unpeeled peaches or nectarines

2 tsp. sugar

2 cups red raspberries

vanilla ice cream

1. Halve and pit peaches or nectarines.

2. Press fresh or thawed raspberries through sieve. Save juice and discard seeds. Sweeten to taste with sugar, if needed.

3. Grill unpeeled peaches cut-side down for approximately 2 minutes. Turn peaches over. With cut-side up, fill each cavity with ½ tsp. sugar, and continue grilling until grill marks appear on skins.

4. Serve immediately with a scoop of vanilla ice cream and drizzle with the raspberry sauce.

Surfside Summer Squash

Ginny Cutler,
Westminster, MD

Makes 6–8 servings
Prep. Time: 25–30 minutes
Baking Time: 30 minutes

5 medium-sized summer squash

2 eggs

½ cup milk

1 medium onion, chopped

½ lb. cheddar or Monterey Jack, cheese, grated

1 tomato, chopped

½ stick (4 Tbsp.) butter, cut in pieces

Parmesan cheese

Italian bread crumbs

1. Cut up or slice squash. Steam or microwave until just tender. Drain and set aside.

2. In a mixing bowl, beat together eggs and milk. Add onion, cheese, and tomato.

3. Add squash to egg /cheese mixture.

4. Pour into a greased 9 × 13 baking dish. Add cut-up butter and stir.

5. Sprinkle with Parmesan cheese and bread crumbs until well covered.

6. Bake uncovered at 400° for 30 minutes.

Vegetables and
Side Dishes

Squash Apple Bake

Lavina Hochstedler,
Grand Blanc, MI

Makes 8 servings
Prep. Time: 20 minutes
Baking Time: 45–50 minutes

3 Tbsp. brown sugar

⅓ cup orange juice, apple juice, or apple cider

4 cups cubed butternut or buttercup squash

salt

2 apples, cored and thinly sliced

¼ cup raisins

cinnamon

1 Tbsp. butter

1. Combine brown sugar and juice in a small mixing bowl. Set aside.

2. Place half the cubed squash in a greased 2-qt. baking dish. Sprinkle with salt.

3. Follow with a layer of half the apples and raisins. Sprinkle generously with cinnamon.

4. Repeat the layers.

5. Pour juice mixture over all. Dot with butter.

6. Cover and bake at 350° for 45–50 minutes, or until tender.

Variation:
Stir 1 Tbsp. orange rind into Step 1.
—Christie Detamore-Hunsberger,
Harrisonburg, VA

Vegetables and
Side Dishes

Acorn Squash Straight Up

Valerie Hertzler,
Weyers Cave, VA

Makes 2 servings
Prep. Time: 5 minutes
Cooking Time: 8–10 hours
Ideal slow-cooker size: 4- or 5-qt.

1 acorn squash
¼ tsp. salt, *divided*
1 tsp. cinnamon, *divided*
2 tsp. butter, *divided*

1. Grease interior of slow-cooker crock.

2. Place whole, rinsed squash in slow cooker.

3. Cover. Cook on Low 8–10 hours, or until it is tender when you poke it with a sharp fork.

4. Split and remove seeds. Sprinkle each half with salt and cinnamon, dot with butter, and serve.

Cranberry Squash

Sara Harter Fredette,
Williamsburg, MA

Makes 4-6 servings
Prep. Time: 20 minutes
Baking Time: 45 minutes

1½ lbs. winter squash, peeled and diced

1 cup fresh cranberries

1 small apple, chopped

juice and peel of 1 orange

1½ Tbsp. honey

1 Tbsp. butter, melted

salt, to taste

1. Place squash, cranberries, and apple in baking pan large enough to spread squash in single layer.

2. Mix orange juice and peel with honey, butter, and salt.

3. Pour over squash.

4. Cover with foil.

5. Bake at 350° for 35 minutes. Remove foil. Bake 10 more minutes until squash is tender.

Vegetables and Side Dishes

Cheesy Zucchini Caterpillar

Delores Gnagey,
Saginaw, MI

Makes 2 servings
Prep. Time: 10 minutes
Baking Time: 35–37 minutes

1 medium zucchini (about 6" long)

1 tsp. olive oil

½ tsp. fresh minced garlic

⅛ tsp. onion powder

2 Tbsp. grated Parmesan cheese

1. Preheat oven to 375°.

2. Trim ends off zucchini and discard. At ½" intervals, slice ¾ of the way through the zucchini, being careful not to cut all the way through (the slices should be connected).

3. Gently dry zucchini with paper towel.

4. Place zucchini on piece of aluminum foil large enough to wrap completely around zucchini.

5. Drizzle top of zucchini with olive oil.

6. Sprinkle with garlic and onion powder.

7. Wrap zucchini in foil and pinch closed. Lay on baking sheet.

8. Bake 30–35 minutes, or until zucchini is tender when poked with fork.

9. Remove from oven, open foil, and sprinkle cheese over zucchini.

10. With foil open, return zucchini to oven for 1–2 minutes. Or turn oven to Broil and lightly brown "caterpillar."

Stir-Fried Broccoli

Vicki Dinkel,
Sharon Springs, KS

Makes 4 servings
Prep. Time: 15 minutes
Cooking Time: 5 minutes

1 onion, diced

1 Tbsp. oil

1 lb. broccoli, cut in pieces

½ cup chicken broth

1 tsp. cornstarch

2 Tbsp. soy sauce

1 tsp. sugar

1. Brown onion in oil in a large skillet. Add broccoli. Stir-fry 3 minutes.

2. In a small bowl, combine chicken broth, cornstarch, soy sauce, and sugar. Add to broccoli. Cook 1–2 minutes until sauce clears.

3. Serve over cooked rice.

Variations:
1. Replace half of broccoli with cauliflower or any other vegetable of your choice.
2. Add strips of boneless skinless chicken breasts to Step 1.

Vegetables and Side Dishes

Zucchini Ribbons

**Delores Gnagey,
Saginaw, MI**

Makes 4 servings
Prep. Time: 15 minutes
Cooking Time: 9 minutes

1 large zucchini, unpeeled, ends trimmed

1 Tbsp. olive oil

3 garlic cloves, minced

1 cup cherry tomato halves

1 tsp. fresh basil, finely chopped

pepper to taste

1. With vegetable peeler, slice zucchini into long, lengthwise strips, thick enough not to bend. (If strips are too thin, they'll get mushy while sautéing.)

2. Heat oil in large skillet over medium heat. Add zucchini ribbons. Sauté 4 minutes.

3. Add garlic and sauté 2 more minutes.

4. Add cherry tomatoes and sauté 2 additional minutes.

5. Sprinkle with basil and pepper to taste. Cook 1 minute.

Italian-Style Broccoli

**Shirley Hedman,
Schenectady, NY**

Makes 4-6 servings
Prep. Time: 10 minutes
Cooking Time: 10 minutes

4 cups broccoli florets

1 Tbsp. olive oil

2 cloves garlic, minced or crushed

¼ tsp. red pepper flakes

1 tsp. grated Parmesan cheese

1. Steam broccoli for 3 minutes in non-stick pan. Remove from pan and wipe pan dry.

2. Add olive oil, garlic, and red pepper flakes to pan. Cook slowly, about 3 minutes.

3. Add broccoli and shake in pan to cook evenly.

4. Sprinkle with grated cheese and serve warm.

Roasted Broccoli

Andrea Cunningham,
Arlington, KS

Makes 4 servings
Prep. Time: 10 minutes
Baking Time: 20 minutes

1 head (about 5 cups) broccoli, cut into long pieces all the way through (you will eat the stems)

1 Tbsp. olive oil

2-3 cloves garlic, sliced thin

pepper

lemon wedges

1. Preheat oven to 400°.

2. Place broccoli in baking pan with sides. Drizzle with olive oil. Toss to coat.

3. Sprinkle garlic and pepper over top.

4. Transfer to oven and roast 15–20 minutes, or until broccoli is crispy on the ends and a little browned.

5. Sprinkle with lemon juice.

Broccoli Dijon

**Jean Butzer,
Batavia, NY**

Makes 4 servings
Prep. Time: 15 minutes
Cooking Time: 10 minutes

1½ lbs. broccoli

2 Tbsp. olive oil

1 medium onion, finely chopped

2 cloves garlic, finely chopped

½ cup fat-free sour cream

1 Tbsp. Dijon mustard

1 Tbsp. fresh lemon juice

pepper to taste

1. Cut broccoli into florets. Peel and slice the stalks. Steam or boil in water in saucepan until tender, but still firm and bright green. Drain, and keep warm.

2. Meanwhile heat oil in a skillet over moderate heat. Sauté onion and garlic until tender but not brown, about 5 minutes.

3. Add remaining ingredients to skillet and stir over low heat.

4. Place broccoli in serving dish. Spoon sauce over top. Serve immediately.

Marge's Cauliflower

Pat Taylor,
Paw Paw, WV

Makes 4 servings
Prep. Time: 30 minutes
Cooking/Baking Time: 25 minutes

1 fresh head of cauliflower

water

½ cup butter, melted

1 cup dry bread crumbs

1 tsp. Italian seasoning

1 cup shredded cheddar cheese

1. Separate cauliflower into florets. Place in microwavable dish. Sprinkle with 1 Tbsp. water. Cover and cook on high for 3–4 minutes.

2. Drain florets and allow to cool until you can handle them.

3. Place melted butter in a shallow dish. Mix the bread crumbs and seasoning together in another shallow dish.

4. Dip each floret into melted butter, and then into the seasoned bread crumbs, rolling to cover well.

5. Place in greased 9 × 13 baking dish. Bake, uncovered, at 375° for 20 minutes. Turn off oven. Sprinkle with shredded cheese and return to oven to melt.

Vegetables and
Side Dishes

Cauliflower Cassoulet

Susie Shenk Wenger,
Lancaster, PA

Makes 6 servings
Prep. Time: 30 minutes
Cooking Time: 4–6 hours
Ideal slow-cooker size: 6-qt.

1 cup uncooked brown rice

½ tsp. kosher salt

2 cups water

1 cup sliced fresh mushrooms

1 large sweet onion, chopped

½ cup chopped red bell pepper

3 cloves garlic, chopped

1 Tbsp. butter

1 Tbsp. olive oil

1 large head cauliflower, chopped

½ cup diced Parmesan cheese

2 tsp. fresh basil, finely chopped

1½ tsp. fresh chopped oregano

salt and pepper, to taste

juice and zest of 1 lemon

1. Put rice and ½ tsp. salt in lightly greased slow cooker. Pour water over rice.

2. Sprinkle in mushrooms, onion, bell pepper, and garlic. Sprinkle lightly with salt and pepper. Dot with butter and drizzle with olive oil.

3. Sprinkle in cauliflower and diced Parmesan. Sprinkle with basil and oregano, adding salt and pepper to taste.

4. Cover and cook on Low for 4–6 hours, until rice is cooked and cauliflower is tender.

5. Drizzle with lemon juice and zest before serving.

Cauliflower Mashed "Potatoes"

Anne Hummel,
Millersburg, OH

Makes 4 servings
Prep. Time: 20 minutes
Cooking Time: 20–30 minutes

1 head cauliflower

1 clove garlic

1 leek, white only, split in 4 pieces

1 Tbsp. soft-tub margarine, nonhydrogenated

pepper to taste

1. Break cauliflower into small pieces.

2. In a good-sized saucepan, steam cauliflower, garlic, and leeks in water until completely tender, about 20–30 minutes.

3. While cauliflower is hot, puree until the vegetables resemble mashed potatoes. (Use a food processor, or if you prefer a smoother texture, use a blender. Process only a small portion at a time, holding the blender lid on firmly with a tea towel.)

4. Add a little hot water if vegetables seem dry.

5. Stir in margarine and pepper to taste.

Peas with Bacon and Crispy Leeks

J. B. Miller,
Indianapolis, IN

Makes 12 servings
Prep. Time: 15 minutes
Cooking Time: 45 minutes

3 large leeks, *divided*

vegetable oil

salt, divided

pepper, divided

6 thick slices of bacon

4 fresh thyme sprigs, or ½ tsp. ground thyme

1 cup chicken broth, *divided*

¾ cup light cream or half-and-half

30 ozs. frozen baby peas, thawed

1 tsp. cornstarch

1 Tbsp. water

1. Using only the white and tender green part of the leeks, slice the leeks crosswise into ¼"-thick pieces. Separate into rings. Wash and pat dry.

2. Heat ¼" of oil in a large saucepan until shimmering. Add all but ½ cup of leeks. Cook over moderate heat, stirring until golden brown.

3. Using a slotted spoon, transfer leeks to a paper-towel-lined plate to drain. Discard oil. Season leeks with salt and pepper.

4. In the same saucepan, cook bacon until brown and crispy. Remove bacon, but reserve its drippings. Place bacon on paper towels. When drained, crumble.

5. Add remaining ½ cup leeks and the thyme to the skillet. Cook until soft.

6. Add ½ cup chicken broth and cook uncovered until broth is reduced by half.

7. Add cream. Cook until the creamy broth is reduced by half.

8. Stir in peas, crumbled bacon, and the remaining ½ cup broth. Bring to a boil.

9. If using fresh thyme sprigs, discard. Season cooked mixture with salt and pepper.

10. In a small bowl, stir cornstarch into water until smooth. Stir into hot sauce. Continue stirring until it thickens slightly.

11. Spoon the peas into a serving dish and top with the reserved crispy leeks just before serving.

Snow Peas with Sesame Seeds

**Sylvia Beiler,
Lowville, NY**

Makes 6 servings
Prep. Time: 15 minutes
Cooking/Baking Time: 10 minutes

3 cups trimmed fresh snow peas

2 Tbsp. diced onions

1 Tbsp. canola oil

3 Tbsp. sesame seeds

¼ tsp. freshly ground pepper

1. Slice each snow pea diagonally into 2–3 pieces.

2. Sauté onions and peas in oil in large skillet until tender.

3. Meanwhile, place sesame seeds in baking pan. Toast in 350° oven for 8 minutes, or until lightly browned.

4. Add sesame seeds to onions and peas. Sauté 1 minute until peas are coated with seeds.

5. Sprinkle with freshly ground pepper.

Roasted Asparagus

Barbara Walker,
Sturgis, SD

Makes 6 servings
Prep. Time: 5 minutes
Cooking Time: 12 minutes

1 lb. fresh asparagus spears

2–3 Tbsp. olive oil

⅛ tsp. pepper

2 Tbsp. balsamic vinegar

1. Place asparagus in bowl with olive oil. Toss together to coat asparagus.

2. Place asparagus spears on a baking sheet in a single layer. Sprinkle with pepper.

3. Roast uncovered at 450°. Shake pan once or twice to turn spears after about 6 minutes.

4. Roast another 6 minutes, or until asparagus is tender-crisp.

5. Put on a plate and drizzle with balsamic vinegar. Serve immediately.

Stir-Fried Asparagus

Sylvia Beiler,
Lowville, NY

Makes 6 servings
Prep. Time: 5 minutes
Cooking Time: 2–3 minutes

1 Tbsp. canola oil

3 cups asparagus, sliced diagonally

4 scallions, sliced diagonally

1 garlic clove, minced, optional

1 tsp. fresh lemon juice

1. Heat oil in pan. Add sliced vegetables.

2. Stir-fry until crisp-tender.

3. Sprinkle with lemon juice. Serve immediately.

Vegetables and Side Dishes

Fresh Green Beans

Lizzie Ann Yoder,
Hartville, OH

Makes 6–8 servings
Prep. Time: 20 minutes
Cooking Time: 6–24 hours
Ideal slow-cooker size: 4- to 5-qt.

¼ lb. ham or bacon pieces

2 lbs. fresh green beans, washed and cut into pieces or frenched

3–4 cups water

1 scant tsp. salt

1. If using bacon, cut it into squares and brown in nonstick skillet. When crispy, drain and set aside.

2. Place all ingredients in slow cooker. Mix together well.

3. Cover and cook on High 6–10 hours or on Low 10–24 hours, or until beans are done to your liking.

Green Beans with Tomatoes and Garlic

Shirley Sears,
Sarasota, FL

Makes 6 servings
Prep. Time: 15 minutes
Cooking Time: 60–70 minutes

1 Tbsp. olive oil

4 cloves garlic, chopped

1½ lbs. green beans, washed and stemmed

2 8-oz. cans crushed tomatoes, no salt added,
   or 5–6 whole tomatoes, peeled and crushed

1 Tbsp. fresh chopped oregano

1. Heat oil in large skillet over medium heat.

2. Add garlic and sauté briefly.

3. Add beans and stir to coat with oil.

4. Add tomatoes.

5. Bring to a boil. Reduce heat to a low simmer.

6. Stir in oregano.

7. Cover and cook 45–60 minutes, or until beans are done to your liking and liquid is nearly absorbed.

Dutch Green Beans

Edwina Stoltzfus,
Narvon, PA

Makes 4–6 servings
Prep. Time: 20 minutes
Cooking Time: 4½ hours
Ideal slow-cooker size: 4- to 5-qt.

½ lb. bacon, or ham chunks

4 medium onions, sliced

2 qts. fresh green beans

4 cups diced fresh tomatoes

½–¾ tsp. salt

¼ tsp. pepper

1. Brown bacon until crisp in skillet. Drain, reserving 2 Tbsp. drippings. Crumble bacon into small pieces.

2. Sauté onions in bacon drippings.

3. Combine all ingredients in slow cooker.

4. Cover. Cook on Low 4½ hours.

Tangy Green Beans

Mary B. Sensenig,
New Holland, PA

Makes 10 servings
Prep. Time: 5 minutes
Cooking Time: 8–10 minutes

1 ½ lbs. fresh green beans

⅓ cup diced red bell peppers

1½ tsp. olive, or canola, oil

1½ tsp. water

1½ tsp. vinegar

1½ tsp. prepared mustard

1 clove garlic, minced

¼ tsp. salt

¼ tsp. pepper

1. Cook beans and red peppers in a steamer basket over water until crisp-tender.

2. Whisk together all remaining ingredients in a small bowl.

3. Transfer beans to a serving bowl. Add dressing and stir to coat.

Vegetables and
Side Dishes

Green Bean Stir-Fry

Sharon Eshleman,
Ephrata, PA

Makes 6 servings
Prep. Time: 10 minutes
Cooking Time: 10 minutes

Vegetables and Side Dishes

¾ lb. fresh green beans

1 Tbsp. canola oil

1 Tbsp. low-sodium soy sauce

2 garlic cloves, minced

1 tsp. sesame seeds, toasted

1 tsp. brown sugar

1 tsp. peanut butter

1. Stir-fry green beans in oil in large skillet until tender. Remove from heat.

2. Mix together remaining ingredients in small bowl.

3. Stir into green beans until well coated.

Southern Green Beans

Pat Bishop,
Bedminster, PA

Makes 4-6 servings
Prep. Time: 10 minutes
Cooking Time: 2-4 hours
Ideal slow-cooker size: 3-4 qt.

2 cups chicken broth

1 lb. fresh cut green beans

1 cup chopped onion

½ cup cooked, chopped bacon

1 Tbsp. white vinegar

1 Tbsp. soy sauce

¼ tsp. pepper

1 clove garlic, minced

1. Toss all ingredients together in slow cooker.

2. Cover and cook on Low for 4 hours or on High for 2 hours.

Steamed Carrots

**Dede Peterson,
Rapid City, SD**

Makes 4 servings
Prep. Time: 15–20 minutes
Cooking Time: 4–6 hours
Ideal slow-cooker size: 4-qt.

8 large carrots, sliced diagonally

¼ cup water

2 Tbsp. butter, cut into pieces

1 tsp. sugar

¼ tsp. salt

1. Layer carrots in slow cooker. Add water and pieces of butter. Sprinkle with sugar and salt.

2. Cover and cook on Low 4–6 hours.

TIP

Stir in 1–2 Tbsp. brown sugar just before serving.

Honey-Glazed Carrots

**Janet Oberholtzer,
Ephrata, PA**

Makes 4 servings
Prep. Time: 5 minutes
Cooking Time: 10-15 minutes

6 medium carrots, peeled and chopped into 2″ chunks

2 tsp. olive oil

1 Tbsp. honey

½ Tbsp. fresh lemon juice

1. Cook carrots in a bit of water in a saucepan until they're as tender as you like.

2. Meanwhile, combine olive oil, honey, and lemon juice in a small microwave-safe dish. Microwave on high 20–30 seconds. Stir.

3. Drain carrots. Pour glaze over top and toss to coat.

Vegetables and Side Dishes

Honey-Orange Glazed Carrots

**Hope Comerford,
Clinton Township, MI**

Makes 12 servings
Prep. Time: 5 minutes I
Cooking Time: 8 hours I
Ideal slow-cooker size: 5-qt.

Vegetables and
Side Dishes

9 medium carrots, peeled and chopped into 2″ chunks

2 Tbsp. freshly squeezed orange juice

½ cup honey

½ tsp. kosher salt

⅛ tsp. pepper

2 Tbsp. coconut oil

½ tsp. orange zest

1. Spray crock with nonstick spray.

2. Place carrots in crock, then add remaining ingredients except orange zest.

3. Cover and cook on Low for 8 hours.

4. Stir in orange zest before serving.

Scalloped Cheesy Tomatoes

**Scarlett Von Bernuth,
Canon City, CO**

Makes 6 servings
Prep. Time: 15 minutes
Baking Time: 35 minutes

4 fresh tomatoes, sliced, *divided*

1 cup soft bread cubes, *divided*

1 Tbsp. fresh parsley, *divided*

2 Tbsp. olive oil, *divided*

½ cup cracker crumbs (made from crackers with unsalted tops)

¼ cup low-sodium, low-fat grated cheese

pepper

1. Fill a lightly greased baking dish with alternate layers of tomatoes and bread cubes.

2. Sprinkle parsley and olive oil over each layer.

3. Cover top with cracker crumbs. Sprinkle with cheese.

4. Bake uncovered in 350°–375° oven for 35 minutes.

Baked Stuffed Tomatoes

Leslie Scott,
Troy, NY

Makes 6 servings
Prep. Time: 30 minutes
Cooking Time: 2–3 hours
Ideal slow-cooker size: 5-qt., oval

6 medium-sized tomatoes

3 Tbsp. butter, melted

2 tsp. chopped fresh basil

2 tsp. chopped fresh oregano

2 tsp. chopped fresh parsley

2 garlic cloves, minced

1 cup grated Parmesan cheese

¾ cup fine bread crumbs

salt and pepper to taste

1. Grease interior of slow-cooker crock.

2. Remove cores from tomatoes, and cut away an additional inch or so underneath the core to make a cavity in each tomato.

3. Mix together butter, herbs, garlic, Parmesan, bread crumbs, and salt and pepper.

4. Gently stuff each tomato with mixture.

5. Set tomatoes in lightly greased slow cooker.

6. Cover and cook on Low 2–3 hours, until tomatoes are soft and heated through.

Variation:
If you don't have fresh herbs, use ⅔ tsp. each of dried basil, oregano, and parsley instead.

Vegetables and
Side Dishes

Stewed Tomatoes

Colleen J. Heatwole,
Burton, MI

Makes 8 servings
Prep. Time: 15 minutes
Cooking Time: 15 minutes

Vegetables and
Side Dishes

½ cup finely chopped onion

½ cup diced green, or red, bell pepper

½ cup diced celery

1 Tbsp. olive, or canola, oil

2 14½-oz. cans low-sodium tomatoes, or 1
quart canned tomatoes (no salt added), or
5–6 whole tomatoes, peeled

1 tsp. sugar

¾ tsp. dry basil

1. In large skillet or saucepan, sauté onion,
bell pepper, and celery in 1 Tbsp. oil until
tender, about 5 minutes.

2. Add rest of ingredients and heat to
boiling.

3. Reduce heat, cover, and simmer 5
minutes.

Baked Corn

Samuel Stoltzfus,
Bird-in-Hand, PA

Makes 8 servings
Prep. Time: 15 minutes
Baking Time: 35–50 minutes

2 cups corn

2 eggs, slightly beaten, or 4 egg whites,
    slightly beaten

1 tsp. sugar

1 Tbsp. soft-tub margarine, melted

2 Tbsp. flour

1 cup skim milk

¼ tsp. salt

1. Mix all ingredients together in a large bowl.

2. Pour into a greased 2-quart baking dish.

3. Bake at 350° for 35–50 minutes, or until corn is firm in the middle and browned around the edges.

Vegetables and
Side Dishes

Corn Extraordinary

Judy Newman,
St. Mary's, ON

Makes 6 servings
Prep. Time: 5-7 minutes
Cooking Time: 4-6 minutes

2 garlic cloves

¼ cup chives

2 tsp. olive oil

4 cups corn (best if cut straight off the cob; if you use canned, it should be without added salt)

pinch of pepper

1. Chop garlic and chives.

2. Heat oil in large skillet over medium heat. Gently sauté garlic. (Reserve chives.)

3. Add corn. Sauté 3–5 minutes.

4. Season to taste with pepper and chives.

Corn on the Cob

Donna Conto,
Saylorsburg, PA

Makes 3–4 servings
Prep. Time: 10 minutes
Cooking Time: 2–3 hours
Ideal slow-cooker size: 5- or 6-qt.

6–8 ears of corn (in husk)

½ cup water

1. Remove silk from corn, as much as possible, but leave husks on.

2. Cut off ends of corn so ears can stand in the cooker.

3. Add water.

4. Cover. Cook on Low 2–3 hours.

Chili Lime Corn on the Cob Slow-Cooked

Hope Comerford,
Clinton Township, MI

Makes 6 servings
Prep. Time: 10 minutes
Cooking Time: 4 hours
Ideal slow-cooker size: 6-qt.

Vegetables and Side Dishes

6 ears of corn, shucked and cleaned

6 Tbsp. butter, at room temperature

2 Tbsp. freshly squeezed lime juice

1 tsp. lime zest

2 tsp. chili powder

1 tsp. salt

½ tsp. pepper

1. Tear off 6 pieces of aluminum foil to fit each ear of corn. Place each ear of corn on a piece of foil.

2. Mix together butter, lime juice, lime zest, chili powder, salt, and pepper.

3. Divide butter mixture evenly between six ears of corn and spread it over ears of corn. Wrap them tightly with foil so they don't leak.

4. Place the foil-wrapped ears of corn into crock. Cover and cook on Low for 4 hours.

Mushrooms in Red Wine

Donna Lantgen,
Rapid City, SD

Makes 4 servings
Prep. Time: 20–30 minutes
Cooking Time: 6 hours
Ideal slow-cooker size: 2- or 3-qt.

1 lb. fresh mushrooms, stemmed, trimmed, and cleaned

4 cloves garlic, minced

¼ cup onion

1 Tbsp. olive oil

1 cup red wine

1. Combine all ingredients in slow cooker.

2. Cook on low 6 hours.

TIPS

1. You can serve this as a side dish or as a condiment.
2. You can also use it as the base for a sauce to which you can add steak tips or ground beef, as well as 2 cups chopped onions, 2 tsp. dried oregano, 1½ tsp. salt, ½ tsp. black pepper, and 4 cloves minced garlic. You can also add a quart of spaghetti sauce and serve the mixture over a pound of your favorite pasta.

Oven Brussels Sprouts

**Gail Martin,
Elkhart, IN**

Makes 6–8 servings
Prep. Time: 15 minutes
Baking Time: 15 minutes

1½ lbs. Brussels sprouts, halved

¼ cup plus 2 Tbsp. olive oil

juice of 1 lemon

½ tsp. salt

½ tsp. pepper

½ tsp. crushed red pepper flakes

1. In a large bowl, toss halved sprouts with 2 Tbsp. olive oil.

2. Place them in a single layer on a rimmed cookie sheet.

3. Roast sprouts in the oven at 470°, stirring twice, until crisp and lightly browned, 10–15 minutes.

4. Whisk together in a large bowl ¼ cup oil, lemon juice, salt, pepper, and red pepper flakes.

5. Toss sprouts with dressing and serve.

Good Go-Alongs:
This is a lovely dish for any meal, but especially nice at Easter with ham and new potatoes.

Saucy Mushrooms

**Donna Lantgen,
Arvada, CO**

Makes 4 servings
Prep. Time: 15 minutes
Cooking Time: 3 ¼–4 ¼ hours
Ideal slow-cooker size: 3- or 4-qt.

1 lb. small, whole, fresh mushrooms, cleaned

4 cloves garlic, minced

¼ cup chopped onion

1 Tbsp. olive oil

¾ cup red wine

¼ tsp. salt

⅛ tsp. pepper

¾ tsp. fresh minced thyme

¼ cup water

2 Tbsp. cornstarch

1. Grease interior of slow-cooker crock.

2. Combine mushrooms, garlic, onion, olive oil, red wine, salt, pepper, and thyme in slow cooker.

3. Cover. Cook on Low 3–4 hours, or until mushrooms are soft but still holding their shape.

4. In a small bowl, whisk together water and cornstarch. Turn cooker to High and stir in cornstarch mixture. Cook, stirring occasionally, until thickened, 10–15 minutes.

5. Serve as a sauce over pasta, or as a side dish with steak and baked potatoes.

Baked Cabbage

Karen Gingrich,
New Holland, PA

Makes 6 servings
Prep. Time: 20 minutes
Cooking/Baking Time: 45 minutes

1 medium-sized head of cabbage

water

½ tsp. salt

1½ cups hot milk

1 Tbsp. flour

1 tsp. salt

½ tsp. pepper

2 Tbsp. butter

½–1 cup grated sharp cheddar cheese

1. Cut cabbage in wedges ¾" thick. Cook, covered, in a saucepan in ½" water, sprinkled with ½ tsp. salt, for 10 minutes. Drain and place cabbage in a greased 2-qt. baking casserole.

2. While cabbage is cooking (Step 1), warm milk in a small saucepan until it forms a skin but does not boil.

3. Sprinkle cabbage with flour, 1 tsp. salt, and pepper.

4. Pour hot milk over, being careful not to wash off the flour and seasonings. Dot with butter. Top with grated cheese.

5. Bake, uncovered, at 350° for 35 minutes.

Vegetables and
Side Dishes

Red Cabbage with Apples

Jean Butzer, Batavia, NY
Louise Thieszen, North Newton, KS

Makes 8 servings
Prep. Time: 15 minutes
Cooking Time: 40 minutes

1 medium head red cabbage, shredded

1 large onion, chopped

2 Tbsp. canola oil

2 medium apples, unpeeled, cored and sliced

¼ cup cider vinegar

¼ tsp. pepper

1 Tbsp. caraway seeds, optional

1. In a large skillet, sauté cabbage and onion in oil 5–8 minutes, or until crisp-tender.

2. Add apples, vinegar, pepper, and caraway seeds if you wish. Bring to a boil.

3. Reduce heat. Cover and simmer 25 minutes, or until cabbage is tender.

Cabbage and Potatoes

Deb Kepiro,
Strasburg, PA

Makes 4 servings
Prep. Time: 15 minutes
Cooking Time: 3–6 hours
Ideal slow-cooker size: 4-qt.

1 small head green cabbage, sliced thinly

14 small red-skinned potatoes, cut in 1" chunks

1 small onion, diced

3 Tbsp. olive oil

2 Tbsp. balsamic vinegar

1 tsp. kosher salt

½ tsp. black pepper

1. Put all ingredients in slow cooker. Mix well.

2. Cover and cook on High for 3 hours, until potatoes are as tender as you like them.

Good go-alongs with this recipe:
Bratwurst in buns with good mustard.

Simply Beets

Colleen Konetzni,
Rio Rancho, NM

Makes 4 servings
Prep. Time: 30 minutes
Cooking Time: 30–45 minutes

6 fresh red beets

water

1 tsp. olive oil

1 Tbsp. fresh dill

¼ tsp. pepper

1. Wash beets and cut off roots and leafy stems. Place in saucepan and cover with water.

2. Boil until beets are fork-tender.

3. Remove from pan and cool. The beets' peels should slip right off.

4. Slice beets ¼" thick. Place back in pan, along with oil.

5. Heat through over low heat.

6. To serve, sprinkle with dill weed and pepper.

Slow-Cooker Beets

Hope Comerford,
Clinton Township, MI

Makes 4-6 servings
Prep. Time: 10 minutes
Cooking Time: 3-4 hours
Ideal slow-cooker size: 3-qt.

4-6 large beets, scrubbed well and tops removed

3 Tbsp. olive oil

1 tsp. sea salt

¼ tsp. pepper

3 Tbsp. balsamic vinegar

1 Tbsp. fresh lemon juice

1. Use foil to make a packet around each beet.

2. Divide the olive oil, salt, pepper, balsamic vinegar, and lemon juice evenly between each packet.

3. Place each beet packet into the slow cooker.

4. Cover and cook on low for 3–4 hours, or until the beets are tender when poked with a knife.

5. Remove each beet packet from the crock and allow to cool and let the steam escape. Once cool enough to handle, use a paring knife to gently peel the skin off each beet. Cut into bite-sized pieces and serve with juice from the packet over the top.

Beets with Capers

**Mary Clair Wenger,
Kimmswick, MO**

Makes 6 servings
Prep. Time: 20 minutes
Cooking Time: 3–4 hours
Ideal slow-cooker size: 3-qt.

Vegetables and
Side Dishes

8 cups diced fresh, uncooked beets, peeled or not

3 Tbsp. olive oil

4 cloves garlic, chopped

¼ tsp. fresh ground pepper

½ tsp. salt

3 tsp. fresh chopped rosemary

1–2 Tbsp. capers with brine

1. Grease interior of slow-cooker crock.

2. In slow cooker, mix together beets, olive oil, garlic, pepper, salt, and rosemary.

3. Cover and cook on High until beets are tender, 3–4 hours.

4. Stir in capers and brine. Taste for salt. Add more if needed.

5. Serve beets hot or at room temperature.

Spinach with Parmesan Cheese

Clarice Williams,
Fairbank, IA

Makes 4 servings
Prep. Time: 10 minutes
Cooking Time: 7½–10 minutes

2 scallions, sliced

1 clove garlic, minced

2 Tbsp. water

1 lb. (about 12 cups) fresh spinach leaves, washed and trimmed

1 Tbsp. grated Parmesan cheese

1 tsp. fresh lemon juice

1. In 3-quart microwave-safe bowl, combine scallions, garlic, and water. Cook in microwave on 100 percent power (High) for 30–60 seconds, or until onions are tender.

2. Add spinach. Cook, covered, on High for 7–9 minutes, or until spinach is tender, stirring once. Drain well.

3. Sprinkle with Parmesan cheese and lemon juice.

Mediterranean Eggplant

**Willard E. Roth,
Elkhart, IN**

Makes 8 servings
Prep. Time: 25–30 minutes
Cooking Time: 5–6 hours
Ideal slow-cooker size: 5-qt.

1 medium-sized red onion, chopped

2 cloves garlic, crushed

1 cup fresh mushrooms, sliced

2 Tbsp. olive oil

1 eggplant, unpeeled, cubed

2 green bell peppers, coarsely chopped

28-oz. can crushed tomatoes, or 10-12 whole
    tomatoes, peeled and crushed

28-oz. can garbanzos, drained and rinsed

2 Tbsp. fresh rosemary

1 cup fresh parsley, chopped

½ cup kalamata olives, pitted and sliced

1. Sauté onion, garlic, and mushrooms in
olive oil in skillet over medium heat. Transfer
to slow cooker coated with nonfat cooking
spray.

2. Add eggplant, peppers, tomatoes,
garbanzos, rosemary, and parsley to cooker.

3. Cover. Cook on low 5–6 hours.

4. Stir in olives just before serving.

5. Serve with couscous or polenta.

Caponata

Katrine Rose,
Woodbridge, VA

Makes 10 servings
Prep. Time: 25–30 minutes
Cooking Time: 5–6 hours
Ideal slow-cooker size: 4-qt.

1 medium-sized eggplant, peeled and cut into
  ½" cubes

14-oz. can low-sodium diced tomatoes

1 medium-sized onion, chopped

1 red bell pepper, cut into ½" pieces

¼ cup fresh salsa

¼ cup olive oil

2 Tbsp. capers, drained

3 Tbsp. balsamic vinegar

3 garlic cloves, minced

1 Tbsp. chopped fresh oregano

⅓ cup chopped fresh basil

1. Combine all ingredients except basil in slow cooker.

2. Cover. Cook on low 5–6 hours, or until vegetables are tender.

3. Stir in basil. Serve over slices of toasted French bread.

Garden Vegetable Medley

Ruth Fisher,
Leicester, NY

Makes 4 servings
Prep. Time: 10 minutes
Cooking Time: 20 minutes

Vegetables and Side Dishes

1 Tbsp. olive oil

4 cups zucchini, chopped into ½" pieces

1 cup chopped onions

1 red or green pepper, chopped

2 medium-sized tomatoes, chopped

2 cloves garlic, minced

½ tsp. salt

4 slices of your favorite cheese

1. Heat oil in stir-fry pan over medium heat. Add zucchini and onions. Heat until tender, about 10 minutes.

2. Add peppers and tomatoes and stir-fry until just tender.

3. Stir in garlic and salt.

4. Lay cheese over top. Turn off heat and let stand until cheese is melted.

Variations:
1. Use only 3 cups zucchini and add 1 baby eggplant, cut up into ½" pieces.
2. Substitute 1–2 tsp. dried Italian seasoning for garlic and salt.
3. Instead of slices of cheese, sprinkle liberally with Parmesan cheese.
   —Stephanie O'Conner, Cheshire, CN

Oven-Roasted Vegetables and Herbs

**Bonnie Goering,
Bridgewater, VA**

Makes 4–5 servings
Prep. Time: 10 minutes
Baking Time: 45–60 minutes

3 potatoes, cut in 1" pieces

3 carrots, cut in 1" pieces

2 onions, cut in wedges

¼ cup olive oil

2 Tbsp. minced fresh rosemary

2 Tbsp. minced fresh thyme

1 Tbsp. fresh chopped parsley

¾ tsp. salt

¼ tsp. freshly ground black pepper

½ lb. fresh mushrooms, cut into halves or quarters

1. Combine potatoes, carrots, and onions in a large mixing bowl.

2. Drizzle olive oil over vegetables.

3. In a small bowl, combine rosemary, thyme, parsley, salt, and pepper. Sprinkle over vegetables.

4. Arrange vegetables in a single layer on a large greased baking sheet.

5. Bake at 400° for 30 minutes.

6. Remove from oven and stir in mushrooms. Return to oven and continue baking for another 15–30 minutes, or until potatoes and carrots are tender.

Vegetables and
Side Dishes

Roasted Summer Vegetables

**Moreen Weaver,
Bath, NY**

Makes 6 servings
Prep. Time: 20–30 minutes
Baking Time: 20 minutes

8-10 cups fresh vegetables: your choice of any summer squash, onions, potatoes, tomatoes, green beans, broccoli, cauliflower, carrots, green or red bell peppers, mild chili peppers, eggplant, mushrooms, or fennel

Seasoning 1:

3 Tbsp. fresh basil, chopped

2 Tbsp. fresh cilantro, chopped

1½ Tbsp. fresh thyme, chopped

1 Tbsp. olive oil

½ tsp. pepper

3 cloves garlic, minced

Seasoning 2:

4 cloves garlic, minced

1 Tbsp. olive oil

2 Tbsp. fresh thyme

2 Tbsp. fresh oregano

2 Tbsp. fresh basil, chopped

2 Tbsp. balsamic vinegar

1 Tbsp. Dijon mustard

¼ tsp. pepper

1. Cut vegetables into bite-size pieces for even cooking. For example, slice potatoes thinly, but chop summer squash in chunks. Place prepared vegetables in large mixing bowl as you go.

2. Toss vegetables with one of the seasoning options.

3. Spread seasoned vegetables in a thin layer on a lightly greased baking sheet with sides.

4. Bake in preheated oven at 425° for 20 minutes. Stir occasionally.

Vegetables and
Side Dishes

Quick Stir-Fried Vegetables

**Judith Govotsos,
Frederick, MD**

Makes 5 servings
Prep. Time: 20 minutes
Cooking Time: 7-10 minutes

4 cloves garlic, sliced thin

4 carrots, sliced thin on angle

1 small yellow squash, sliced thin on angle

1 small green zucchini squash, sliced thin on angle

1 large onion, sliced thin

1 Tbsp. olive oil

¼ tsp. salt

⅛ tsp. pepper

1. Prepare all vegetables. Do not mix together.

2. Place olive oil in large nonstick skillet.

3. Add garlic and carrots. Stir-fry 2–3 minutes.

4. Add remainder of vegetables. Cook and stir until just lightly cooked, about 5–7 more minutes.

5. Stir in seasonings and serve.

Italian Veggie Bake

Orpha Herr,
Andover, NY

Makes 8 servings
Prep. Time: 20 minutes
Cooking/Baking Time: 45–50 minutes

⅓ cup reduced-fat Italian dressing

1 large onion, chopped

1 small unpeeled eggplant, cubed

2 medium zucchini, sliced thin

1 large red bell pepper, chopped

6-oz. pkg. fresh mushrooms, sliced

2 cups freshly diced tomatoes

⅓ cup shredded Parmesan cheese

1 Tbsp. chopped fresh parsley

1. Heat dressing in large skillet over medium-high heat.

2. Add onion and steam or stir-fry 5 minutes, or until just tender.

3. Add eggplant and steam or stir-fry 5 minutes.

4. Add zucchini, pepper, and mushrooms. Steam or stir-fry 5 minutes more.

5. Add tomatoes and bring to a boil.

6. Pour mixture into lightly greased baking dish. Sprinkle with cheese.

7. Bake uncovered at 350° for 25–30 minutes, or until bubbly.

8. Sprinkle with parsley just before serving.

Quinoa with Vegetables

Hope Comerford,
Clinton Township, MI

Makes 4–6 servings
Prep. Time: 10 minutes
Cooking Time: 4–6 hours
Ideal slow-cooker size: 3-qt.

Vegetables and Side Dishes

2 cups quinoa

4 cups vegetable stock

½ cup chopped onion

1 Tbsp. olive oil

1 medium red pepper, chopped

1 medium yellow pepper, chopped

1 medium carrot, chopped

3 garlic cloves, minced

½ tsp. sea salt

¼ tsp. pepper

1 Tbsp. fresh cilantro, chopped

1. Place quinoa, vegetable stock, onion, olive oil, red pepper, yellow pepper, carrot, garlic, salt, and pepper into crock and stir.

2. Cook on low for 4–6 hours or until liquid is absorbed and quinoa is tender.

3. Top with fresh cilantro to serve.

Oven-Fried Potatoes

**Robin Schrock,
Millersburg, OH**

Makes 8 servings
Prep. Time: 10 minutes
Baking Time: 1 hour

4 large baking potatoes, unpeeled

⅓ cup vegetable oil

2 Tbsp. Parmesan cheese

½ tsp. salt

¼ tsp. garlic powder

¼ tsp. paprika

⅛ tsp. pepper

1. Cut each potato lengthwise into 6 wedges.

2. Place wedges skin-side down in a greased 9 × 13 baking dish.

3. In a mixing bowl, combine oil, cheese, salt, garlic powder, paprika, and pepper. Brush over potatoes. Or, mix all ingredients except the potatoes in a large mixing bowl. When thoroughly blended, stir in potato wedges. Stir until they're well covered. Then place in a single layer in the baking dish.

4. Bake at 375° for 1 hour.

Variations:
To create a crustier finish on the potatoes, add 3 Tbsp. flour to Step 3. And increase the Parmesan cheese to ⅓ cup.

—Jere Zimmerman, Reinholds, PA
—Jena Hammond, Traverse City, MI
—Sara Wilson, Blairstown, MO

Vegetables and
Side Dishes

Rosemary New Potatoes

Carol Shirk,
Leola, PA

Makes 4–5 servings
Prep. Time: 15 minutes
Cooking Time: 2–5 hours
Ideal slow-cooker size: 3- or 4-qt.

1½ lbs. new red potatoes, uncooked and unpeeled

1 Tbsp. olive oil

1 Tbsp. fresh chopped rosemary

1 large clove garlic, minced

½ tsp. salt

¼ tsp. pepper

1. Grease interior of slow-cooker crock.

2. If potatoes are larger than golf balls, cut them in half or in quarters.

3. Toss potatoes with olive oil in slow cooker, coating well.

4. Add rosemary, minced garlic, salt and pepper. Toss again until the potatoes are well coated.

5. Cover. Cook on High 2–3 hours, or on Low 4–5 hours, or until potatoes are tender but not mushy or dry.

Lemon Red Potatoes

Joyce Shackelford,
Green Bay, WI

Makes 6 servings
Prep. Time: 15–20 minutes
Cooking Time: 2½–3 hours
Ideal slow-cooker size: 4-qt.

1½ lbs. medium-sized red potatoes

¼ cup water

2 Tbsp. butter, melted

1 Tbsp. lemon juice

3 Tbsp. fresh chives, snipped

3 Tbsp, chopped fresh parsley

1 tsp. salt

½ tsp. black pepper

1. Cut a strip of peel from around the middle of each potato. Place potatoes and water in slow cooker.

2. Cover. Cook on high 2½–3 hours.

3. Drain.

4. Combine butter, lemon juice, chives, and parsley. Pour over potatoes. Toss to coat.

5. Season with salt and pepper.

Baked Basil Fries

Sharon Brubaker,
Myerstown, PA

Makes 6 servings
Prep. Time: 15 minutes
Baking Time: 30 minutes

2 Tbsp. Parmesan cheese

2 tsp. olive oil

¼ cup chopped fresh basil

¼ tsp. garlic powder

4 medium red potatoes

1. Combine first 4 ingredients in a good-sized bowl.

2. Cut potatoes into ¼"-thick matchsticks. Toss with cheese mixture in bowl.

3. Place in jelly-roll baking pan, lightly coated with nonstick cooking spray.

4. Bake at 425° for 15 minutes.

5. Turn potatoes with a metal spatula. Bake an additional 15 minutes, or until potatoes are crisp-tender.

Irish Mashed Potatoes

Esther J. Yoder,
Hartville, OH

Makes 9 servings
Prep. Time: 30–45 minutes
Cooking Time: 2½–4 hours
Ideal slow-cooker size: 5-qt.

3 lbs. peeled Yukon gold, or red potatoes, cubed

2½ cups chopped cabbage

3-6 garlic cloves, peeled, according to your taste preference

2 cups fat-free, low-sodium chicken broth

½ cup (4 ozs.) low-fat cream cheese, at room temperature

⅓ cup fat-free, or low-fat, sour cream

¼ cup skim, or 2%, milk

½ tsp. kosher salt

¼ tsp. black pepper

1. Combine potatoes, cabbage, garlic cloves, and chicken broth in slow cooker.

2. Cook on high 2½–4 hours, or until vegetables are soft.

3. Drain. Add remaining ingredients and mash.

4. The potatoes are now ready to serve, or you may pour them back into the slow cooker and set the cooker on low until you're ready to serve.

Vegetables and Side Dishes

Creamy Scalloped Potatoes

Dede Peterson,
Rapid City, SD

Makes 8–10 servings
Prep. Time: 15 minutes
Cooking Time: 6–7 hours
Ideal slow-cooker size: 6-qt.

5 lbs. uncooked red potatoes, peeled or unpeeled and sliced, *divided*

2 cups water

1 tsp. cream of tartar

¼ lb. bacon, cut in 1-inch squares, browned until crisp, and drained

dash of salt

½ pt. whipping cream

1 pt. half-and-half

1. Grease interior of slow-cooker crock.

2. In a large bowl, toss sliced potatoes in water and cream of tartar. Drain.

3. Layer half of potatoes and half of bacon in large slow cooker. Sprinkle each layer with salt.

4. Mix whipping cream and half-and-half in bowl. Pour over potatoes.

5. Cover. Cook on Low 6–7 hours, or until potatoes feel tender when you poke those in the center of the crock.

Golden Potato Casserole

Andrea Igoe,
Poughkeepsie, NY

Makes 8 servings
Prep. Time: 20 minutes
Cooking/Baking Time: 1½–2 hours
Chilling Time: 3–4 hours, or overnight

8 large potatoes

8 ozs. cheddar cheese, grated

1 bunch of scallions, chopped fine

1 tsp. salt

⅛ tsp. pepper

2 cups (1 pt.) sour cream

3–4 Tbsp. milk

¾ cup bread crumbs

4 Tbsp. butter, melted

1. Boil potatoes until tender but firm. Chill thoroughly 3–4 hours or overnight. Peel and grate.

2. In a large mixing bowl, stir cheese and grated potatoes together.

3. Fold in scallions, salt, pepper, sour cream, and milk. Mix well.

4. Spread in a greased 9 × 13 baking dish.

5. Combine bread crumbs and butter. Sprinkle over potatoes.

6. Bake at 350° for 60 minutes.

Vegetables and Side Dishes

Sweet Potato Casserole

Joyce Shackelford,
Green Bay, WI

Makes 6 servings
Prep. Time: 20 minutes
Cooking/Baking Time: 1 hour

4 medium sweet potatoes

1 Tbsp. olive oil

¼ cup freshly squeezed orange juice

2 Tbsp. chopped walnuts, plus 2 tsp. for garnish

¼ tsp. nutmeg

1. Cook whole sweet potatoes in boiling water in a covered saucepan 25–30 minutes, or until tender. Drain.

2. Allow potatoes to cool enough to hold. Then peel and mash in a mixer or with a hand held ricer.

3. Add olive oil, orange juice, 2 Tbsp. chopped walnuts, and nutmeg. Mix thoroughly.

4. Place in lightly greased 1-quart baking dish. Garnish with 2 tsp. chopped walnuts.

5. Bake uncovered at 375° for 25 minutes.

Honey Maple Sweet Potatoes

**Lorraine Kratz,
Sinking Spring, PA**

Makes 6-8 servings
Prep. Time: 30 minutes
Cooking/Baking Time: 50 minutes

6-8 medium sweet potatoes

½ cup honey

½ cup maple syrup

½ cup milk

4 Tbsp. butter

1. Cook sweet potatoes in a pot with water to cover. Test with a fork and remove from heat when they are becoming soft. Do not overcook.

2. Run cold water over the sweet potatoes. Peel them.

3. Place the honey, maple syrup, milk, and butter in a pan and bring to a boil for about 30 seconds.

4. Place sweet potatoes in a 9" square pan. Pour the sauce over them.

5. Bake at 350° for 30 minutes.

Thyme Roasted Sweet Potatoes

**Hope Comerford,
Clinton Township, MI**

Makes 6 servings
Prep. Time: 20 minutes
Cooking Time: 2–3 hours
Ideal slow-cooker size: 4-qt.

Vegetables and
Side Dishes

4–6 medium sweet potatoes, peeled, cubed

3 Tbsp. olive oil

5–6 large garlic cloves, minced

⅓ cup fresh thyme leaves

½ tsp. kosher salt

¼ tsp. red pepper flakes

1. Place all ingredients into the crock and stir.

2. Cover and cook on low for 7 hours, or until potatoes are tender.

Healthy Sweet Potato Fries

**Gladys M. High,
Ephrata, PA**

Makes 4 servings
Prep. Time: 15 minutes
Baking Time: 30 minutes

olive oil cooking spray

2 large sweet potatoes, peeled and cut into wedges

¼ tsp. salt

¼ tsp. black pepper

freshly chopped oregano, thyme, rosemary, and garlic, optional

1. Preheat oven to 400°.

2. Coat baking sheet with olive oil cooking spray.

3. Arrange sweet potato wedges on baking sheet in a single layer. Coat with cooking spray.

4. Sprinkle sweet potatoes with salt, pepper, and any additional optional seasoning of your choice.

5. Roast 30 minutes, or until tender and golden brown.

Yam Fries

Kathy Keener Shantz,
Lancaster, PA

Makes 6 servings
Prep. Time: 10 minutes
Baking Time: 20 minutes

2 Tbsp. olive oil

1 tsp. salt

1 tsp. pepper

1 tsp. curry powder

½ tsp. hot sauce

4 medium-sized yams, sliced like French fries

1. In a large mixing bowl, combine oil, salt, pepper, curry powder, and hot sauce.

2. Stir in sliced yams.

3. When thoroughly coated, spread on lightly greased baking sheet.

4. Bake at 375° for 20 minutes, or until tender.

Fresh Herb Stuffing

Barbara J. Fabel,
Wausau, WI

Makes 8 servings
Prep. Time: 30–45 minutes
Cooking Time: 4–5 hours
Ideal slow-cooker size: 6-qt.

3 onions, chopped

4 celery ribs, chopped

3 Tbsp. butter

½ cup chopped fresh parsley

1 Tbsp. chopped fresh rosemary

1 Tbsp. chopped fresh thyme

1 Tbsp. chopped fresh marjoram

1 Tbsp. chopped fresh sage

1 tsp. salt

½ tsp. freshly ground black pepper

1 loaf stale low-fat sourdough bread, cut in
   1-inch cubes

2 cups fat-free chicken broth

1. Sauté onions and celery in butter in skillet until transparent. Remove from heat and stir in fresh herbs and seasonings.

2. Place bread cubes in large bowl. Add onion/herb mixture. Add enough broth to moisten. Mix well but gently. Turn into greased slow cooker.

3. Cover. Cook on high 1 hour. Reduce heat to low and continue cooking 3–4 hours.

Vegetables and
Side Dishes

Potato Herb Stuffing

**Lewis J. Matt III,
Holbrook, PA**

Makes 8 servings
Prep. Time: 30 minutes
Cooking Time: 6–8 hours
Ideal slow-cooker size: 6-qt.

4 ribs celery with leaves, chopped

1 large onion, chopped

½ cup (1 stick) butter

4 large potatoes, cooked and diced

10 slices whole wheat bread, diced

5 eggs

½ cup chopped fresh parsley

1 tsp. finely chopped fresh basil

1½ tsp. chopped fresh thyme

½ tsp. chopped fresh rosemary

1 tsp. freshly ground pepper

1 tsp. salt

3-4 cups vegetable broth

1. In a skillet, sauté celery and onion in butter until softened. Transfer to slow cooker, being sure to get all the butter.

2. Add to slow cooker the potatoes, bread, eggs, parsley, basil, thyme, rosemary, pepper, and salt. Mix gently.

3. Add 3 cups broth and mix again. If stuffing is not moist enough, add up to another cup broth.

4. Cover and cook on Low for 6–8 hours, until firm and browning around edges.

Moist Poultry Dressing

Virginia Bender, Dover, DE
Josie Boilman, Maumee, OH
Sharon Brubaker, Myerstown, PA
Joette Droz, Kalona, IA
Jacqueline Stefl, E. Bethany, NY

Makes 14 servings
Prep. Time: 25 minutes
Cooking Time: 5 hours
Ideal slow-cooker size: 5-qt.

16-oz. fresh button mushrooms, diced

4 celery ribs, chopped (about 2 cups)

2 medium onions, chopped

¼ cup minced fresh parsley

¼–¾ cup margarine (enough to flavor bread)

13 cups cubed day-old bread

1½ tsp. salt

3 tsp. fresh sage

1 tsp. poultry seasoning

3 tsp. fresh chopped thyme

½ tsp. pepper

2 eggs

1 or 2 14½-oz. cans chicken broth (enough to moisten bread)

1. In large skillet, sauté mushrooms, celery, onions, and parsley in margarine until vegetables are tender.

2. Toss together bread cubes, salt, sage, poultry seasoning, thyme, and pepper. Add mushroom mixture.

3. Combine eggs and broth and add to bread mixture. Mix well.

4. Pour into greased slow cooker. Cook on Low 5 hours, or until meat thermometer reaches 160°.

Variations:

1. Use 2 bags bread cubes for stuffing. Make one mixed bread (white and wheat) and the other corn bread cubes.
2. Add ½ tsp. dried marjoram to Step 2.
   —Arlene Miller, Hutchinson, KS

NOTE

This is a good way to free up the oven when you're making a turkey.

Homemade Refried Beans

Emily Fox,
Bethel, PA

Makes 15 servings
Prep. Time: 15 minutes
Cooking Time: 8 hours
Ideal slow-cooker size: 5-qt.

1 onion, peeled and halved

3 cups dry pinto or black beans, rinsed

½ fresh or frozen jalapeño, chopped

2 cloves garlic

3–4 tsp. salt

1¾ tsp. black pepper

⅛ tsp. ground cumin

9 cups water

1. Place all ingredients in slow cooker and stir to combine.

2. Cook on High for 8 hours.

3. Drain off liquid, reserving it. Mash beans with potato masher, adding liquid as needed to get consistency you want.

TIP

Much better than canned! Eat alone or with rice and tortillas, or use in recipes.

Basil Refried Beans

Jacqueline Swift,
Perrysburg, NY

Makes 6–8 servings
Prep. Time: 20 minutes
Cooking Time: 5–7 hours
Ideal slow-cooker size: 3-qt.

2 Tbsp. butter

1½ cups diced onion

4 cups cooked pinto beans

½ cup vegetable broth

2 cloves garlic, minced

1 tsp. cumin

½ cup chopped fresh basil

1½ tsp. fresh chopped rosemary

pinch cayenne pepper, or to taste

1 tsp. salt

½ cup shredded sharp cheddar cheese

1. Combine butter and onions in slow cooker.

2. Cover and cook on High for 1 hour.

3. Add beans, broth, garlic, cumin, basil, rosemary, cayenne, and salt.

4. Cover and cook on Low for 4–6 hours.

5. Mash beans with potato masher. Stir in cheese until melted. Taste for seasoning before serving.

Simple Black Beans

Carolyn Spohn,
Shawnee, KS

Makes 6 servings
Prep. Time: 10 minutes
Cooking Time: 4–6 on High, depending on age of slow cooker.
Standing Time: 6–10 hours
Ideal slow-cooker size: 5-qt.

2 cups dry black beans

¼ cup chopped onion

1-2 cloves garlic, chopped

1 Tbsp. brown sugar

1 Tbsp. olive oil

4 cups water or chicken broth

salt, to taste

1. Place beans in bowl and cover with water about 2" over beans. Soak for 6–10 hours.

2. Drain off water. Put soaked beans in slow cooker.

3. Add rest of ingredients to slow cooker except salt.

4. Cover and cook on High for 4–6 hours, until beans are soft. Add salt.

Good go-alongs with this recipe:
Rice or other mild-flavored grain to make a complete protein.

Greek Salad

Ruth Feister,
Narvon, PA

Makes 8 servings
Prep. Time: 20 minutes

Dressing:

¼ cup chicken stock

2 Tbsp. red wine vinegar

2 tsp. lemon juice

1 tsp. sugar

1 tsp. fresh minced basil

¾ tsp. fresh minced oregano

Salad:

head of torn romaine lettuce

1 medium-sized cucumber sliced thin

2 medium-sized tomatoes, cut in pieces

half a red onion, finely chopped

¼ cup chopped fresh parsley

4-oz. can sliced black olives, drained

3–4 ozs. crumbled feta cheese

several artichoke hearts, quartered

1. Combine dressing ingredients in a jar with a tightly fitting lid. Shake until mixed well.

2. Place lettuce, cucumber, tomatoes, onions, and parsley in a large serving bowl.

3. Just before serving, drizzle with dressing and toss.

4. Top with olives, cheese, and artichoke hearts.

Caesar Salad

**Colleen Heatwole,
Burton, MI**

Makes 8 servings
Prep. Time: 15–20 minutes

8-12 cups romaine lettuce, or spring mix, torn
   into bite-sized pieces

⅓ cup oil

3 Tbsp. red wine vinegar

1 tsp. Worcestershire sauce

½ tsp. salt

¾ tsp. dry mustard powder

1 large garlic clove, minced

1½-2 Tbsp. fresh lemon juice

dash of pepper

¼-½ cup grated Parmesan cheese

2 cups Caesar-flavored, or garlic, croutons

1. Place lettuce in a large bowl.

2. Combine next 6 ingredients in a blender
or food processor.

3. Add fresh lemon juice and process until
smooth.

4. Just before serving, toss with lettuce.

5. Sprinkle with pepper. Add Parmesan
cheese and toss well. Serve croutons
separately.

TIPS

1. I have made this on more Sundays
   than I can count. I prepare the
   lettuce, blend the 6 ingredients,
   and get the hard cheese ready for
   my son to grate. I always use fresh
   lemon or fresh lime.
2. My family prefers a tart dressing.
   My friend adds 1 Tbsp. sugar.

Colorful Lettuce Salad

**Anna Wise,
Seneca Falls, NY**

Makes 8 servings
Prep. Time: 20 minutes

6 cups red leaf lettuce

1 bell pepper, chopped or sliced

½ cup shredded carrots

4 radishes, sliced

1 onion, minced

½ cup shredded low-fat cheddar, or Colby, cheese

2½ Tbsp. honey

1 tsp. prepared mustard

2 Tbsp. skim milk

2 Tbsp. vinegar

½ cup fat-free mayonnaise

1. Wash lettuce and pull apart coarsely into 2-quart bowl. Add bell pepper, carrots, radishes, onion, and cheese.

2. In another bowl, whisk together honey, mustard, and milk. Add vinegar and mayonnaise and whisk until smooth.

3. Pour dressing over salad greens and mix lightly. Serve immediately.

Apple Blue Cheese Salad

**Judy Houser,
Hershey, PA**

Makes 6 servings
Prep. Time: 15–20 minutes

⅓ cup broken walnuts, or pecans

1 bunch red or green leaf lettuce

1-2 apples

3 ozs. crumbled blue cheese

⅓ cup raisins, optional

Greek salad dressing

1. Toast coarsely chopped nuts in dry skillet over medium heat. Stir frequently to prevent burning. Set toasted nuts aside to cool.

2. Wash lettuce and tear into salad bowl.

3. Dice unpeeled apples.

4. Add apples to lettuce, along with nuts and crumbled cheese, and raisins if you wish.

5. Drizzle with Greek dressing when ready to serve.

Salads

Orange Pecan Salad

Mary Lynn Miller,
Reinholds, PA

Makes 4 servings
Prep. Time: 10 minutes.

2 oranges, peeled and sectioned

1 head, or bunch, leaf lettuce, torn

¼ cup pecan halves, toasted

½ cup peach yogurt

3 Tbsp. mayonnaise

1. Toss oranges, lettuce, and pecans in a large salad bowl. Set aside.

2. Combine yogurt and mayonnaise in a small bowl.

3. Pour dressing over salad just before serving. Toss.

Salads

Bibb Lettuce with Pecans and Oranges

Betty K. Drescher,
Quakertown, PA

Makes 8 servings
Prep. Time: 10-15 minutes

4 heads Bibb lettuce

¾ cup pecan halves, toasted

2 oranges, peeled and sliced

Dressing:

⅓ cup vinegar

½ cup sugar

1 cup vegetable oil

½ tsp. salt

half a small onion, chopped

1 tsp. dry mustard

2 Tbsp. water

1. Place lettuce, pecans, and oranges in a salad bowl.

2. Combine dressing ingredients in blender. (You can make this ahead of time and refrigerate it.)

3. Toss dressing with salad ingredients just before serving.

Asparagus Tossed Salad

Carolyn Baer,
Conrath, WI

Makes 8 servings
Prep. Time: 15 minutes
Cooking Time: 5 minutes
Standing Time: 30 minutes

4 cups water

2 medium carrots, sliced

1 lb. fresh asparagus, cut into 1" pieces

8 cups torn Bibb lettuce

Orange Ginger Vinaigrette:
¼ cup orange juice

4½ tsp. olive, or canola, oil

2 Tbsp. white wine vinegar, rice vinegar, or cider vinegar

1 Tbsp. honey

1 tsp. Dijon mustard

1 Tbsp. freshly grated ginger

½ tsp. grated orange peel

⅛ tsp. salt

1. In a large saucepan, bring 4 cups water to a boil. Add carrots. Cover and boil 1 minute.

2. Add asparagus. Cover and boil 3 minutes longer.

3. Drain and immediately place vegetables in ice water. Drain and pat dry. Place in large mixing bowl.

4. In a jar with a tight-fitting lid, combine the vinaigrette ingredients. Shake well.

5. Drizzle over vegetables and toss to coat.

6. Let stand 30 minutes to allow dressing flavors to penetrate vegetables.

7. Combine lettuce, carrots, asparagus, and dressing. Serve immediately.

Beet Walnut Salad

**Jenny Kennedy,
Driggs, ID**

Makes 8 servings
Prep. Time: 20 minutes
Cooking Time: 45 minutes

1 small bunch beets, or enough canned beets
(no salt added) to make 3 cups, drained

¼ cup red wine vinegar

¼ cup chopped apple

¼ cup chopped celery

3 Tbsp. balsamic vinegar

1 Tbsp. olive oil

1 Tbsp. water

8 cups fresh salad greens

freshly ground pepper

3 Tbsp. chopped walnuts

¼ cup Gorgonzola cheese, crumbled

1. Steam raw beets in water in saucepan until tender. Slip off skins. Rinse to cool.

2. Slice in ½" rounds. In a medium bowl, toss with red wine vinegar.

3. Add apples and celery. Toss together.

4. In a large bowl, combine balsamic vinegar, olive oil, and water. Add salad greens and toss.

5. Put greens onto individual salad plates. Top with sliced beet mixture.

6. Sprinkle with pepper, walnuts, and cheese. Serve immediately.

Salads

Blueberry Spinach Salad

**Judi Robb,
Manhattan, KS**

Makes 6–8 servings
Prep. Time: 15–20 minutes

½ cup vegetable oil

¼ cup raspberry vinegar

2 tsp. Dijon mustard

1 tsp.-1 Tbsp. sugar, according to your taste
  preference

½ tsp. salt

10-oz. pkg. fresh torn spinach

4-oz. pkg. blue cheese, crumbled

1 cup fresh blueberries

½ cup chopped pecans, tasted

1. In a jar with a tight-fitting lid, combine oil, vinegar, mustard, sugar, and salt. Shake well.

2. In a large salad bowl, toss spinach, blue cheese, blueberries, and pecans.

3. Just before serving, add dressing and toss gently.

Spinach Salad with Walnut Dressing

Dolores Metzler,
Lewistown, PA

Makes 8 servings
Prep. Time: 15 minutes
Standing Time: 30 minutes

Dressing:

¼ cup vegetable oil

1 Tbsp. honey

¼ tsp. salt

2 Tbsp. lemon juice

2 tsp. Dijon mustard

dash of pepper

⅔ cup walnuts, chopped

2 Tbsp. sliced scallions

Salad:

4-6 cups spinach and/or other greens

1 cup diced Swiss cheese

1 cup diced fresh fruit (apples, peaches, and pears are all good, dipped in lemon juice to keep from discoloring)

1. Mix oil, honey, salt, lemon juice, mustard, pepper, walnuts, and scallions in a jar with a tight-fitting lid.

2. Cover and shake until well mixed. Then let stand for 30 minutes to enhance flavor.

3. Mix spinach, Swiss cheese, and diced fruit in a large mixing bowl.

4. Just before serving, add dressing to salad and toss together.

Salads

Spinach Salad Caprese

Jan Moore. Wellsville, KS

Makes 4 servings
Prep. Time: 10-20 minutes

6 cups fresh spinach

12 cherry tomatoes, halved

½ cup chopped fresh basil

4 ozs. fresh mozzarella cheese, cubed

¼ cup light olive oil

1. Gently combine all ingredients.

2. Toss to mix.

3. Serve immediately.

Tabbouleh with Blueberries and Mint

**Pat Bechtel,
Dillsburg, PA**

Makes 4 main-dish servings
Prep. Time: 20–25 minutes
Marinating Time: 2 hours

2 cups water

1 cup uncooked bulgur wheat, medium grind

½ lb. (about 2) fresh tomatoes, peeled and
   diced

half a cucumber, diced

4 scallions, white and green parts, minced

2 cups fresh blueberries

5 Tbsp. fresh lemon juice

¼ cup olive oil

½ cup shredded fresh mint leaves

1 Tbsp. chopped fresh parsley

¼ tsp. ground cumin

¼ tsp. salt

¼ tsp. freshly ground black pepper

1. Bring 2 cups water to a boil. Add bulgur
and allow to stand 5 minutes.

2. Turn soaked bulgur onto a cloth. Pick
up cloth with bulgur inside and squeeze out
excess moisture.

3. Combine all ingredients in a large bowl,
tossing gently.

4. Cover and refrigerate. Allow to marinate
2 hours before serving.

5. Serve at room temperature.

Salads

Refreshing Summer Salad

**Kathleen A. Rogge,
Alexandria, IN**

Makes 4 servings
Prep. Time: 20 minutes
Cooking Time: 10 minutes

2 lbs. fresh asparagus, tough ends trimmed

2 oranges, preferably Valencia

1 Tbsp. orange juice

¼ cup extra-virgin olive oil

1 cup crumbled blue cheese

1. Fill a large bowl with ice water; set it aside.

2. Bring large pot of water to a boil. Add asparagus to boiling water and cook until crisp tender, about 4 minutes.

3. Transfer asparagus to ice bath and let sit for 1 minute. Drain and set aside.

4. Meanwhile, peel oranges, cutting off white pith. Cut between membranes to release segments. Set aside.

5. In a small bowl or jar, whisk or shake together the orange juice and olive oil.

6. To serve, divide asparagus, blue cheese, and oranges among four salad plates. Drizzle each with about 1 Tbsp. of the dressing.

Broccoli Salad

Sherlyn Hess,
Millersville, PA
Ruth Zendt,
Mifflintown, PA

Makes 6-8 servings
Prep. Time: 20 minutes
Chilling Time: 2 hours

1 cup raisins

2 cups boiling water

6 cups chopped broccoli tops

⅔ cup chopped red onions

10 strips of bacon, cooked and crumbled

¼ cup shredded carrots

½ cup salad dressing

½ cup mayonnaise

2 Tbsp. vinegar

½ cup sugar

1. Soak raisins for a few minutes in boiling water. Drain.

2. Combine plumped raisins, broccoli, onions, bacon, and carrots.

3. Whisk together remaining ingredients in a separate bowl. Pour over broccoli mixture. Toss to mix.

4. Refrigerate at least 2 hours before serving.

Variations:
1. Add 1 cup grated cheese and/or ½ cup chopped peanuts to Step 2.
   —Ruth Zendt, Mifflintown, PA
2. Add 1 cup chopped celery and ½ cup hulled sunflower seeds to Step 2.
   —Jean Butzer, Batavia, NY

Salads

Apple Broccoli Salad

Melanie Mohler,
Ephrata, PA

Makes 6 servings
Prep. Time: 20 minutes

2 McIntosh, Empire, or Cortland apples, unpeeled, but cored and chopped

3 cups fresh raw broccoli, cut up

¼ cup chopped walnuts

1 Tbsp. chopped red onion

⅓ cup raisins

½ cup fat-free vanilla yogurt, sweetened with low-calorie sweetener

lettuce leaves

1. Mix all ingredients, except lettuce, together in a large bowl.

2. Serve on a bed of lettuce.

Trees and Seeds Salad

**Nanci Keatley,
Salem, OR**

Makes 8–10 servings
Prep. Time: 10–20 minutes
Chilling Time: 30 minutes

4 cups cauliflower florets

3 cups cut-up broccoli

1 cup diced red onions

2 pts. cherry tomatoes, halved

½–1 lb. bacon, cooked and diced, according
   to your preference

3 Tbsp. sesame seeds

¼ cup sunflower seeds

¼ cup slivered almonds

Dressing:

1 cup mayonnaise

½ cup sugar or sugar substitute

3 Tbsp. cider vinegar

½ tsp. salt

½ tsp. pepper

1. In a large serving bowl, combine cauliflower, broccoli, onions, tomatoes, bacon, seeds, and nuts.

2. In a separate bowl, mix together mayonnaise, sugar, vinegar, salt, and pepper. Pour over vegetables.

3. Refrigerate at least 30 minutes to blend flavors.

Variations:

1. Change the "green" base of this salad to: 3 cups shredded cabbage or coleslaw mix; 2 cups broken cauliflower; 2 cups chopped broccoli.
    —Teresa Martin, Gordonville, PA

2. Add ⅓ cup grated Parmesan cheese to the Dressing in Step 2.
    —Phyllis Smith, Goshen, IN

3. Add 8 sliced radishes to Step 1.
    —Sara Wilson, Blairstown, MO

TIP

This is great to make ahead. Mix all ingredients together except the dressing. Chill, then add the dressing half an hour before serving. Refrigerate until serving time.

Mixed Vegetables Salad

**Kathleen Johnson,
Rolfe, IA**

Makes 4 servings
Prep. Time: 20–30 minutes

1½ cups cauliflower, cut into small pieces

½ cup celery, diced

1 cup shredded carrot

1½ cup broccoli, cut into small pieces

low-calorie Italian dressing

1. Mix vegetables in a bowl.

2. Mix in just enough dressing to coat vegetables.

Green Bean Salad

**Jean H. Robinson,
Cinnaminson, NJ**

Makes 6–8 servings
Prep. Time: 20 minutes
Cooking Time: 10 minutes
Chilling Time: 2 hours

4 cups water

1 Tbsp. salt

2 lbs. fresh green beans, cut into 2" pieces

1 rib celery, chopped fine

½ cup chopped scallions

2 cups cherry tomatoes, halved

½ cup feta cheese

Dressing:
½ cup oil

2 Tbsp. rice vinegar

1 tsp. Dijon mustard

salt to taste

pepper to taste

1. Bring water and salt to a boil in a large stockpot. Place beans into boiling water and cook for 6 minutes. Remove from stove and drain. Plunge beans immediately into ice water. Drain.

2. In a large mixing bowl, combine beans, celery, scallions, tomatoes, and cheese.

3. In a jar with a tight-fitting lid, combine oil, vinegar, mustard, salt, and pepper. Shake well.

4. Pour dressing over bean mixture. Toss.

5. Chill for at least 2 hours before serving.

Edamame/Soybean Salad

Esther Porter,
Minneapolis, MN

Makes 4 servings
Prep. Time: 15-20 minutes

16 ozs. fresh, or frozen, green soybeans
(thawed if frozen)

¼ cup seasoned rice vinegar

1 Tbsp. corn oil

⅛ tsp. black pepper

sliced radishes and fresh
cilantro leaves for garnishing

1. Mix together rice vinegar, oil, and black pepper. Pour over soybeans in a large bowl.

2. Garnish with radishes and cilantro.

3. Chill and serve.

Lime Cucumbers

Norma I. Gehman,
Ephrata, PA

Makes 4 servings
Prep. Time: 10 minutes

½ tsp. grated lime rind

1 Tbsp. lime juice

2 Tbsp. olive oil

¼ tsp. salt

⅛ tsp. pepper

1 large burpless, seedless cucumber, thinly
   sliced

1. Whisk together first 5 ingredients in a bowl.

2. Add cucumber and mix well.

Refreshing Cucumber Salad

**Kathy Alderfer,
Broadway, VA**

Makes 4 servings
Prep. Time: 15 minutes
Chilling Time: 1 hour

¼ cup mayonnaise

¼ cup sour cream

1 Tbsp. sugar

1 Tbsp. vinegar

3 tsp. fresh chopped dill

salt and pepper to taste

3 cups thinly sliced cucumbers (about 3 medium-sized ones)

1 cup grape tomatoes, halved

2–4 small scallions, sliced into rings, amount according to your preference

1. In a medium-sized mixing bowl, mix mayonnaise, sour cream, sugar, vinegar, dill, salt, and pepper. Blend thoroughly.

2. Add cucumbers, tomatoes, and scallions to creamy mixture and stir together.

3. Allow to marinate in refrigerator for at least 1 hour before serving.

Salads

Marinated Garden Tomatoes

Bonnie Goering,
Bridgewater, VA

Makes 10 servings
Prep. Time: 10 minutes
Chilling Time: 1 hour or more

6 large firm tomatoes, cut in wedges

½ cup sliced onions

½ cup sliced green bell pepper

¼ cup olive oil

2 Tbsp. red wine vinegar

¼ tsp. garlic powder

½ tsp. salt

¼ tsp. pepper

2 Tbsp. sugar

2 Tbsp. minced fresh parsley flakes

1 Tbsp. snipped fresh thyme

1. Arrange tomatoes, onions, and peppers in a flat dish.

2. In a jar with a tight-fitting lid, mix together oil, vinegar, garlic powder, salt, pepper, and sugar. Pour over vegetables.

3. In a small bowl, combine parsley and thyme and sprinkle on top.

4. Refrigerate for one hour or more before serving.

Mozzarella/Tomato/Basil Salad

Phyllis Good,
Lancaster, PA

Makes 6 servings
Prep. Time: 8 minutes

1 pint buffalo mozzarella cheese balls, or
¼–½ lb. buffalo mozzarella cheese, sliced

2 large tomatoes, sliced and quartered

½ cup black olives, sliced

½ cup basil leaves, torn

1 Tbsp. olive oil

1 Tbsp. red wine vinegar

¼ tsp. salt

⅛ tsp. pepper

1. If the mozzarella balls are in liquid, rinse and drain them. Place in a mixing bowl.

2. Add tomatoes, black olives, and basil leaves. Mix together gently.

3. Mix olive oil, vinegar, salt, and pepper together. Pour over salad ingredients and mix gently.

Variations:
1. Add 1 sweet Vidalia onion, sliced, to Step 2.
2. Serve the dressed salad on a bed of arugula leaves.
   —Bonita Ensenberger, Albuquerque, NM

Salads

Bulgarian Salad

Gail Martin,
Elkhart, IN

Makes 2 servings
Prep. Time: 8–10 minutes

1 tomato, diced

2 scallions, chopped

¼ cup chopped parsley

half a green bell pepper, chopped, optional

salt and pepper, optional

vinaigrette dressing

Bulgarian, or other, feta cheese

1. Mound tomato, scallions, and parsley on two salad plates. Add chopped green pepper if you wish.

2. Sprinkle with salt and pepper if you wish.

3. Drizzle with dressing.

4. Crumble feta over top.

Flavorful Coleslaw

Sara Kinsinger,
Stuarts Draft, VA

Makes 10 servings
Prep. Time: 20 minutes

1 head green cabbage, shredded

1 cucumber, peeled and diced

1 cup fresh pineapple, chopped

1 jalapeño pepper, minced

2 Tbsp. extra-virgin cold-pressed olive oil

2 Tbsp. water

1 avocado, pit removed, peeled, and coarsely
   chopped

2 Tbsp. pine nuts

1 Tbsp. cider vinegar

2 tsp. celery seed

1. Combine prepared cabbage, cucumber, pineapple, and pepper in a bowl.

2. In a blender, combine olive oil, water, avocado, pine nuts, vinegar, and celery seed.

3. Blend well. Pour over cabbage mixture and mix together thoroughly.

Creamy Coleslaw

Tammy Yoder,
Belleville, PA

Makes 6 servings
Prep. Time: 10 minutes
Chilling Time: 30 minutes

half a head of cabbage

½ cup mayonnaise

2 Tbsp. vinegar

⅓ cup sugar

pinch of salt

pinch of pepper

1 Tbsp. celery seed, or to taste

¼ cup grated carrots

1. Shred cabbage. Place in a large mixing bowl.

2. Mix all remaining ingredients together in another bowl.

3. Stir dressing into shredded cabbage, mixing well.

4. Chill for 30 minutes before serving.

Variations:
1. If you're short on time, use a bag of prepared shredded cabbage with carrots.
2. For added zest, stir ½ tsp. dry mustard into the dressing in Step 2.
   —Maricarol Magill, Freehold, NJ

Salads

Cabbage Slaw with Vinegar Dressing

**Betty Hostetler,
Allensville, PA**

Makes 10-12 servings
Prep. Time: 30-45 minutes
Chilling Time: 3-4 hours

8 cups grated cabbage

¼ cup grated carrots

¼ cup diced celery

¼ cup chopped red pepper

¼ cup chopped yellow pepper

⅛ cup chopped green pepper

1 Tbsp. celery seed

¾-1 cup sugar

1 tsp. salt

½ cup white vinegar

¼ cup, plus 2 Tbsp., oil

Variations:
1. Add 1 medium-sized onion, chopped to the vegetables in Step 1.
2. Reduce celery seed to 1 tsp. and add 1½ tsp. mustard seed and ½ tsp. turmeric.
   —Emilie Kimpel, Arcadia, MI

1. Combine vegetables, celery seed, sugar, and salt in a large mixing bowl. Mix well.

2. In a small saucepan, bring vinegar to a boil. Add oil. Pour over vegetables. Mix well.

3. Refrigerate for 3–4 hours before serving.

Salads

Cranberry Coleslaw

**Carolyn A. Baer,
Conrath, WI**

Makes 6 servings
Prep. Time: 15 minutes
Chilling Time: 45 minutes

¼ cup mayonnaise

1–2 Tbsp. honey

1 Tbsp. vinegar

¼ cup fresh chopped cranberries

small head (5 cups) cabbage, shredded

1. Stir together mayonnaise, honey, and vinegar. Stir in cranberries.

2. Place shredded cabbage in large serving bowl. Pour dressing over cabbage. Toss to coat.

3. Cover and chill 45 minutes.

Salads

Summer Squash Salad

Colleen J. Heatwole,
Burton, MI

Makes 6 servings
Prep. Time: 15 minutes
Chilling Time: 1 hour

4 medium zucchini, or summer squash,
   julienned

3 Tbsp. fresh basil

3 Tbsp. freshly grated Parmesan cheese

Dressing:

¼ cup olive oil

2 Tbsp. rice vinegar

2 Tbsp. red wine vinegar

2 tsp. fresh minced garlic

½ tsp. salt

¼ tsp. pepper

¼ tsp. sugar

1. Toss together squash, fresh basil, and Parmesan cheese in a large mixing bowl.

2. Combine dressing ingredients in a separate bowl and pour over salad.

3. Mix together well.

4. Cover and chill at least 1 hour before serving. The salad is best if eaten the same day it's made.

Tuscan Bean Salad

Eileen B. Jarvis,
St. Augustine, FL

Makes 8 servings
Prep. Time: 20 minutes
Chilling Time: 8 hours

3 Tbsp. fresh lemon juice

2 Tbsp. red wine vinegar

2 Tbsp. olive oil

2 tsp. grated lemon zest

1 tsp. honey

½ tsp. freshly ground pepper

3 garlic cloves, minced

2 anchovy fillets, minced, optional

1 cup halved grape tomatoes

¾ cup (about ¼ medium) English cucumber, chopped

½ cup chopped celery

½ cup thinly sliced red onion

¼ cup chopped fresh flat leaf parsley

1 Tbsp. chopped fresh sage

15½-oz. can garbanzo beans (chickpeas), rinsed and drained

15½-oz. can white beans, rinsed and drained

1. Combine first 7 ingredients (plus anchovies if you wish) in a small bowl. Stir well with a whisk.

2. Combine tomatoes and next 7 ingredients in a large bowl.

3. Add dressing. Toss gently.

4. Cover and chill at least 8 hours, stirring occasionally.

My Brother's Black Bean Salad

Shirley Hedman,
Schenectady, NY

Makes 16 servings
Prep. Time: 20 minutes

3 cups black beans (2 15-oz. cans, drained and rinsed)

1½ cups corn fresh off the cob

1 cup chopped red bell pepper

¾ cup chopped red onion

4-6 cloves minced garlic, according to your taste preference

½ cup chopped fresh cilantro

1 minced jalapeño

⅓ cup olive oil

½ cup lemon juice

¼ tsp. white pepper

1. Drain and rinse the beans, and the corn if it's canned. (If you're using fresh or frozen corn, you don't need to cook it.)

2. Mix all ingredients in a large bowl.

3. Serve immediately, or refrigerate until 2 hours before serving. Remove from fridge and serve at room temperature.

Chickpea Salad

Elaine Gibbel,
Lititz, PA

Makes 8 servings
Prep. Time: 20-25 minutes
Chilling Time: 4-24 hours

3 cups coarsely chopped fresh tomatoes (about 4 medium)

15-oz. can chickpeas (garbanzo beans), rinsed and drained

half a large cucumber, peeled, quartered, and sliced (about 1 cup)

1 cup chopped green bell pepper

¼ cup finely chopped onion

½ cup snipped parsley, or cilantro

¼ cup olive oil

3 Tbsp. red wine vinegar

1 clove garlic, minced

pinch of sugar (about ⅛ tsp.)

mixed salad greens, optional

lemon wedges, optional

1. In a large bowl combine vegetables and parsley or cilantro.

2. To make dressing, combine oil, vinegar, garlic, and sugar in a jar and shake well.

3. Pour dressing over vegetables and toss. Cover and chill 4–24 hours.

4. Before serving, let stand at room temperature 15 minutes.

5. Serve alone or with mixed greens. Serve with lemon wedges to squeeze over salad.

Lentil Salad

**Sharon Brubaker,
Myerstown, PA**

Makes 8 servings
Prep. Time: 20 minutes
Cooking Time: 15–25 minutes
Chilling Time: 30 minutes

½ cup dry lentils

1½ cups water

15-oz. can garbanzo beans, rinsed and drained

4 scallions, chopped

1 green bell pepper, julienned

1 red bell pepper, julienned

1 yellow bell pepper, julienned

1 Tbsp. fresh lemon juice

⅓ cup olive oil

½ cup vinegar

⅓ cup sugar

1. Place lentils and water in saucepan and bring to a boil. Reduce to simmer, cover, and cook 15–25 minutes, or until lentils are tender.

2. Drain lentils. Combine with remaining vegetables in a mixing bowl.

3. Mix dressing ingredients (lemon juice, olive oil, vinegar, and sugar) until thoroughly blended.

4. Stir dressing into vegetables.

5. Chill at least 30 minutes. Serve chilled.

Potato Salad

Gladys Shank,
Harrisonburg, VA
Sheila Soldner,
Lititz, PA
Sue Suter,
Millersville, PA

Makes 8–10 servings
Prep. Time: 20–30 minutes
Cooking Time: 45 minutes
Cooling Time: 3–4 hours

8 medium-sized potatoes, diced, peeled or
   unpeeled

1½ tsp. salt

water

4 hard-boiled eggs, diced

½–1 cup celery, chopped

¼–1 cup onions, chopped

Dressing:
2 eggs, beaten

¾ cup sugar

1 tsp. cornstarch

⅓ cup vinegar

⅓ cup milk

3 Tbsp. butter

1 tsp. prepared mustard

1 cup mayonnaise

1. Cooked diced potatoes in salt water to a firm softness (don't let them get mushy). Cool.

2. Cook eggs. Cool, peel, and dice.

3. Mix cooled potatoes and eggs with celery and onions.

4. Mix eggs, sugar, cornstarch, vinegar and milk in a saucepan and cook until thickened. Add butter, mustard, and mayonnaise. Cool.

5. Pour cooled dressing over potatoes, eggs, celery, and onions.

6. Refrigerate and chill for several hours before serving.

Variations:
1. Stir 1 tsp. celery seed into the dressing (Step 4), or substitute celery seed for the celery if you wish.
        —Ruth Schrock, Shipshewana, IN

2. Shred the potatoes after they're cooked, instead of cubing them before they're cooked. And substitute ⅓ cup sour cream for the milk in the dressing.
        —Martha Belle Burkholder,
        Waynesboro, VA

Salads

Easy Red Potato Salad

**Becky Harder,
Monument, CO**

Makes 6 servings
Prep. Time: 20 minutes
Cooking Time: 20 minutes
Standing Time: 30 minutes

2 lbs. red potatoes

⅓ cup cider vinegar

2 medium-sized ribs of celery, chopped

⅓ cup sliced scallions, including some green tops

½ cup mayonnaise

½ cup sour cream

1½ tsp. salt

½ tsp. pepper

sprinkle of paprika

1. Place potatoes in pot and cover with water. Cover and bring to a boil over high heat. Reduce heat to medium-low. Cover and simmer 10 minutes, or until potatoes are tender in the center. Drain and cool.

2. Cut potatoes into quarters, or eighths if they're large. Place in large mixing bowl. Pour vinegar over them and stir.

3. Let the potatoes stand for 30 minutes while you prepare the celery and onions. Stir the potatoes occasionally.

4. Mix mayonnaise, sour cream, salt, and pepper together in a small bowl.

5. Add the celery and scallions to the potatoes. Toss gently.

6. Stir in dressing and mix together gently. Sprinkle with a dash of paprika. Chill until ready to serve.

Variations:
1. Add 3 hard-cooked eggs, chopped, to Step 5.
2. Use ¾ tsp. celery seed instead of the chopped celery.
   —Lori Newswanger, Lancaster, PA

Salads

Creamy Dill Pasta Salad

Jan Mast,
Lancaster, PA

Makes 10 servings
Prep. Time: 15 minutes
Cooking Time: 12–15 minutes

3 cups uncooked tricolor spiral pasta

6-oz. can black olives, halved and drained

½ cup red pepper, chopped

½ cup green pepper, chopped

½ cup onions, chopped

2 tomatoes, chopped

3 Tbsp. fresh chopped dill

Dressing:
¾ cup mayonnaise

2 Tbsp. prepared mustard

¼ cup vinegar

⅓ cup sugar

1. Cook pasta according to package directions, being careful not to overcook. Rinse in cool water. Drain well. Place in large mixing bowl.

2. Add vegetables and dill weed and toss.

3. In a mixing bowl, combine mayonnaise, mustard, vinegar, and sugar.

4. Pour over pasta and vegetables and stir to coat.

5. Chill and serve.

Salads

Greek Orzo Salad

Lavina Hochstedler,
Grand Blanc, MI

Makes 8 servings
Prep. Time: 20 minutes
Cooking Time: 12 minutes
Chilling Time: 2–24 hours

1 cup uncooked orzo pasta

6 tsp. olive oil, *divided*

1 medium-sized red onion, finely chopped

/₂ cup minced fresh parsley

/₃ cup cider vinegar

4½ tsp. fresh chopped oregano

1 tsp. salt

1 tsp. sugar

/₈ tsp. pepper

1 large tomato, chopped

1 large red pepper, chopped

1 medium-sized cucumber, peeled, seeded, and chopped

½ cup black olives, sliced and drained, optional

½ cup crumbled feta cheese

1. Cook pasta according to directions. Drain.

2. In a large mixing bowl, toss cooked orzo with 2 tsp. olive oil.

3. In a separate bowl, combine the onion, parsley, vinegar, oregano, salt, sugar, pepper, and remaining oil. Pour over orzo and toss to coat.

4. Cover and refrigerate 2–24 hours.

5. Just before serving, gently stir in tomato, red pepper, cucumber, olives, and cheese.

Salads

Orzo and Corn off the Cob

Karen Kay Tucker,
Manteca, CA

Makes 6-8 servings
Prep. Time: 30 minutes
Cooking Time: 8-9 minutes

4 fresh ears of corn

1¼ cups uncooked orzo

1 cup black olives, pitted and halved

1 medium-sized red bell pepper, chopped

¼ cup thinly sliced scallions

¼ cup finely snipped fresh basil

¼ cup finely snipped fresh parsley

¼ cup olive oil

2 Tbsp. white wine vinegar

¼ tsp. salt

¼ tsp. pepper

1. Cut corn off the cob, about 2 cups' worth. Set aside.

2. Bring a large pot of lightly salted water to a boil. Add orzo and cook, stirring occasionally for 8 to 9 minutes, or until tender, adding corn during the last 3 minutes of cooking time. Drain and place in a large serving bowl.

3. Stir in the olives, bell pepper, scallions, basil, and parsley.

4. In a small bowl, combine the olive oil, vinegar, salt, and pepper. Whisk together.

5. Pour dressing over orzo mixture. Toss gently to combine.

Salads

Fresh Corn Salsa

J. B. Miller,
Indianapolis, IN

Makes about 3½–4 cups
Prep. Time: 20 minutes
Cooking Time: 15 minutes
Marinating Time: 3–4 hours, or overnight

Dressing:

1 tsp. chili powder

1 clove garlic, crushed

black pepper to taste

1 Tbsp. water

2 Tbsp. fresh lime juice

5 Tbsp. corn or vegetable oil

1 tsp. sugar

½ tsp. salt, *divided*

Salsa:

3 ears sweet corn

1 bell pepper

1 jalapeno pepper, cored, seeded, and minced

½ cup chopped tomatoes

¼ cup (about 3–4) scallions, sliced

cilantro to taste, optional

1. To make dressing, mix chili powder, garlic, and black pepper with 1 Tbsp. water in a small bowl. Let stand 5 minutes.

2. Add lime juice, oil, sugar, and ¼ tsp. salt.

3. Whisk to combine and set aside.

4. Place husked corn in a large pot of rapidly boiling water and cook 10 minutes. Rinse with cold water and drain.

5. While corn is boiling, roast the bell pepper; then chop.

6. Cut off cooked corn kernels, cutting as deeply as possible without getting cob.

7. Place kernels in a large bowl, along with the chopped roasted bell pepper. Add jalapeno, tomatoes, and scallions.

8. Pour the mixed dressing over the salsa and toss gently to combine. Refrigerate 3–4 hours or overnight.

9. Just before serving, toss again, taste, and adjust seasoning to your liking. Add ¼ tsp. salt and cilantro, if you wish.

10. Serve with white and yellow corn chips.

Salads

Peachy Chicken Salad

Pat Unternahrer,
Wayland, IA

Makes 4-6 servings
Prep. Time: 10-15 minutes

⅓ cup mayonnaise

2 Tbsp. milk

¼ tsp. pepper

½ tsp. salt

1 tsp. chopped fresh tarragon

2½ cups cubed cooked chicken

1 cup seedless red grapes, halved

1 cup frozen peas, thawed

2 large peaches, peeled, pitted and chopped

1 cup pecan halves, toasted lettuce leaves, optional

1. In a large bowl, stir the mayonnaise, milk, pepper, salt, and tarragon together until smooth.

2. Add chicken and toss to coat.

3. Stir in grapes, peas, peaches, and pecans.

4. Serve in a lettuce-lined bowl if you wish.

Salads

Asparagus, Apple, and Chicken Salad

Betty Salch,
Bloomington, IL
Wilma Stoltzfus,
Honey Brook, PA

Makes 3–4 servings
Prep. Time: 20 minutes
Cooking Time: 3–4 minutes, if using pre-cooked chicken

1 cup fresh asparagus, cut into 1"-long pieces

2 Tbsp. cider vinegar

2 Tbsp. vegetable oil

2 tsp. honey

2 tsp. minced fresh parsley

½ tsp. salt

¼ tsp. pepper

1 cup cubed cooked chicken

½ cup diced red apples, unpeeled

2 cups torn mixed greens alfalfa sprouts, optional

1. In a small saucepan, cook asparagus in a small amount of water until crisp-tender, about 3–4 minutes. Drain and cool.

2. In a good-sized mixing bowl, combine the next 6 ingredients.

3. Stir in the chicken, apples, and asparagus. Toss.

4. Serve over greens. Garnish with alfalfa sprouts if you wish.

Pasta Salad with Tuna

Sheila Soldner,
Lititz, PA

Makes 6–8 servings
Prep. Time: 15 minutes
Cooking Time: 15 minutes

½ lb. uncooked rotini pasta

12.5-oz. can solid white tuna, drained and flaked

2 cups thinly sliced cucumber

1 large tomato, seeded and sliced, or ½ pint cherry or grape tomatoes

½ cup sliced celery

¼ cup chopped green pepper

¼ cup sliced scallions

1 cup bottled Italian dressing

¼ cup mayonnaise

1 Tbsp. prepared mustard

1 Tbsp. fresh chopped dill

1 tsp. salt

⅛ tsp. pepper

1. Prepare rotini according to package directions. Drain.

2. In a large bowl, combine rotini, tuna, cucumber, tomato, celery, green pepper, and scallions.

3. In a small bowl, blend together Italian dressing, mayonnaise, mustard, and seasonings. Add to salad mixture. Toss to coat.

4. Cover and chill. Toss gently before serving.

Tofu Salad

**Sara Harter Fredette,
Goshen, MA**

Makes 4–6 servings
Prep. Time: 10 minutes
Cooking Time: 10 minutes
Chilling Time: 2–3 hours

1 pkg. extra-firm tofu, cubed

1 carrot, grated

1 scallion, sliced

1 clove garlic, minced

⅓–½ cup sunflower seeds

1 Tbsp. soy sauce

2 Tbsp. lemon juice and rind

2 Tbsp. olive oil

¼ tsp. salt

⅛ tsp. pepper

1. In a saucepan, steam tofu in 1" of water for 10 minutes.

2. Drain and cool. Crumble with fork.

3. Place crumbled tofu, carrot, scallion, garlic, and seeds in a large mixing bowl. Combine gently.

4. In a jar with a tight-fitting lid, combine all remaining ingredients.

5. Pour dressing over the tofu/veggies mixture. Combine well.

6. Cover and chill for 1–2 hours.

Citrus Salad

Sue Williams,
Gulfport, MS

Makes 6 servings
Prep. Time: 20 minutes
Chilling Time: 2–8 hours

1 pink grapefruit

2 navel oranges

2 tangerines

1 Tbsp. honey

⅓ cup chopped pecans, or walnuts

1. Over a large bowl, peel and section grapefruit, oranges, and tangerines. Remove membranes.

2. Stir honey into fruit.

3. Cover and refrigerate 2 hours, or overnight.

4. Sprinkle each individual serving with nuts just before serving.

Mango Tango Salad

Karen Ceneviva,
New Haven, CT

Makes 6 servings
Prep. Time: 25 minutes
Standing Time: 10 minutes

3 ripe mangos, pitted and cubed

juice of 1 lime

1 tsp. minced red onion

2 Tbsp. chopped fresh cilantro leaves

half of one jalapeño pepper, seeded and
   minced

1. Combine all ingredients in a mixing
bowl. Let stand 10 minutes.

2. Toss just before serving.

Cranberry Salad

**Mary Lynn Miller,
Reinholds, PA**

Makes 6-8 servings
Prep. Time: 30-40 minutes
Chilling Time: 6-8 hours, or overnight

4 cups fresh cranberries, rinsed and drained

4 oranges (2 peeled, 2 unpeeled)

4 apples, peeled and cut into quarters

2 cups sugar

1. Grind or puree cranberries, oranges, and apples. Mix well.

2. Pour sugar over fruit and mix well.

3. Refrigerate for 6–8 hours before serving.

Salads

Fresh Peach Salad

Barbara Sparks,
Glen Burnie, MD

Makes 4-6 servings
Prep. Time: 20 minutes
Chilling Time: 2 hours, or more

¼ cup sugar

1 Tbsp. mayonnaise

1 cup sour cream

9 fresh peaches, peeled, pitted and sliced

lettuce leaves

1. Mix together sugar, mayonnaise, and sour cream in a small bowl.

2. Pour over peaches in a large mixing bowl.

3. Cover and chill for at least 2 hours to allow flavors to blend.

4. Serve on a bed of lettuce, either on a large platter, or on individual salad plates.

Want More Salad

Sherry H. Kauffman,
Minot, ND

Makes 4 servings
Prep. Time: 20 minutes

2 Granny Smith apples, unpeeled and cut fine

3 ribs celery, chopped fine

¼ cup raisins

2 Tbsp. sunflower seeds

1 cup pineapple chunks

½ cup pineapple juice

Dressing:

¼ cup light mayonnaise

¼ cup plain nonfat yogurt

2 Tbsp. orange juice, or liquid from canned pineapple

2 tsp. honey

1. Combine first five ingredients in a salad bowl.

2. Combine dressing ingredients in a separate bowl.

3. Pour dressing over fruit. Toss and refrigerate until ready to serve.

Fresh Pickles

Arleta Petersheim,
Haven, KS

Makes about 5 cups
Prep. Time: 15 minutes
Chilling Time: 8 hours, or overnight

6 small to medium-sized cucumbers

1 cup water

¼ cup vinegar

1 Tbsp. salt

½ cup sugar

1. Wash, peel, and slice fresh cucumbers into ¼"-thick slices.

2. In a small bowl, mix other ingredients together. Pour over sliced cucumbers.

3. Cover. Refrigerate 8 hours, or overnight.

TIP

Add some onion slices to the brine for more flavor.

Salads

Barb's Fresh Pickles

Carna Reitz,
Remington, VA

Makes 1-2 cups
Prep. Time: 5-10 minutes
Chilling Time: 1-12 hours

½ cup white vinegar

½ cup water

½ cup sugar

1 Tbsp. chopped fresh dill weed

1-2 cucumbers, sliced about ¼" thick

1. Mix first 3 ingredients in a medium-sized mixing bowl. Stir until sugar is dissolved.

2. Mix in dill and cucumber slices.

3. Cover. Refrigerate for at least 1 hour for lightly flavored pickles, or up to 1 day for more pickled pickles.

TIP

When the pickle slices are all eaten, you can use the leftover liquid for up to three more batches of fresh pickles.

Salads

New Dill Slices

Mary E. Wheatley,
Mashpee, MA

Makes 4–5 cups
Prep. Time: 20–30 minutes
Standing Time: 1 hour
Chilling Time: 2–9 hours

4-6 medium-sized pickling cucumbers (about 1 lb.)

1 Tbsp., plus 1 tsp., kosher salt, *divided*

cold water

3 Tbsp. cider vinegar

1½ tsp. fresh chopped dill

1 garlic clove, thinly sliced

bay leaf and fresh dill sprigs, optional

1. Cut cucumbers into ⅛" thick slices.

2. In a large bowl, toss cucumbers with 1 Tbsp. salt. Let stand 1 hour, tossing occasionally. Rinse and drain 3 times with cold water.

3. Meanwhile, in a saucepan, combine vinegar with dill, garlic, 1 tsp. salt, and 1 cup water, along with bay leaf if used. Bring to boil. Boil 1 minute. Cool to room temperature.

4. With your hands, squeeze out excess moisture from pickle slices. Place in a small (glass) bowl. Add fresh dill sprigs, if you wish, and cooled brine.

5. Cover. Refrigerate for at least one hour before serving, or for 8 hours, or overnight.

Chopped Apple Cake

**Sherri McCauley,
Lakeway, TX**

Makes 8 servings
Prep. Time: 15 minutes
Baking Time: 30–35 minutes

3-4 medium apples, unpeeled, chopped

1 cup sugar

1½ cups all-purpose flour

1 tsp. baking soda

½ tsp. cinnamon

½ cup oil

1 egg, beaten

½ cup chopped nuts

½ cup raisins

1. Put apples in a bowl with sugar. Stir.

2. In another bowl, sift flour, baking soda, and cinnamon together.

3. Blend oil and beaten egg into apples.

4. Add dry ingredients all at once and blend well.

5. Stir in nuts and raisins. Mix well.

6. Spread batter in a greased 8 × 8 square baking pan.

7. Bake at 350° for 30–35 minutes, or until tester inserted in middle comes out clean.

TIPS

1. Use an apple slicer to save time on cutting the apples. Feel free to use your favorite nuts to make this recipe your own.
2. If there is any cake left over, store it in the refrigerator for a refreshing treat later.

Go-Along:
This cake tastes great warm with some vanilla ice cream on top!

Desserts

Perfectly Peach Cake

Ruthie Schiefer,
Vassar, MI

Makes 4–6 servings
Prep. Time: 20 minutes
Cooking Time: 6–8 hours
Ideal slow-cooker size: 3-qt.

¾ cup biscuit baking mix

¼ cup brown sugar, packed

⅓ cup sugar

2 eggs, beaten

2 tsp. vanilla

¼ cup evaporated milk

2 Tbsp. butter, melted

3 peaches, peeled, pitted, and mashed

¾ tsp. ground cinnamon

vanilla ice cream or whipped cream, for serving

1. In large bowl, combine baking mix and sugars.

2. Stir in eggs and vanilla until blended. Mix in milk and butter.

3. Fold in peaches and cinnamon until well mixed.

4. Spoon mixture into lightly greased slow cooker. Lay a double layer of paper towels across the top of the cooker (to absorb condensation).

5. Cover and cook on Low 6–8 hours.

6. Serve warm with a scoop of ice cream or a dollop of whipped cream.

Coconut Buttermilk Pound Cake

Janie Canupp,
Millersville, MD

Makes 20 servings
Prep. Time: 30 minutes
Baking Time: 1 hour 35 minutes

1 cup shortening

3 cups sugar

6 eggs

½ tsp. salt

¼ tsp. baking soda

1 cup buttermilk

3 cups all-purpose flour

2 tsp. lemon flakes or lemon zest

1 cup shredded coconut

1. In blender or food processor, mix shortening and sugar until well blended.

2. Add eggs, one at a time, and blend well after each one.

3. Mix salt, baking soda, and buttermilk together in a separate bowl.

4. Add buttermilk mixture alternately with flour to egg mixture.

5. Beat well after each addition.

6. Stir in lemon and coconut.

7. Place batter in greased and floured tube pan.

8. Bake at 325° for 1 hour and 35 minutes, or until cake tests done.

Desserts

Dark Chocolate Indulgence Cake

**Sharon Wantland,
Menomonee Falls, WI**

Makes 8 servings
Prep. Time: 15 minutes
Cooking/Baking Time: 30 minutes

1 pkg. (6 squares) Baker's bittersweet
    chocolate

1½ sticks (¾ cup) butter

4 eggs

1 cup sugar

½ cup flour

1. Heat oven to 350°.

2. Melt butter and chocolate together. Cool and set aside.

3. In a mixing bowl, beat eggs and sugar until smooth.

4. Add chocolate and flour and stir until smooth.

5. Pour into a 9"-round greased and floured pan.

6. Bake 30 minutes.

Optional Toppings:
Sprinkle with confectioners' sugar, or drizzle melted chocolate on top.

Desserts

Lemon Cheesecake

Meg Suter,
Goshen, IN

Makes 8 servings
Prep. Time: 20–25 minutes
Baking Time: 50–55 minutes
Standing Time: 1 hour
Chilling Time: 2–24 hours

1¼ cups crushed graham crackers (about 10 whole crackers)

¾ cups crushed gingersnaps (about 15 cookies)

¼ cup sugar

5 Tbsp. buttery spread

4½ tsp. egg substitute

6 Tbsp. water

24 oz. non dairy cream cheese, softened and cut in small cubes

1 cup sugar

½ tsp. vanilla

4–6 Tbsp. fresh lemon juice

2 Tbsp. lemon zest

fresh strawberries for serving, optional

1. In a food processor, crush graham crackers and gingersnaps. Add sugar and buttery spread. Pulse until mixed.

2. Press into a lightly oiled 9-inch springform pan.

3. Bake crust at 350° for 10 minutes, until golden. Set aside to cool.

4. Using electric hand mixer in a large bowl, whip egg substitute and water together until thick and creamy.

5. Beat in cream cheese for 30 seconds— don't go longer!

6. Beat in sugar, vanilla, lemon juice and lemon zest just until smooth. Don't overbeat— this will cause cracking on the surface during baking.

7. Pour batter into crust. Smooth top with a spatula.

8. Bake at 350°, until center barely jiggles when pan is tapped, 50–55 minutes. It is fine if it puffs up a bit and turns golden brown; it will settle as it cools.

9. Cool completely in pan on rack for at least one hour.

10. Refrigerate for at least two hours, but preferably 24 hours, before serving. This is lovely garnished with strawberries when ready to serve.

Desserts

Slow-Cooker Berry Cobbler

**Wilma Haberkamp,
Fairbank, IA
Virginia Graybill,
Hershey, PA**

Makes 8 servings
Prep. Time: 15–20 minutes
Cooking Time: 2–2½ hours
Ideal slow-cooker size: 5-qt.

1¼ cups all-purpose flour, *divided*

2 Tbsp. sugar, plus 1 cup sugar, *divided*

1 tsp. baking powder

¼ tsp. ground cinnamon

1 egg, lightly beaten

¼ cup skim milk

2 Tbsp. canola oil

⅛ tsp. salt

2 cups raspberries

2 cups blueberries

1. In mixing bowl, combine 1 cup flour, 2 Tbsp. sugar, baking powder, and cinnamon.

2. In a separate bowl, combine egg, milk, and oil. Stir into dry ingredients until moistened. Batter will be thick.

3. Spray slow cooker with cooking spray. Spread batter evenly on bottom of slow cooker.

4. In another bowl combine salt, remaining flour, remaining sugar, and berries. Toss to coat berries.

5. Spread berries over batter.

6. Cook on high 2–2½ hours, or until toothpick inserted into cobbler comes out clean.

Texas Peach Cobbler

Edna Good,
Richland Center, WI

Makes 9 servings
Prep. Time: 20 minutes
Baking Time: 50 minutes

6 Tbsp. butter

1¼ cups all-purpose flour

¾ cup, plus 2 Tbsp., sugar, *divided*

2 tsp. baking powder

⅛ tsp. salt

dash cinnamon

1 tsp. vanilla, *divided*

1 cup milk

4 cups peaches, peeled, pitted and sliced

1 tsp. fresh lemon juice

1. Turn oven on to 350°. Place butter in 8 × 8 baking dish. Place dish in oven to melt butter.

2. In mixing bowl, combine flour, sugar, baking powder, salt, cinnamon, ½ tsp. vanilla and milk. Stir just until combined.

3. Spoon batter over melted butter. Do not mix!

4. In a bowl, combine peaches, 1 Tbsp. sugar, lemon juice and remaining ½ tsp. vanilla.

5. Spoon peach mixture over batter, gently pressing peaches into batter.

6. Bake at 350° for 40 minutes.

7. Sprinkle with remaining 1 Tbsp. sugar and bake 10 minutes longer.

Desserts

Blackberry Cobbler

**Virginia R. Bender,
Dover, DE**

Makes 6 servings
Prep. Time: 15 minutes
Cooking/Baking Time: 40 minutes

½ cup sugar

1 cup flour

½ cup milk

1 tsp. baking powder

2 cups blackberries

1. Mix sugar, flour, milk, and baking powder together in a medium-sized mixing bowl until well blended.

2. Pour into a lightly greased 9 × 9 baking dish.

3. Spoon fresh or frozen blackberries over top.

4. Bake at 350° for 40 minutes, or until a toothpick inserted in center comes out clean. Crust will rise to the top.

5. Serve warm.

Aunt Annabelle's Fruit Cobbler

Shirley Unternahrer,
Wayland, IA

Makes 12 servings
Prep. Time: 15–20 minutes
Baking Time: 45 minutes

6 cups diced rhubarb, blueberries,
blackberries, or cherries

2½ cups sugar, *divided*

2 cups plus 2 Tbsp. all-purpose flour, *divided*

1 tsp. salt

⅓ cup canola oil

2 tsp. baking powder

1 cup milk

2 Tbsp. flour

scant 2 cups boiling water

1. Spread fruit across bottom of greased 9 × 13 baking pan.

2. In a mixing bowl, mix 1 cup sugar, 2 cups flour, salt, oil, baking powder and milk. Mix until smooth.

3. Pour evenly over fruit.

4. Next mix remaining 1½ cups sugar with remaining 2 Tbsp. flour.

5. Sprinkle mixture over dough.

6. Slowly and evenly pour boiling water over top. Do not stir!

7. Bake at 375° for 40–50 minutes, until lightly browned.

Variation:
You can use fruit such as peaches, but then reduce fruit amount to 5 cups instead of 6.

Desserts

Apple Crunch

Anita Troyer,
Fairview, MI

Makes 6 servings
Prep. Time: 30 minutes
Cooking Time: 2½–3 hours
Ideal slow-cooker size: 6-qt.

Crumb:

1 cup flour

½ cup brown sugar

½ tsp. cinnamon

6 Tbsp. butter

Filling:

6 large Granny Smith apples

½ tsp. lemon juice

⅓ cup sugar

3 Tbsp. flour

½ tsp. cinnamon

⅛ tsp. nutmeg

⅛ tsp. salt

1. Spray crock very well with nonstick spray, or grease the inside of the crock very well with butter.

2. Mix all the crumb ingredients together. Set aside.

3. Peel, core, and cut the apples into ¼-inch slices.

4. In a bowl, mix the apples together with the other filling ingredients. Dump this mixture into the crock.

5. Place the crumb mixture over the top of the apple mixture in the crock.

6. Cover with a lid, placing a fork between lid and crock so that extra moisture can escape and crumbs will bake nicely. Cook on High for 2½–3 hours. Use care when removing the lid so that moisture on it will not drip on the crumbs.

Serving suggestion:
Serve with vanilla ice cream.

Desserts

Extra-Crisp Apple Crisp

Christina Gerber,
Apple Creek, OH

Makes 4 servings
Prep. Time: 15 minutes
Cooking Time: 3–6 hours
Ideal slow-cooker size: 6-qt.

5–6 cups tart apples, sliced

¾ cup (1½ sticks) butter

1 cup rolled or quick oats

1½ cups flour

1 cup brown sugar, packed

3 tsp. ground cinnamon

1. Place apples in lightly greased slow cooker.

2. Separately, melt butter. Add rest of ingredients and mix well.

3. Crumble topping over apples.

4. Cover and cook on High for 3 hours or Low for 4–6 hours. Allow cooker to sit, turned off with lid removed, for about 30 minutes before serving, so Crisp is nicely warm for serving.

TIP

This is the recipe for people who can never get enough crisp topping on their apple crisp!

Variations:
Add 1 tsp. salt to topping in Step 2.

Serving suggestion:
Serve with ice cream or whipped cream.

Desserts

1-2-3 Apple Crisp

**Lavina Hochstedler,
Grand Blanc, MI**

Makes 8 servings
Prep. Time: 15 minutes
Baking Time: 35–45 minutes

8 apples, peeled and cored

1½ cups brown sugar

1 cup all-purpose flour

1 cup quick or rolled oats

1 tsp. cinnamon

1 tsp. nutmeg

1 stick (½ cup) butter, softened

1. Lightly grease a 9 × 13 glass baking pan.

2. Cut apples into slices and layer in bottom of pan.

3. In a medium bowl, mix together brown sugar, flour, oats, cinnamon and nutmeg.

4. Cut in butter with a pastry blender until crumbly.

5. Sprinkle mixture over apples.

6. Bake at 375° for 35–45 minutes, or until the top is browned.

Go-Along:
Serve with ice cream or whipped topping.
This follows a bowl of soup well!

TIP

Because of using a glass pan, I often like to cook this in the microwave for 10–15 minutes before I put the crumbs on. It shortens the baking time in the oven. Bake just until the topping browns, about 15–20 minutes.

Desserts

Apple Cranberry Crisp

Charlotte Burkholder,
East Petersburg, PA

Makes 8 servings
Prep. Time: 25 minutes
Baking Time: 60–75 minutes

8 large baking apples

8 oz. fresh cranberries

juice of 1 lemon

¾ cup brown sugar, packed, *divided*

2½ tsp. cinnamon, *divided*

2 Tbsp. whole wheat flour

1¾ cups rolled oats

⅓ cups canola oil

Variation:
Before adding topping, sprinkle with walnuts and raisins.

Go-Along:
Serve warm with ice cream or whipped cream.

1. Peel, core and slice apples into a bowl. Add cranberries and lemon juice. Set aside.

2. Mix ¼ cup brown sugar, 1 tsp. cinnamon and whole wheat flour. Stir into apple mixture.

3. Put into a 8 × 10 greased baking pan

4. To make topping, mix rolled oats, remaining 1½ tsp. cinnamon, and remaining ½ cup brown sugar. Then add oil and mix until crumbly. Sprinkle over apples.

5. Cover with foil. Bake at 350° for 30 minutes. Remove foil and bake 30–45 minutes longer, until apples are soft.

Desserts

Strawberry Mint Crisp

Hope Comerford,
Clinton Township, MI

Makes 4 servings
Prep. Time: 20 minutes
Cooking Time: 2 hours
Ideal slow-cooker size: 2- or 3-qt.

2½–3 cups sliced strawberries

1 tsp. cinnamon

½ tsp. mint extract

1 tsp. vanilla

3 Tbsp. fresh chopped mint

Crumble:

½ cup gluten-free oats

¼ cup gluten-free oat flour

½ tsp. cinnamon

¼ tsp. salt

1 Tbsp. honey

1 Tbsp. coconut oil, melted

1–2 Tbsp. unsweetened almond or coconut
   milk

1. Spray crock with nonstick spray.

2. In the crock, combine strawberries,
cinnamon, mint extract, vanilla extract, and
fresh chopped mint.

3. In a bowl, combine all the crumble
ingredients. If it's too dry, add a bit more
honey or milk of your choice. Pour this
mixture into the crock.

4. Cover and cook on low for 2 hours.

Serving suggestion:
Serve with vanilla Greek yogurt.

Desserts

Strawberry Rhubarb Crisp

Hope Comerford,
Clinton Township, MI

Makes 6–8 servings
Prep. Time: 30 minutes
Cooking Time: 2–3 hours
Ideal slow-cooker size: 2½-qt.

Filling:
1 lb. strawberries, quartered if medium or large
3 rhubarb stalks, halved and sliced
½ cup sugar
2 Tbsp. flour
2 tsp. vanilla extract

Crisp:
½ cup sugar
2 Tbsp. flour
½ tsp. cinnamon
Pinch of salt
3 Tbsp. unsalted butter, cold and sliced
½ cup old-fashioned oats
2 Tbsp. chopped pecans
2 Tbsp. chopped almonds

1. Spray your crock with nonstick spray.

2. Place the strawberries and rhubarb into the crock.

3. In a bowl, mix together the sugar, flour, and vanilla. Pour this over the strawberries and rhubarb and stir to coat evenly.

4. In another bowl, start on the crisp. Mix together the sugar, flour, cinnamon, and salt. Cut the butter in with a pastry cutter.

5. Stir in the oats, pecans, and almonds. Pour this mixture over the contents of the crock.

6. Cover and cook on Low for 2–3 hours.

7. The last half hour of cooking, remove the lid to help the crisp thicken.

Serving suggestion:
Serve over vanilla ice cream or on yogurt.

Nectarine Almond Crisp

Hope Comerford,
Clinton Township, MI

Makes 8–9 servings
Prep. Time: 10 minutes
Cooking Time: 2 hours
Ideal slow-cooker size: 3- or 4-qt.

5 nectarines, pitted and sliced

¼ cup slivered almonds

1 tsp. cinnamon

¼ tsp. nutmeg

¼ tsp. ginger

1 tsp. vanilla

Crumble:

1 cup gluten-free oats

½ cup almond flour

½ cup slivered almonds

1 tsp. cinnamon

1 Tbsp. freshly grated ginger

½ tsp. sea salt

2 Tbsp. honey

2 Tbsp. coconut oil, melted

2–3 Tbsp. unsweetened almond milk

1. Spray crock with nonstick spray.

2. In the crock, combine nectarines, almonds, cinnamon, nutmeg, ginger, and vanilla.

3. In a medium bowl, combine all the crumble ingredients. If the mixture is too dry, add a bit more honey or almond milk. Pour over the top of the nectarine mixture.

4. Cover and cook on low for 2 hours.

Serving suggestion:
Serve over frozen vanilla Greek yogurt.

Fruit Mixture Crisp

Willard Swartley,
Elkhart, IN

Makes 6–8 servings
Prep. Time: 30 minutes
Baking Time: 40 minutes

2 cups sour cherries, peaches or rhubarb

3 cups mulberries or blackberries, or 2 cups strawberries

1/2–3/4 cup sugar, according to your taste preference

1/4 cup water

3 Tbsp. cornstarch or minute tapioca

1 3/4 cups quick oats

1 cup flour

3/4 cup brown sugar

1/2 tsp. baking soda

3 Tbsp. butter, softened

1/2 cup chopped walnuts

1. Pit the sour cherries. Cut up chosen fruits.

2. In a saucepan over low heat, cook the chosen fruits, sugar, water and cornstarch until thickened.

3. Pour into a greased 2-quart casserole dish.

4. Mix together oats, flour, brown sugar, baking soda, butter and nuts. Sprinkle over top of casserole dish.

5. Bake at 350° for 30 minutes, or until top is slightly browned and edges are bubbling.

Go-Along:
Serve warm, topped with frozen yogurt or ice cream.

Desserts

Blueberry Crinkle

**Phyllis Good,
Lancaster, PA**

Makes 6–8 servings
Prep. Time: 15–20 minutes
Cooking Time: 2–3 hours
Ideal slow-cooker size: 3- or 4-qt.

⅓ cup turbinado sugar

¾ cup gluten-free oats

½ cup gluten-free flour

½ tsp. cinnamon

dash of kosher salt

6 Tbsp. coconut oil, cold

4 cups blueberries

2 Tbsp. maple syrup

2 Tbsp. instant tapioca

2 Tbsp. fresh lemon juice

½ tsp. lemon zest

1. Grease interior of slow-cooker crock.

2. In a large bowl, combine turbinado sugar, oats, gluten-free flour, cinnamon, and salt.

3. Using two knives, a pastry cutter, or your fingers, work coconut oil into dry ingredients until small crumbs form.

4. In a separate bowl, stir together blueberries, maple syrup, tapioca, lemon juice, and lemon zest.

5. Spoon blueberry mixture into slow cooker crock.

6. Sprinkle crumbs over blueberries.

7. Cover. Cook 2–3 hours on low, or until firm in the middle with juice bubbling up around the edges.

8. Remove lid with a giant swoop away from yourself so condensation on inside of lid doesn't drip on the crumbs.

9. Lift crock out of cooker. Let cool until either warm or room temperature before eating.

Quick Apple Pie

Vivian Benner,
Dayton, VA

Makes 6 servings
Prep. Time: 30 minutes
Baking Time: 30–35 minutes

5 McIntosh apples, peeled and sliced

1 Tbsp. plus 1 cup sugar, *divided*

1 tsp. cinnamon

1 stick (½ cup) butter, softened

1 egg, beaten

1 tsp. vanilla

1 cup flour

½ cup chopped nuts

whipped cream or ice cream, optional

1. In a large bowl, combine apples, 1 Tbsp. sugar and cinnamon.

2. Transfer to a greased 9" pie plate.

3. In a small bowl, cream the butter and 1 cup sugar with an electric mixer.

4. Beat in egg and vanilla.

5. Add flour. Mix well until blended.

6. By hand, stir in the nuts.

7. Spread mixture over apples.

8. Bake at 350° for 30–35 minutes, or until apples are tender and crust is brown.

9. Serve warm with whipped cream or ice cream.

Creamy Apple Pie

Mary Hackenberger,
Thompsontown, PA

Makes 8 servings
Prep. Time: 45 minutes
Baking Time: 45 minutes

1 stick (½ cup) plus 1 Tbsp. butter, at room temperature, *divided*

¾ cup plus 2 Tbsp. sugar, *divided*

1 tsp. vanilla, *divided*

1 cup flour

8-oz. pkg. cream cheese, at room temperature

1 egg

4 cups thinly sliced apples, peeled or unpeeled

½ tsp. cinnamon

½ cup chopped pecans

1. To make crust, use an electric mixer to beat 1 stick butter, ¼ cup sugar and ½ tsp. vanilla in mixing bowl.

2. Gradually add flour, until mixture forms soft dough.

3. Press into bottom and up sides of a deep-dish 9" pie pan.

4. In a mixing bowl, use an electric mixer to beat cream cheese, 2 Tbsp. sugar, egg and remaining ½ tsp. vanilla.

5. Spread cream cheese mixture evenly over crust.

6. By hand, gently mix together apples, cinnamon, and remaining ½ cup sugar.

7. Layer apple filling evenly over cream-cheese filling.

8. Dot with remaining one tablespoon butter. Sprinkle with nuts.

9. Make a loose tent of foil to cover pie while baking.

10. Bake at 400° for 15 minutes. Lower heat to 350° and bake an additional 20 minutes. Remove foil tent. Bake 10 minutes longer, or until apples are done.

Fresh Peach Pie

Jan Mast,
Lancaster, PA

Makes 8 servings
Prep. Time: 15 minutes
Chilling Time: 3–5 hours
Cooking/Baking Time: 5–10 minutes

½–¾ cup sugar

2 Tbsp. clear gel

¼ cup peach-flavored gelatin∗

1 cup water

1 qt. fresh peaches, peeled, pitted and sliced

9" prepared pastry or graham cracker, crust

frozen whipped topping, thawed, optional

1. Mix the sugar, clear gel, and gelatin in a small mixing bowl. Stir in water.

2. Microwave to a full boil. Cook briefly at that heat until gel become clear.

3. Cool at room temperature for several hours.

4. Fold in peaches.

5. Spoon into baked pie shell.

6. Refrigerate 1 hour or more before serving.

7. If you wish, top with whipped topping just before serving.

Desserts

Raspberry Custard Pie

**Laura R. Showalter,
Dayton, VA**

Makes 6–8 serivngs
Prep. Time: 7–10 minutes
Cooking/Baking Time: 45–55 minutes
Cooling Time: 30 minutes

9" unbaked pie shell

3 cups fresh black raspberries

¾ cup sugar

3 Tbsp. flour

¾ cup half-and-half

½ tsp. cinnamon, optional

1. Wash berries. Dry by blotting with a paper towel. Place in pie shell.

2. Mix remaining ingredients in a small mixing bowl until smooth. Pour over berries.

3. Bake at 375° for 15 minutes. Turn oven back to 300°. Bake 30–40 minutes more, or until center is set.

4. Allow to cool before slicing and serving.

Variation:
Use peaches or other berries instead of raspberries.

Desserts

Maple Peach Crumble Pie

Judy Newman,
St. Marys, ON

Makes 8 servings
Prep. Time: 30 minutes
Baking Time: 45-50 minutes

½ cup flour

½ cup maple sugar or brown sugar

½ tsp. cinnamon

¼ cup butter-flavored shortening

3 eggs

1 Tbsp. fresh lemon juice

¼ cup maple syrup

4 cups sliced peaches, peeled and pitted

⅓ cup sliced almonds

9" unbaked pie shell

1. In a small mixing bowl, combine flour, sugar and cinnamon.

2. Cut in shortening with a pastry cutter. Set aside.

3. To make filling beat eggs, lemon juice and syrup together in a medium mixing bowl.

4. Fold in peaches.

5. Pour into pie shell. Top with flour mixture and almonds.

6. Bake at 375° for 45–50 minutes, or until set and lightly browned.

Desserts

Grandma's Spring Rhubarb Pie

**Eleya Raisn,
Oxford, IA**

Makes 6 servings
Prep. Time: 30 minutes
Cooking/Baking Time: 45 minutes

1 cup sugar

3 Tbsp. flour

2 egg yolks, beaten

3 cups diced rhubarb

9" unbaked piecrust

1. In a mixing bowl, stir sugar, flour, and egg yolks together until crumbly. Set aside ¾ cup of the crumbs for topping.

2. Stir cut-up rhubarb into remaining crumbs.

3. Spoon rhubarb mixture into pie shell.

4. Sprinkle reserved crumbs on top of pie filling.

5. Bake at 400° for 25 minutes.

6. Reduce heat to 350° and bake an additional 20 minutes, or until rhubarb filling is bubbling.

7. Allow to cool before slicing and serving.

Mom's Fresh Fruit Pie

Stacy Stoltzfus,
Grantham, PA
Jean A. Shaner,
York, PA
Janet Oberholtzer,
Ephrata, PA
Eunice Fisher,
Clarksville, MI
Carolyn Lehman Henry,
Clinton, NY
Monica ByDeley,
Annville, PA

Makes 8 servings
Prep. Time: 15 minutes
Chilling Time: 4-8 hours

3-4 cups fresh fruit of your choice: berries, peaches, or a mixture of fruits

9" baked pie shell

.3-oz. pkg. strawberry gelatin (or other flavor to match the fruit)

¾-1¼ cups sugar, depending on the sweetness of the fruit

3 rounded Tbsp. cornstarch

2 cups warm water

whipped topping, optional

1. Wash and pat dry fresh fruit. Slice if necessary.

2. Arrange fruit in baked pie shell and set aside.

3. In a saucepan mix the gelatin, sugar, and cornstarch. Add 2 cups warm water. Cook and stir until thickened and clear.

4. Pour over fruit. Refrigerate several hours until set.

5. When time to serve, top with whipped topping if you wish.

Desserts

Pecan Pumpkin Pie

**Nancy Leatherman,
Hamburg, PA**

Makes 8 servings
Prep. Time: 15 minutes
Baking Time: 50 minutes

3 eggs, slightly beaten

1 cup sugar

½ cup corn syrup

1 cup cooked pumpkin

¼ tsp. salt

1 tsp. vanilla

½ tsp. cinnamon

9" unbaked pie shell

1 cup chopped pecans

1. In a mixing bowl, mix eggs and sugar.

2. Add syrup, pumpkin, salt, vanilla and cinnamon.

3. Beat well.

4. Pour into 9" pie shell.

5. Sprinkle with pecans.

6. Bake at 425° for 15 minutes.

7. Reduce heat to 350° and bake 30 minutes, or until set in the middle.

Barbara's Apple Bubble

**Mabel Eshelman,
Lancaster, PA**

Makes 8 servings
Prep. Time: 30 minutes
Baking Time: 1 hour

4 cups water

1 cup sugar

1 Tbsp. butter or margarine

1 tsp. cinnamon

3 cups all-purpose flour

2 tsp. salt

4 tsp. baking powder

2 Tbsp. shortening

¾ cup milk

4 cups sliced apples

½ cup brown sugar

TIP

This is a good stand-in for apple dumplings.

1. In a small pan, bring water, sugar, butter, and cinnamon to a boil. Pour into greased 9 × 13 baking pan.

2. In a bowl, combine flour, salt, baking powder, shortening and milk to form dough.

3. On floured surface, roll dough into 12 × 18 oblong shape.

4. In a bowl, mix apples and brown sugar. Spread on dough.

5. Roll jelly-roll fashion, starting with a long side. Pinch seam to seal.

6. Cut roll into 1" slices with a sharp knife and lay flat in syrup in baking pan.

7. Cover. Bake at 375° for 30 minutes.

8. Remove cover and bake an additional 30 minutes.

9. Serve warm with milk.

Rhubarb Custard Dessert with Streusel

**Ruthie Schiefer,
Vassar, MI**

Makes 12–15 servings
Prep. Time: 35 minutes
Baking Time: 1 hour 15 minutes

Crust:
2 cups all-purpose flour

½ cup confectioners' sugar

¼ tsp. salt

2 sticks (1 cup) butter, softened

Custard Filling:
6 cups diced rhubarb

4 eggs, slightly beaten

1½ cups sugar

½ tsp. salt

3 Tbsp. all-purpose flour

Streusel Topping:
1 stick (½ cup) butter, softened

1 cup sugar

⅔ cup flour

dash cinnamon

1. With pastry blender, cut together flour, powdered sugar, salt, and butter.

2. Press into 9 × 13 baking pan.

3. Bake at 325° for 15 minutes.

4. Spread rhubarb on crust.

5. In a mixing bowl, beat eggs, sugar, salt, and flour. Pour over rhubarb.

6. With pastry blender, cut together butter, sugar, flour, and cinnamon.

7. Sprinkle over top of pan.

8. Bake at 350° for 1 hour, or until top is lightly brown and knife inserted in center comes out clean.

Almond Pear Torte

Martha Mullet,
Sugarcreek, OH

Makes 8 servings
Prep. Time: 20–25 minutes
Cooking/Baking Time: 20 minutes

pastry for 9" single-crust pie

¾ cup plus 2 tsp. sugar, *divided*

3 Tbsp. all-purpose flour

4 cups sliced peeled fresh pears
(about 4 medium-sized pears)

3 Tbsp. sliced almonds

1. Roll out pastry into a 10" circle. Fold lightly into quarters, and place on an ungreased baking sheet with sides. (The sides are important in case the pastry develops a tear and the filling leaks out while baking.)

2. In a small bowl, combine ¾ cup sugar and flour.

3. Add pears. Toss to coat.

4. Place pear mixture in center of pastry, spreading to within 2" of edges. Fold edges up and slightly crimp.

5. Sprinkle with remaining sugar.

6. Bake at 450° for 15 minutes, or until pears are tender.

7. Sprinkle with almonds. Bake 5 minutes longer.

8. Cool slightly before cutting into wedges.

Desserts

Honey Pecan Cookies

MaryAnn Beachy,
Dover, OH

Makes 48 cookies
Prep. Time: 20 minutes
Baking Time: 13 minutes

1 stick (½ cup) butter, softened

½ cup shortening

1½ cups sugar, plus more for rolling dough

½ cup honey

2 eggs

2 Tbsp. fresh lemon juice

4 cups all-purpose flour

2½ tsp. baking soda

½ tsp. ground cloves

1 tsp. cinnamon

2 Tbsp. freshy grated ginger

½ tsp. salt

1 cup chopped pecans

1. Cream butter, shortening, and sugar together in mixing bowl until fluffy.

2. Add honey, eggs, and lemon juice and beat well.

3. In a separate bowl, combine flour, baking soda, cloves, cinnamon, ginger, and salt. Gradually add to creamed mixture.

4. Fold in pecans.

5. Shape dough into 1" balls. Roll in sugar.

6. Place on ungreased baking sheets.

7. Bake at 350° for 12–13 minutes, or until light brown. Do not overbake.

8. Cool slightly before removing from baking sheets.

Rhubarb Crunch

**Kathryn Yoder,
Minot, ND**

Makes 10 servings
Prep. Time: 20 minutes
Baking Time: 35–40 minutes

2 cups whole wheat flour

¾ cup quick or rolled oats

1 cup brown sugar, packed

1½ sticks (¾ cup) butter, melted

1 tsp. cinnamon

1 cup sugar

2 Tbsp. cornstarch

1 cup water

1 tsp. vanilla

4 cups diced rhubarb

TIP

This may be served hot or cold, but is best served the day it's made.

1. In a bowl, mix flour, oats, brown sugar, butter, and cinnamon until crumbly.

2. Press ½ of crumbs in 9 × 9 baking dish. Set aside.

3. In medium saucepan, mix sugar, cornstarch, water, and vanilla.

4. Bring to rolling boil.

5. Add rhubarb and cook 2 minutes.

6. Pour rhubarb mixture over crumb crust.

7. Sprinkle remaining crumbs on top of rhubarb mixture.

8. Bake at 350° for 35–40 minutes.

9. Cut in squares and serve.

Zucchini Brownies

**Laraine Good,
Bernville, PA
Debra Kilheffer,
Millersville, PA**

Makes 12 brownies
Prep. Time: 20 minutes
Baking Time: 35 minutes

1 egg

1 tsp. vanilla

½ cup oil

¾ cup sugar

¾ cup brown sugar

1 cup flour

¾ cup whole wheat flour

⅓ cup unsweetened cocoa powder

½ tsp. baking soda

¼ tsp. salt

½ cup sour cream or plain yogurt

2-3 cups finely grated zucchini, peeled or unpeeled

1 cup chocolate chips

½ cups chopped pecans or walnuts

1. Combine egg, vanilla, oil, sugar, and brown sugar in a bowl.

2. In a separate bowl combine flour, whole wheat flour, cocoa powder, baking soda, and salt.

3. Add to egg mixture alternately with the sour cream, stirring each time.

4. Add zucchini.

5. Pour into a greased 9 × 13 baking pan. Sprinkle with chocolate chips and pecans.

6. Bake at 350° for 35 minutes, or until tester inserted in middle comes out clean.

7. Cool. Cut into bars.

Zucchini Chocolate-Chip Bars

Hope Comerford,
Clinton Township, MI

Makes 8–10 servings
Prep. Time: 10 minutes
Cooking Time: 2–3 hours
Cooling Time: 30 minutes
Ideal slow-cooker size: 3-qt.

3 eggs

¾ cup turbinado sugar

1 cup all-natural applesauce

3 tsp. vanilla

3 cups whole wheat flour

1 tsp. baking soda

½ tsp. baking powder

2 tsp. cinnamon

¼ tsp. salt

2 cups peeled and grated zucchini

1 cup dark chocolate chips

1. Spray the crock with nonstick spray.

2. Mix together the eggs, sugar, applesauce, and vanilla.

3. In a separate bowl, mix together the flour, baking soda, baking powder, cinnamon, and salt. Add this to the wet mixture and stir just until everything is mixed well.

4. Stir in the zucchini and chocolate chips

5. Pour this mixture into the crock.

6. Cover and cook on low for 2–3 hours. Let it cool in crock for about 30 minutes, then flip it over onto a serving platter or plate. It should come right out.

Desserts

Zucchini Bars

Jane Geigley,
Lancaster, PA

Makes 8 servings
Prep. Time: 30 minutes
Cooking Time: 4–6 hours
Ideal slow-cooker size: 4-qt.

Bars:

2 cups sugar

1 cup olive oil

4 eggs

2 cups flour

1 tsp. baking soda

1 tsp. baking powder

1 tsp. cinnamon

¼ tsp. salt

3 tsp. vanilla extract

½ tsp. nutmeg

2 cups shredded zucchini

Frosting:

2 cups confectioners' sugar

3 ozs. softened cream cheese

½ cup softened butter

1 tsp. milk

1 tsp. vanilla extract

1. Mix sugar and oil.

2. Beat in eggs.

3. Add the rest of bar ingredients except for the zucchini and blend until smooth.

4. Fold in zucchini.

5. Pour into greased slow cooker.

6. Cook on Low for 4–6 hours.

7. Prepare frosting by creaming sugar, cream cheese, and butter.

8. Beat in milk and vanilla.

9. Once bars are baked, pour frosting over them, cut, and serve warm.

Desserts

Caramel Custard

Nadine L. Martinitz,
Salina, KS

Makes 8 servings
Prep. Time: 20 minutes
Cooking/Baking Time: 40–45 minutes
Standing/Cooling Time: 30 minutes–2 hours

1½ cups sugar, *divided*

6 eggs

2 tsp. vanilla extract

3 cups milk

1. In a heavy saucepan over low heat, cook and stir ¾ cup sugar just until melted and golden. Stir frequently to prevent burning.

2. Divide caramelized sugar into eight 6-oz. custard cups. Tilt each cup after you've poured in the sugar to coat bottom of cup. Let stand for 10 minutes.

3. In a large mixing bowl, beat eggs, vanilla, milk, and remaining sugar until combined but not foamy. Divide among the eight custard cups, pouring over caramelized sugar.

4. Place the cups in two 8"-square baking pans. Pour boiling water in pans to a depth of 1".

5. Bake at 350° for 40–45 minutes, or until a knife inserted in center of custards comes out clean. Remove cups from pans to cool on wire racks.

6. To unmold, run a knife around rim of cup and invert custard onto dessert plate.

7. Serve warm or chilled.

Desserts

Simple Egg Custard

Paula Winchester,
Kansas City, MO

Makes 6 servings
Prep. Time: 25 minutes
Cooking Time: 2–3 hours
Ideal slow-cooker size: 6-qt.

1½ cups whole milk

1 cup half-and-half

3 eggs

⅓ cup sugar

½ tsp. vanilla extract

pinch salt

1. In mixing bowl, whisk ingredients well until smooth and totally combined.

2. Prepare slow cooker by finding a shallow oval baking dish that can fit inside. Place jar rings or lids or trivets on the floor of the crock so the baking dish is not touching the bottom or sides of the crock.

3. Pour custard liquid in baking dish. Set in crock.

4. Carefully pour water into the crock (not the baking dish!) to reach halfway up the side of the baking dish.

5. Cover slow cooker. Cook on High for 2–4 hours, or until custard is set in the middle.

6. Wearing oven gloves to protect your knuckles, remove baking dish from cooker. Allow to cool for at least 20 minutes before serving warm. May also serve chilled.

Variations:
May use 4–5 baking ramekins instead of 1 shallow baking dish.

Serving suggestion:
Serve with any fresh fruit, especially berries that have been lightly sugared. Lovely served chilled with sliced peaches and buttered toast for a summer breakfast.

TIP

There are different ways to flavor the custard. Heat the milk and add 1 bay leaf. Allow to steep and cool. Remove bay leaf and proceed with Step 1. Alternatively, sprinkle top of custard with ½ tsp. ground nutmeg or cinnamon in Step 3.

Desserts

Slow-Cooker Tapioca

Nancy W. Huber,
Green Park, PA

Makes 12 servings
Prep. Time: 10 minutes
Cooking Time: 3½ hours
Chilling Time: minimum 4 hours
Ideal slow-cooker size: 4-qt.

2 quarts fat-free milk

1 cup small pearl tapioca

½ cup honey

4 eggs, beaten

1 tsp. vanilla

fruit of choice, optional

1. Combine milk, tapioca, and honey in slow cooker. Cook on high 3 hours.

2. Mix together eggs, vanilla, and a little hot milk from slow cooker. Add to slow cooker. Mix. Cook on high 20 more minutes.

3. Chill thoroughly, at least 4 hours. Serve with fruit.

Orange Tapioca

Karla Baer,
North Lima, OH

Makes 6-8 servings
Prep. Time: 10 minutes
Cooking/Baking Time: 15-20 minutes
Chilling Time: 3-4 hours

3-4 fresh oranges

1 cup sugar, *divided*

1 qt. water

½ cup granulated tapioca

¼ tsp. salt, optional

1 small can frozen orange juice concentrate

1. Several hours before preparing tapioca, peel oranges. Cut into small pieces. Sprinkle with 3 Tbsp. sugar. Chill.

2. Pour water and tapioca into medium-sized saucepan. Cook over medium/medium-high heat until tapioca is clear, about 15 minutes. Stir frequently.

3. Stir remaining sugar, salt if you wish, orange juice concentrate, and chilled oranges into tapioca.

4. When well blended, pour into a serving dish.

5. Cover and chill until firm.

Strawberry Dessert

**Glenda Weaver,
Manheim, PA
Joyce Nolt,
Richland, PA**

Makes 6-8 servings
Prep. Time: 15-20 minutes
Cooking/Baking Time: 4-8 hours

4 cups water

⅔ cup granulated tapioca

1-1½ cups sugar, according to your taste
  preferences

2 qts. crushed strawberries

8-oz. container frozen whipped topping,
  thawed

1. Place water and tapioca in a large saucepan. Stir. Bring to a boil.

2. Cook until mixture is clear and slightly thickened.

3. Stir in sugar.

4. Cool.

5. Add crushed strawberries, mixing well.

6. Fold in whipped topping.

7. Refrigerate until thoroughly chilled and thickened.

Peach Tapioca Dessert

**Sharon Shank,
Bridgewater, VA**

Makes 12 servings
Prep. Time: 15 minutes
Cooking/Baking Time: 10–15 minutes
Chilling Time: 2–3 hours

2 qts. water

¾ cup minute tapioca

12-oz. can frozen orange juice concentrate

1 cup sugar

½ tsp. salt

2 qts. sliced peaches, fresh or frozen

1½–2 cups bananas and/or grapes, optional

1. In a large saucepan, cook water and tapioca together, stirring constantly, until tapioca softens and becomes clear.

2. Remove from heat and stir in the orange juice, sugar, and salt.

3. Mix together well until the sugar is dissolved.

4. Stir in the peaches, and the bananas and grapes if you wish.

5. Refrigerate. Stir after 1 hour to make sure the fruit is well distributed throughout the tapioca as it gels.

Cherries Jubilee

Hope Comerford,
Clinton Township, MI

Makes 4 servings
Prep. Time: 15 minutes
Cooking Time: 3–4 hours
Ideal slow-cooker size: 2 or 3-qt.

1 lb. fresh cherries, pitted

½ cup turbinado sugar

1 tsp. fresh lemon juice

1 tsp. lemon zest

1 tsp. vanilla extract

⅓ cup coconut rum

2 Tbsp. cornstarch

2 Tbsp. water

Vanilla ice cream, for serving

1. Spray crock with nonstick spray.

2. Place cherries in crock with turbinado sugar, lemon juice, lemon zest, vanilla, and coconut rum.

3. Mix together the cornstarch and water, then stir this mixture into the contents of the crock.

4. Cook on Low for 3–4 hours.

5. Serve over vanilla ice cream.

Country Apples

Betty K. Drescher,
Quakertown, PA

Makes 8 servings
Prep. Time: 25 minutes
Cooking Time: 4–6 hours
Ideal slow-cooker size: 2½-qt.

4–5 cups apples, peeled and sliced

2 Tbsp. flour

¼ cup sugar

⅓ cup raisins

¼ tsp. ground cinnamon

⅔ cup dry oatmeal, rolled or quick

1 cup water

2 Tbsp. butter, melted

⅓ cup brown sugar

1. Coat apples in flour and white sugar. Stir in raisins, cinnamon, and oatmeal.

2. Pour water into slow cooker. Add apple mix.

3. Pour melted butter over apples. Sprinkle with brown sugar.

4. Cover. Cook on low 4–6 hours.

5. Serve over vanilla ice cream as a dessert, over oatmeal for breakfast, or use as a filling for crepes.

Desserts

Drunken Fruit

Dena Mell-Dorchy,
Royal Oak, MI

Makes 14 servings
Prep. Time: 25 minutes
Cooking Time: 3½–4 hours
Ideal slow-cooker size: 3- or 4-qt.

¼ cup honey

¼ cup melted coconut oil

½ cup coconut rum

2 Tbsp. quick-cooking tapioca, crushed

¼ tsp. salt

2½ cups fresh pineapple chunks

3 firm ripe plums, pitted and cut into wedges

2 medium Granny Smith apples, cored and cut into 1-inch pieces

2 medium pears, cored and cut into 1-inch pieces

2 medium peaches, pitted and cut into wedges

1. In a small bowl combine honey, coconut oil, coconut rum, tapioca, and salt.

2. Combine all fruit in the slow cooker

3. Pour rum mixture over fruit; stir to combine.

4. Cover and cook on low for 3½–4 hours.

Caramel Pears 'n' Wine Sauce

**Sharon Timpe,
Jackson, WI**

Makes 6 servings
Prep. Time: 20–30 minutes
Cooking Time: 4–6 hours
Ideal slow-cooker size: 6-qt.

6 medium-sized fresh pears with stems

1 cup white wine (Sauternes works well)∗

½ cup sugar

½ cup water

3 Tbsp. fresh lemon juice

2 apple cinnamon sticks, each about
2½–3" long

3 whole dried cloves

¼ tsp. ground nutmeg

6 Tbsp. fat-free caramel apple dip

1. Peel pears, leaving whole with stems intact.

2. Place upright in slow cooker. Shave bottom if needed to level fruit.

3. Combine wine, sugar, water, lemon juice, cinnamon, cloves, and nutmeg. Pour over pears.

4. Cook on Low 4–6 hours, or until pears are tender.

5. Cool pears in liquid.

6. Transfer pears to individual serving dishes. Place 2 tsp. cooking liquid in bottom of each dish.

7. Microwave caramel dip for 20 seconds and stir. Repeat until heated through.

8. Drizzle caramel over pears and serve.

NOTE

For a nonalcoholic option, use apple juice or white grape juice instead of white wine.

Desserts

Marinated Strawberries

Barbara Sparks,
Glen Burnie, MD

Makes 4 servings
Prep. Time: 20–25 minutes
Chilling Time: 2 hours

3 pints fresh strawberries

½ cup superfine or granulated sugar

juice of 2 large oranges

zest of 1 orange

⅓ cup orange-flavored liqueur

whipped topping or whipped cream, optional

1 Tbsp. chopped fresh mint leaves, optional

1. Hull strawberries and place in large bowl. If berries are large, cut in half. Do not overcrowd.

2. Sprinkle with sugar and orange zest. Add juice and liqueur. Carefully fold into berries.

3. Cover bowl. Refrigerate for about 2 hours, stirring carefully once or twice.

4. Serve chilled, topped with whipped topping or cream and mint leaves, if you wish.

Desserts

Strawberry Rhubarb Sauce

**Tina Snyder,
Manheim, PA**

Makes 8 servings
Prep. Time: 25 minutes
Cooking Time: 6–7 hours
Ideal slow-cooker size: 3½-qt.

6 cups sliced rhubarb

¾ cup sugar

1 cinnamon stick, optional

½ cup white grape juice

2 cups sliced strawberries, unsweetened

1. Place rhubarb in slow cooker. Pour sugar over. Add cinnamon stick if you wish, and grape juice. Stir well.

2. Cover and cook on low 5–6 hours, or until rhubarb is tender.

3. Stir in strawberries. Cook 1 hour longer.

4. Remove cinnamon stick if you've used it. Chill.

Chocolate Strawberry Salad

**Lucy O'Connell,
Northampton, MA**

Makes 8 servings
Prep Time: 15 minutes

2 lbs. fresh strawberries, sliced and slightly
  mashed

1 cup milk chocolate chips or chunks

½ cup sugar, or to taste

½ cup toasted coconut, optional

1. Combine berries, chocolate, and sugar.

2. Top with toasted coconut, if you wish.

Creamy Grape Salad

Nettie J. Miller,
Millersburg, OH

Makes 8–10 servings
Prep. Time: 20–30 minutes
Chilling Time: 1–2 hours, or more

8-oz. pkg. cream cheese, at room temperature

2 cups sour cream

½ cup brown sugar

½ tsp. vanilla

6 cups stemmed and washed seedless grapes,
red or green

1. In a large mixing bowl, blend the first three ingredients together until smooth.

2. Add vanilla.

3. Fold in grapes.

4. Cover and chill in the refrigerator for 1–2 hours, or more.

Peach Sherbert Popsicles

Leanne Yoder,
Tucson, AZ

Makes 10 servings
Prep. Time: 20 minutes
Chilling Time: 4 hours

2 egg whites

pinch of salt

6 Tbsp., plus ½ cup, sugar, *divided*

3 cups fresh peach purée

½ cup sugar

⅛ tsp. almond flavoring

1 cup milk

1. Use electric mixer to beat egg whites until foamy. Add salt. Continue beating until soft peaks form.

2. Add 6 Tbsp. sugar, one tablespoon at a time, beating well after each addition.

3. In a separate mixing bowl, mix together puréed peaches, ½ cup sugar, almond flavoring, and milk. Fold peach mixture into egg whites.

4. Pour into popsicle molds and freeze at least 4 hours.

Desserts

Cranberry Ice

Patricia Howard,
Green Valley, AL

Makes 6 servings
Prep. Time: 10 minutes
Cooking/Baking Time: 10 minutes
Freezing Time: 3-4 hours or more

2 cups fresh cranberries

1 cup very hot water additional water

1 cup sugar

2 cups tart apples, grated

1. In a medium-sized saucepan, cook cranberries in 1 cup partially boiling water until skins burst, about 5 minutes. Strain through a medium sieve. Discard skins.

2. Measure and add enough water to make 2 cups pulp and juice. Return to pan and cook 2 minutes.

3. Stir in sugar and simmer gently until it dissolves. Stir frequently.

4. Cool until room temperature.

5. Stir in 2 cups grated tart apples. Pour into refrigerator tray and freeze for 1–2 hours.

6. Stir. Return to freezer and continue freezing until firm.

7. To serve, place in refrigerator until partially thawed. Stir, or scratch up with fork tines before placing in serving bowl or individual dessert bowls.

Desserts

Metric Equivalent Measurements

If you're accustomed to using metric measurements, I don't want you to be inconvenienced by the imperial measurements I use in this book.

Use this handy chart, too, to figure out the size of the slow cooker you'll need for each recipe.

Weight (Dry Ingredients)

1 oz		30 g
4 oz	¼ lb	120 g
8 oz	½ lb	240 g
12 oz	¾ lb	360 g
16 oz	1 lb	480 g
32 oz	2 lbs	960 g

Volume (Liquid Ingredients)

½ tsp.		2 ml
1 tsp.		5 ml
1 Tbsp.	½ fl oz	15 ml
2 Tbsp.	1 fl oz	30 ml
¼ cup	2 fl oz	60 ml
⅓ cup	3 fl oz	80 ml
½ cup	4 fl oz	120 ml
⅔ cup	5 fl oz	160 ml
¾ cup	6 fl oz	180 ml
1 cup	8 fl oz	240 ml
1 pt	16 fl oz	480 ml
1 qt	32 fl oz	960 ml

Slow Cooker Sizes

1-quart	0.96 l
2-quart	1.92 l
3-quart	2.88 l
4-quart	3.84 l
5-quart	4.80 l
6-quart	5.76 l
7-quart	6.72 l
8-quart	7.68 l

Length

¼ in	6 mm
½ in	13 mm
¾ in	19 mm
1 in	25 mm
6 in	15 cm
12 in	30 cm

Abbreviations, Assumptions, and Equivalents

Abbreviations Used in This Cookbook

lb. = pound
oz. = ounce
pkg. = package
pt. = pint
qt. = quart
Tbsp. = tablespoon
tsp. = teaspoon
9 × 13 baking pan = 9 inches wide by 13 inches long
8 × 8 baking pan = 8 inches wide by 8 inches long
5 × 9 loaf pan = 5 inches wide by 9 inches long

Assumptions

flour = unbleached or white, and all-purpose
oatmeal or oats = dry, quick or rolled (old-fashioned),unless specified
pepper = black, finely ground
rice = regular, long-grain (not minute or instant)
salt = table salt
shortening = solid, not liquid
spices = all ground, unless specified otherwise
sugar = granulated sugar (not brown and not confectioners')

Equivalents

dash = little less than $\frac{1}{8}$ tsp.

3 teaspoons = 1 Tablespoon
2 Tablespoons = 1 oz.
4 Tablespoons = ¼ cup
5 Tablespoons plus 1 tsp. = ⅓ cup
8 Tablespoons = ½ cup
12 Tablespoons = ¾ cup
16 Tablespoons = 1 cup
1 cup = 8 ozs. liquid
2 cups = 1 pint
4 cups = 1 quart
4 quarts = 1 gallon
1 stick butter = ¼ lb.
1 stick butter = ½ cup
1 stick butter = 8 Tbsp.
Beans, 1 lb. dried = 2–2½ cups (depending upon the size of the beans)
Bell peppers, 1 large = 1 cup chopped
Cheese, hard (for example, cheddar, Swiss, Monterey Jack, mozzarella),
    1 lb. grated = 4 cups
Cheese, cottage, 1 lb. = 2 cups
Chocolate chips, 6-oz. pkg. = 1 scant cup
Coconut, 3-oz. pkg., grated = 1 cup, lightly filled
Crackers, graham, 12 single crackers = 1 cup crumbs
Crackers (butter, saltines, snack), 20 single crackers = 1 cup crumbs
Herbs, 1 Tbsp. fresh = 1 tsp. dried
Lemon, 1 medium-sized = 2–3 Tbsp. juice
Lemon, 1 medium-sized = 2–3 tsp. grated rind
Mustard, 1 Tbsp. prepared = 1 tsp. dry or ground mustard
Oatmeal, 1 lb. dry = about 5 cups dry
Onion, 1 medium-sized = ½ cup chopped
Pasta- Macaronis, penne, and other small or tubular shapes, 1 lb. dry = 4 cups
    uncooked Noodles, 1 lb. dry = 6 cups uncooked Spaghetti, linguine, fettucine,
    1 lb. dry = 4 cups uncooked
Potatoes, white, 1 lb. = 3 medium-sized potatoes = 2 cups mashed
Potatoes, sweet, 1 lb. = 3 medium-sized potatoes = 2 cups mashed
Rice, 1 lb. dry = 2 cups uncooked
Sugar, confectioners', 1 lb. = 3½ cups sifted
Whipping cream, 1 cup un-whipped = 2 cups whipped
Whipped topping, 8-oz. container = 3 cups
Yeast, dry, 1 envelope (¼ oz.) = 1 Tbsp.

About the Author

Growing up, Hope spent many hours in the kitchen with her Meme (grandmother) and her love for cooking grew from there. While working on her master's degree when her daughter was young, Hope turned to her slow cookers for some salvation and sanity. It was from there she began truly experimenting with recipes and quickly learned she had the ability to get a little more creative in the kitchen and develop her own recipes.

In 2010, Hope started her blog, *A Busy Mom's Slow Cooker Adventures*, to simply share the recipes she was making with her family and friends. She never imagined people all over the world would begin visiting her page and sharing her recipes with others as well. In 2013, Hope self-published her first cookbook, *Slow Cooker Recipes 10 Ingredients or Less and Gluten-Free*, and then later wrote *The Gluten-Free Slow Cooker*.

Hope Comerford is a mom, wife, elementary music teacher, blogger, recipe developer, public speaker, ALM Zone fit leader, Young Living Essential Oils essential oil enthusiast/educator, and published author. In 2013, she was diagnosed with a severe gluten intolerance and since then has spent many hours creating easy, practical and delicious gluten-free recipes that can be enjoyed by both those who are affected by gluten and those who are not.

Hope became the new brand ambassador and author of Fix-It and Forget-It in mid-2016. Since then, she has brought her excitement and creativeness to the Fix-It and Forget-It brand. Through Fix-It and Forget-It, she has written *Fix-It and Forget-It Lazy & Slow*, *Fix-It and Forget-It Healthy Slow Cooker Cookbook*, *Fix-It and Forget-It Favorite Slow Cooker Recipes for Mom*, *Fix-It and Forget-It Favorite Slow Cooker Recipes for Dad*, *Fix-

It and Enjoy-It Welcome Home Cookbook, Fix-It and Forget-It Holiday Favorites and *Fix-It and Forget-It Cooking for Two, Fix-It and Forget-It Crowd Pleasers for the American Summer* and *Fix-It and Forget-It Dump Dinners and Dump Desserts,* and *Welcome Home Diabetic Cookbook.*

Hope lives in the city of Clinton Township, Michigan, near Metro Detroit.

She's been a native of Michigan her whole life. She has been happily married to her husband and best friend, Justin, since 2008. Together they have two children, Ella and Gavin, who are her motivation, inspiration, and heart. In her spare time, Hope enjoys traveling, singing, cooking, reading books, spending time with friends and family, and relaxing.